# PRAISE FOR *BROADS, SISTERS, EXES*

"In this detailed, insightful, intelligent, sharply researched book, Vincent L. Stephens has assembled an argument that is relevant, timely, precise, and deftly analytical. He brilliantly investigates how feminist television has manifested and transformed over the decades. Meticulously integrating historical, sociological, anthropological, rhetorical, philosophical, and cultural works to provide a convincing and compelling narrative that will be a valuable resource for popular culture scholars across multiple disciplines in the humanities and social sciences as well as journalists and those in the larger public who are avid consumers of popular media."

—Elwood Watson, author of *Keepin' It Real: Essays on Race in Contemporary America*

"*Broads, Sisters, Exes* brings a long-overdue intersectionalist-feminist lens to twenty-first-century US television, centering diverse women creators' roles in bringing about the Millennial women–centric shows cumulatively hailed as the 'Golden Age of Feminist TV.' Steeped in deep understanding of its roots in American indie film and television history alongside its broader cultural influences and industrial impacts, Stephens's study offers cogent and compelling analyses of nine pivotal series created by Millennial women stretching from the groundbreaking *Girls* to the iconoclastic *I May Destroy You*."

—Maria San Filippo, editor of *After "Happily Ever After": Romantic Comedy in the Post-Romantic Age* (Wayne State University Press)

"This book is a timely and insightful entry into the growing body of scholarship that thinks through the prominence of women on US television screens and their ties to feminism. Thinking through the relationships between authorship, industrial conditions, and media feminisms, *Broads, Sisters, Exes* offers critical insight into the diverse and distinct women that populate television today."

—Jessica Ford, senior lecturer in media, The University of Adelaide, Australia

"*Broads, Sisters, Exes* is a wonderful addition to contemporary scholarship on women's television creation. Exploring key issues in feminist television criticism, the book provides thoughtful analyses of narrative, genre, visual style, and industrial contexts."

—Yael Levy, author of *Chick TV: Antiheroines and Time Unbound*

# BROADS, SISTERS, EXES

**Contemporary Approaches to Film and Media Series**

A complete listing of the books in this series can be found online at wsupress.wayne.edu.

# BROADS, SISTERS, EXES

## FEMINIST MILLENNIAL TELEVISION

Vincent L. Stephens

WAYNE STATE UNIVERSITY PRESS
DETROIT

ISBN 9780814350263 (paperback)
ISBN 9780814350270 (hardcover)
ISBN 9780814350287 (ebook)

Library of Congress Control Number: 2024942827

Cover illustration and design by Lindsey Cleworth.

Published with the assistance of a fund established by Thelma Gray James of Wayne State University for the publication of folklore and English studies.

Wayne State University Press rests on Waawiyaataanong, also referred to as Detroit, the ancestral and contemporary homeland of the Three Fires Confederacy. These sovereign lands were granted by the Ojibwe, Odawa, Potawatomi, and Wyandot Nations, in 1807, through the Treaty of Detroit. Wayne State University Press affirms Indigenous sovereignty and honors all tribes with a connection to Detroit. With our Native neighbors, the press works to advance educational equity and promote a better future for the earth and all people.

Wayne State University Press
Leonard N. Simons Building
4809 Woodward Avenue
Detroit, Michigan 48201-1309

Visit us online at wsupress.wayne.edu.

# CONTENTS

# PREFACE

When the cable network TV Land aired reruns of the series *Mary Hartman, Mary Hartman* (1976–77, syndicated; referred to hereafter as *MH2*) in 2002, I was fascinated by its unusualness. As an aficionado of 1970s television comedies, I was taken aback by its soap operatic style, including its lush theme song and low-budget sets. Further, its topicality, dry wit, deadpan acting, and lack of a laugh track distinguished it from any other 1970s comedy in my memory. Everything about it defied common sense about what constituted typical sitcoms of the era, and I was intrigued. Seeking to know more about this oddball series, I read vintage articles on the series, located ephemeral paperbacks about the show, and scrolled online fan sites about how to access the series on DVD. Both the 2007 DVD release of the first twenty-five episodes and the publication of Elana Levine's 2007 book *Wallowing in Sex: The New Sexual Culture of 1970s American Television*, which discusses the series in various chapters, increased my fascination.[1]

Emboldened by my newfound access to the first twenty-five of its 325 episodes, I showed the pilot episode, which focuses on a heterosexual married couple struggling with sexual impotence, to undergraduate students enrolled in a course on family relations in popular media. As part of a generation accustomed to slickly produced network sitcoms, fantasy series, and dramedies, my students found *MH2* off-putting and called it the "worst show they had ever seen" . . . which they followed up with the question: "What happens in the next episode?" The combination of *MH2*'s highly stylized aesthetics and intriguing cliffhangers—What will happen to Mary and her husband Tom? When will they discover the identity of the Fernwood Flasher? Who killed the Lombardi family and their brood of animals? Will Loretta become a major country singer?—did exactly what was intended: it made you want to see more.

Thirty years after it ended, the series still had the power to capture an audience's attention. When prompted, students immediately picked up on the gender norms that played out among *MH2*'s various couples, especially the angst Mary felt as a spouse, mother, and daughter, who also wanted to be seen as a person independent of those roles. *MH2* was an anomaly for the time; it aired five days a week, was syndicated because no network understood it or wanted to risk airing it, and occupied an odd space between comedy, parody, and satire. In 2013, Shout Factory! released the entire series, with bonus episodes of its spin-off series *Fernwood 2-Night* (1977), and though I soldiered through most of it my initial viewing was incomplete.[2]

Then the COVID-19 pandemic forced the nation into lockdown in March 2020, and I had more solitary free time. Watching the entire series from the pilot to its final episode was illuminating and inspiring in two notable ways. First, the series was created by members of a generation born before the Depression, including Ann Marcus (b. 1921) and Norman Lear (b. 1922), who focused, primarily, on the way members of the "Silent Generation" (1928–45) and "Baby Boomers" (1946–64) navigated American life in mid-1970s America. The interactions Mary's generation had with her parents, and grandfather, pointed to different generational perspectives about relationships, consumerism, sexuality, and human existence that tend to be overlooked. Second, the second season (September 1976–May 1977) introduced a significant plotline about the infiltration of a White supremacist organization in the show's fictional Ohio small town. The resurgence of these groups during the 1970s was historically accurate, and its depiction provided a fictional window into attempts to undo the progress several generations, including the Baby Boomers, made against anti-Black racism and toward civil rights and greater social inclusion.[3]

Writers from one generation telling a story about another generation is a common phenomenon in television. Less common, however, is when a generation has the opportunity to reflect on its experiences in its own voice. The issue of generational authorship has fascinated me since the mid-2010s when I noticed a proliferation of television series written, directed, and/or creatively led by women, about women. Throughout television history, many of television's most iconic women characters or women-centered series were developed by men. Though a number of women showrunners such as producers Marcy Carsey, Linda Bloodworth Thomason, and Mara Brock Akil, expanded the range of female producers in television, they were a rarity. Since the 2010s, a generation of mostly Millennial-era women creatives, including Lena Dunham, Rachel Bloom, Issa Rae, Michaela Coel, and Phoebe Waller-Bridge, were writing, starring in, and often producing and directing, some of the most captivating contemporary television series. Nine series form the foundation of this book's inquiry. My academic interest began with the stylistic scope of *Crazy Ex-Girlfriend* (2015–19, CW), starring Bloom, and then grew into a more comparative inquiry about the way women creatives were changing how women were seen and understood in comedies and dramedies. *Girls* (2012–17, HBO), *Insecure* (2016–21, HBO), *Fleabag* (2016, 2019, BBC and Amazon Prime Video), *Broad City* (2016–20, Comedy Central), *Shrill* (2018–20, Hulu), and *I May Destroy You* (2020, HBO), focus primarily on Millennial-generation (1981–96) women, push representational boundaries of television, and subvert familiar formulas of genre. The Millennials featured on the ensemble series *Orange Is the New Black* (2013–19, Netflix) and *Jane the Virgin* (2014–19, CW) were equally relevant. Collectively, these series offer a challenge to the television comedy as a form and demand a closer look at how Millennial women-centric shows transformed television from the early 2010s through 2020.

Among these nine series, women's authorship shows up in different ways. *Broad City*, *Crazy Ex-Girlfriend*, *Fleabag*, *Insecure*, and *I May Destroy You* feature their Millennial showrunner/executive producers as leads. *Jane the Virgin* was adapted from a Venezuelan series by producer Jennie Snyder Urman, who is not a Millennial but leads the creative team behind the Millennial lead character. Urman wrote the pilot and final episode of each of its five seasons. *Orange Is the New Black* and *Shrill* are adaptations of popular books centered on women whose respective authors, Piper Kerman and Lindy West, are differently involved in the series.[4] Showrunner Jenji Kohan, who also produced *Weeds* (2005–12, Showtime), serves as the executive producer and showrunner of *Orange*. Kerman is not involved in its writing or production. Author Lindy West is one of the executive producers of *Shrill* and wrote or cowrote six of its twenty-two episodes.

My interest in women's authorship is less about reducing authentic narrative voices to gender than expanding the conversation about what constitutes authenticity. Each series has a unique focus and a distinctive range of narrative arcs. Having a multigender and optimally multiracial creative team opens up space for telling new stories differently.

While these creative developments of the early 2010s–2020 were fostered by the shift from a mass audience to a niche audience, storytelling remains vulnerable to how the television industry compensates writers. Both the 2008 and 2023 Writers Guild of America (WGA) strikes, and the 2023 SAG-AFTRA strike, which buttress the 2010–20 era under discussion, amplify the challenges of making a living in popular media industries. This is particularly true for minoritized writers from social groups only beginning to get their foot in the door. The strikes highlight the particularity of that period and the threat of regression.

I hope the book helps readers understand the unique way these creatives and their shows push boundaries. The emergence of post-2020 series like *Run the World* (2021–23, Starz), *Harlem* (2021–present, Amazon Prime), *Somebody Somewhere* (2022–present, HBO), *Single Drunk Female* (2022–23, Freeform), *Feel Good* (2020–21, Channel 4), *Everything's Trash* (2022, Freeform), and *Rap Sh!t* (2022–24, HBO Max), illustrate the ways the nine series in this book opened doors creatively and structurally for women producers. Relatedly, many producers and showrunners have intentionally created structures to incubate emerging creative voices from women, from offering them opportunities as writers, producers, and directors to sponsoring fellowship programs and scholarships. For example, Rae and Lena Waithe (*The Chi*, *Boomerang*) are Black women writer-producer-actresses who have provided multiple opportunities for emerging creatives from minoritized communities, especially women of color, to develop industry experience.

Writing this book inspired me to reflect on the nature of close readings of popular culture and future possibilities. When your formal education has equipped you with critical frameworks to identify and interrogate various types of bias structuring our contemporary world, writing about popular culture critically, and with a semblance of optimism, feels almost foreboding. For many scholars who view themselves as conscientious and progressive, a melancholic, despairing, and hypercritical perspective on media hovers like a default expectation. Enthusiastic, passionate, optimistic, and joyful engagement with popular culture can easily seem naive, deluded, and complicit with the "neoliberal" turn many scholars frequently invoke to explain domestic and global injustices.

*Broads, Sisters, Exes* is a work of cautious optimism. History repeatedly reveals that there is nothing inevitable or teleological about artists' access to the means to create art and have it distributed widely. Nonetheless, there seemed to be an opening up in the television industry for women in the early 2010s–early 2020s. Creatives as privileged and connected as Dunham, who grew up in a prominent New York artistic family, and as emergent as Coel, who was better known in Britain than the United States prior to *I May Destroy You* of the 2020s, had a new access to tell stories about the Millennial generation. Though Kohan and Snyder Urman are Generation X-ers, as seasoned producers, writers, and showrunners they shepherded shows that have contributed to the mythmaking about the varied complexities of Millennial womanhood.

Critical and cultural theories offer useful tools for tackling some key aspects of representation, power, and politics. I find these most useful when paired with "close analysis of the stylistic and narrative histories of the medium," which media scholar Jeffrey Sconce has identified as crucial for a medium as dynamic as television.[5] The industrial context, technological apparatus, and creative processes entailed in the genesis and execution of television has changed considerably since the medium emerged, and its malleability remains one of its strengths. In that spirit, this book addresses the marriage of innovative narrative approaches with social and cultural observations and critique, especially about gender and its intersections.

This book captures a rupture in what stories got told, how they were told, and who was and was not represented in the telling. We're accustomed to men as auteurs in television. Names like Norman Lear, Steve Bochco, J. J. Abrams, Joss Whedon, and Damon Lindelof are known to many television fans, but, with the exception of Joy Press's 2018 book *Stealing the Show*, less attention has been paid to the women in front, behind, and beyond the camera who are (re)shaping the medium in the early twenty-first century.[6] I am excited to recognize and analyze their creative leadership as storytellers, artists, and feminists.

# ACKNOWLEDGMENTS

Scholarly writing is an act of humility requiring one to engage deeply with established conversations and aim to contribute meaningfully. In that spirit I am indebted to multiple generations of scholars in feminist media studies, television studies, and related fields who have established the study of women on television as an essential area of inquiry. I was continually inspired by the thoughtful scholars cited in this work and hope it gives them their proper due.

I am equally appreciative of the individuals whose advice, guidance, and support made this study possible, including the following:

Stephanie Hewitt for watching and discussing the first few episodes of *Crazy Ex-Girlfriend* with me in 2015.

Elaine M. Hayes for encouraging me to pursue this project early on, and for offering me informed and insightful feedback during the early stages of the book's development.

Maria Bruno, Say Burgin, Dee Dragani, Anne Marie Stewart, Meg Winchester, and Amaury Sosa for their time and insights as my ideas took shape.

Olivia Riordan for her invaluable research assistance funded by two research grants from Dickinson College, and Hannah Youmans for her musical insights.

Jerry Philogene, Susan Lombardi-Verticelli, and Jonathan Foltz who each offered very helpful advice for moving this study forward.

Domino Perez for naming and clarifying the value of the "slow approach," which has transformed my approach to research and writing.

Carian Diaz, Sonja Paulson, and Trent Masiki for their positive presence during my writing weekends in Providence, Rhode Island, and Northampton, Massachusetts.

Eric Nelson, Alyssa Baker, Carolyn Snell, Karl Kirchwey, Tamzen Flanders, Alice Tseng for listening and for ongoing encouragement.

Indara Suarez and Malika Jeffries-El for keeping me company during very productive coffee shop sessions.

Paula Davis and Gary Steiner for hosting me during a reinvigorating visit to Los Angeles County.

Kyna Hamill for expert advice and feedback.

Kat Wright for helping me clarify the book's images.

Two anonymous reviewers and Barry Keith Grant whose thoughtful insights helped me refine, reconsider, and elevate my ideas.

Marie Sweetman, my acquisitions editor, for championing this work from the beginning and providing expert advice.

Finally, I dedicate this book to my dear late friend and colleague Carmen Renee Gillespie. Carmen was an amazing thought partner with whom I discussed many of the themes of this book continuously over the years with great tenacity and fervor. She was a genuine champion of my work and I miss her immensely. I am eternally thankful to her for introducing me to her wonderful daughters Chelsea and Delaney, and to Chelsea for bringing her lovely wife Emily, and their daughter Remi, into my life.

This book was partially funded by a Publication Production Award from the Boston University Center for the Humanities (BUCH).

# INTRODUCTION

## *Women Creatives Redefine the Grammars of Contemporary Television*

The proliferation of television comedies centered on Black women ensembles in the 2020s, including Amazon Prime's *Harlem* (2022–present), Starz's *Run the World* (2021–present), BET's *Twenties* (2020–21), and Freeform's *Everything's Trash* (2022), is a significant change in representation from the 1990s. As is the fact that each was created and run by Black women showrunners, including Leigh Davenport (*Run the World*), Tracie Oliver (*Harlem*), Phoebe Robinson (*Everything's Trash*), and Lena Waithe (*Twenties*).

Their existence is not the result of benevolence or a sudden industry turn toward equity. Rather, these shows came into being during the postnetwork era when the television audience became more fragmented than ever, broadcast networks declined in dominance, especially as they faced competition from streaming services and cable, and the notion of what constituted television was up for debate. The proliferation of women-centric web-based series such as Issa Rae's *The Misadventures of Awkward Black Girl* (2011–13) and Jen Richards's *Her Story* (2016) exemplifies how more contemporary understandings of television have served as an incubator for emerging talents in the industry.[1]

Though we can point to *Living Single* (1993–98, FOX), *Sex and the City* (1998–2004, HBO), and *Girlfriends* (2000–2008, UPN and CW) as generic precedents for these series, their aesthetic and thematic "genealogy" is also indebted to the newer series this book addresses, including surreal aspects of women-centric comedies like *Broad City* (2014–19, Comedy Central), *Crazy Ex-Girlfriend* (2015–19, CW), and *Insecure* (2016–21, HBO). Collectively, their stylistic choices, as well as those of similarly stylized series, have gradually expanded the aesthetic vocabulary of television since the 2010s, especially its relationship to film, genre conventions, and depictions of narrative time, and ushered in women-centric storylines most broadcast networks would have been reluctant to air in the 1990s and '00s.

More recently, however, the television industry has had to shift from an imagined "monoculture" that was content to digest stories primarily told from straight, White, cisgender men's creative perspectives, and find ways to maintain relevance to a diverse audience that has more choices in what, how, and when they view television. As such, we have witnessed more diversity in what stories are being told on television and who gets to tell those stories, and thus the voices of women across difference in race, gender, sexuality, class background, political commitment, and other areas are more prominent. The discernible rise in women-centric content is promising, but as the *Inclusion or Invisibility?* report of 2016 indicated, the industry has a long way to go to achieve gender and racial equity.[2] *Broads, Sisters, Exes* is a critical intervention into some key creative developments that emerged from 2010 to 2020 and significantly expanded what seemed possible for the vocabulary of television as a medium, and specifically for women-identified creatives seeking to tell women-centric stories. Though my book is composed of close readings that place television series in conversation with media studies and feminist thought, it also seeks to chronicle a period of creative growth and transition—with hope that the phenomenon it analyzes develops into something more enduring for future audiences and creatives.

Comedic and dramedic series focused on women-identified lead characters with predominantly women-identified creative team, proliferated from the 2010s to the early 2020s. Many of these series, such as *Girls* and *Insecure*, have inspired a wide range of scholarship. This book takes a comparative approach that examines the relationship between formal elements of a select group of dramedies and contemporary feminist thought to tell a larger story about how television is made and by whom. Women-led creative teams have shaped a discernible new aesthetic grammar in television that is stylistically innovative, thematically daring, and deeply reflective of the ethos of the early '00s. The chapters to come focus on *Broad City*, *Crazy Ex-Girlfriend*, *Fleabag*, *Girls*, *I May Destroy You*, *Insecure*, *Jane the Virgin*, *Orange Is the New Black*, and *Shrill*, women-centric series linked by their fusing of comedic and dramatic elements, innovative approaches to genre, and focus on Millennial-generation characters living in the twenty-first century. Millennials describes a generation born between the early 1980s and '00s who are notable for being the first digital natives and holding progressive social values, among other characteristics.[3] Compared to previous generations, Millennials have been slower in forming households, more likely to delay marriage, and start families at a later age, among other general characteristics.[4] Many of these elements surface in the living arrangements depicted in the series and characters', especially women's, complex relationships to social expectations.

Aesthetically, each series is both "good" and "complex." These terms are a mash-up of Cardwell's and Mittell's stirring conversations about the range of qualities that make television programs "good" for viewers aesthetically, and Mittell's definition of "narrative complexity" as "a new paradigm of television storytelling [that] has emerged over the past two decades, redefining the boundary between episodic and serial forms, with a heightened degree of self-consciousness in storytelling mechanics and demanding intensified viewer engagement focused on both diegetic pleasures and formal awareness."[5] These qualities speak specifically to the best qualities of television programs—from various forums, including broadcast networks, cable, and streaming services—without privileging other mediums, like film, above television or limiting notions of excellence to one genre (e.g., men-centered dramas) or production style. Because "complexity" is an aesthetic characteristic rather than a genre, I proceed with the claim that the nine series under analysis in this book are "good," and in this specific instance a key element of this quality is their "complexity."

Each series engages with feminism in a dynamic and pluralized manner rather than privileging one specific wave. The tension between "pessimistic" and "optimistic" perspectives on postfeminism have led me to embrace Keller's and Ryan's notion of "emergent feminisms," which aspires to "bring together some of the complex and contradictory ways in which feminisms are emerging within media cultures that remain shaped by patriarchy, racism, classism, heterosexism, and other forms of oppression."[6] Embracing tensions and contradictions is a more expansive and authentic way of addressing the diverse subject positions and experiences of women, and their representations. While the postfeminist temporal frame is valid and relevant for engaging with the new generation of innovative women-centric, post-network-era series, they have more compelling critical possibilities than a narrow focus on an amorphous political metric would allow. Thus, the study here pivots from the "Is it 'authentically' feminist?" question to questions that are critical and relevant for a televisual analysis.

My embrace of emerging feminism is informed by Johnson's observation that television shows mix "feminist, postfeminist, antifeminist, and pseudofeminist motifs," which does not absolve critics from paying attention but rather requires attending to these contradictions.[7] Similarly, Sobande's analysis of *Insecure* and the British series *Chewing Gum* (2015–17, E4) discusses how they juxtapose "various postfeminist, Black feminist, and even—Black postfeminist television qualities."[8] By considering the coexistence of ideological and formal elements in texts, we can engage in reading practices that allow us to explore the form and content of the series in a manner that considers feminist content when its relevant but resists reducing women-authored series to thinly veiled comments on feminism.

This book asks three critical questions: What are the industrial and sociocultural contexts fostering the rise of women-identified televisual authorship during the 2010s–20s? What formal innovations do these series offer that advances comedic and dramedic forms, especially those representing women? How do their formal and thematic choices help us understand women's diverse identities and experiences in new and different ways than before?

The introduction articulates the relationship of the nine series to different forms of feminist thought and situates them in relation to their aesthetic women-centric forebears. After placing them in a genealogy of women-centric series I discuss the concept and implications of postfeminism, unpack "goodness" and "complexity" in the discourse of contemporary television aesthetics, and consider how these series honor and build from the pivotal generic and thematic innovations of *Ally McBeal*, *Buffy the Vampire Slayer*, and *Sex and the City*.

## The Genealogy of Women's Television

Several foundational genealogies of women-centric television from the 1950s through the first decade of the twenty-first century offer critical approaches for framing this book's nine series in relation to women's lived experiences.[9] Three major strands of feminist television criticism, outlined by McCabe and Akass, includes scholars who examine tensions between domesticity and femininity and feminism, reception studies focused on how women watch and use television, and the endurance of patriarchal ideas about women's lives that pervade television of the "postfeminist" era.[10] The era of programming this book examines lies within the "postfeminist" era, and I explore the trends preceding it to properly contextualize my analysis.

Television of the 1950s and 1960s focused primarily on male characters; those focused on women emphasized their domestic roles as wives and mothers and naturalized White, female suburban domesticity, including *I Love Lucy* (1951–57), *Leave It to Beaver* (1957–63) and *Father Knows Best* (1954–62). Though several series of the 1960s, such as *That Girl* (1966–71, ABC) and *Julia* (1968–71, NBC), centered on independent women characters, the 1970s offers the clearest breakthrough for female representation. Both television's aspiration toward social "relevance," via depictions informed by racial and gender social movements, and its increasing awareness of women as a viable consumer demographic, informed the production of CBS series such as *The Mary Tyler Moore Show* (1970–77), *Maude* (1972–78), *Rhoda* (1974–78), *One Day at a Time* (1975–84), and *Alice* (1976–85). These characters represent "new woman" roles focused on professional achievement rather than domestic roles confining them to the home.[11]

These "new woman" series presented women in a broader range of domestic and intimate situations, including sexually active single career women and single mothers. They focused primarily on White women, however, and reflected liberal feminist values, which tend to be less critical of power relationships within domestic spaces, including patriarchal values, and presume existing systems inevitably foster justice and equality.[12] Aside from the characters Gloria Stivic (portrayed by Sally Struthers on *All in the Family*, 1971–79, CBS) and Maude Finley (portrayed by Beatrice Arthur on *Maude*), the characters were rarely overtly political in dialogue or action.

Women-centric series of the 1980s presented "superwomen" who were "capable of balancing a successful career and a conventional family life, with little redistribution of women's, or men's, traditional responsibilities within the homes," demonstrated in such characters as Claire Huxtable, *The Cosby Show* (1984–92, NBC), Angela Bower, *Who's the Boss* (1984–92, ABC), and Maggie Seaver, *Growing Pains* (1985–92, ABC). Several series emerged later in the decade that presented the balance with more complexity and nuance, such as those on *thirtysomething* (1987–91, ABC). Some also challenged the conservative cultural climate of the 1980s and early 1990s, including the frequently topical approaches of *Designing Women* (1986–93, CBS) and *Murphy Brown* (1988–98; 2018–19, CBS). Similarly, several scholars offer frameworks that explore representation of women quite intricately, including D'Acci's analysis of the different kinds of feminism evident in *Cagney & Lacey* (1982–88, CBS) and Rowe's discussion of "unruly" women in series such as *Roseanne* (1988–97, ABC). Rowe's framework is especially relevant to the series in this study.[13]

The late 1990s–early '00s yielded critical concerns and anxieties about how feminist ideas were represented in iconic series such as *Ally McBeal* (1998–2002, FOX), *Buffy the Vampire Slayer* (1997–2003, WB and UPN), *Desperate Housewives* (2004–12, ABC), and *Sex and the City*. Whereas second-wave feminism was the primary anchor for most previous scholarship on women on television, the rise of newer feminist discourses, such as postfeminism and third-wave feminism, complicated "feminism" as a referent. Many scholars questioned how liberated characters were when their pursuit of men to complete them was so central. More recent women-centric series such as NBC's *30 Rock* (2006–13) and *Parks and Recreation* (2009–15) have also inspired critical discussions about the infusion of postfeminism into comedic series as have several 2006–16 British series.[14]

In contrast to questions of what constitutes legitimate feminism (e.g., what it demands of women's intimate desires), Lotz embraces the era's complexity more overtly, noting how in contemporary television, "No one character emerges as the unflawed poster woman for contemporary feminists, but this is not an appropriate standard, nor does it account for the internal complexity and contradiction common to television representations and discourses." In place of a generic metric for assessing feminist authenticity, which simply dismisses them as "part of a hegemonic, patriarchal, capitalist system," she examines what constitutes the postfeminist television landscape. Among her observations are how these contemporary narratives explore diverse relations to power women inhabit, their depictions of varied feminist solutions and loose organizations of activism, conscious efforts to deconstruct binary categories of gender and sexuality, and treat them as flexible and indistinct, and the way situations illustrating the contemporary struggles faced by women and feminists are raised and examined within the series.[15]

In addition to Lotz's observations from 2001, I also want to consider the specific ways women interact with media in the convergence era of media.[16] The rise of digital technologies has changed how women artists develop their voices and build audiences, including content sites like YouTube and streaming services. The pervasiveness of these technologies also normalized digital communication as core to how television characters communicate and interact with the fictional worlds they inhabit and fostered a greater sense of formal experimentation among creative staffs. These shifts in technology, production, and reception operate in tandem with more recent theorizations of popular, celebrity, and fourth-wave feminism. As such, I see critical value in further unpacking the implications of "postfeminist" and other feminist possibilities.

## Emergent Feminisms and Media Studies

Exploring how innovative women-centric television programs of the postnetwork era illuminate our understandings of women's lives in the early twenty-first century is my critical focus. Before delving further into my critical focus, structure, and approach, I briefly discuss the study's relationship to emergent feminisms in media studies and locate it in the contemporary aesthetic landscape.

Since the early 1990s postfeminism as a concept has remained a contentious discussion topic in media studies.[17] The pessimistic view contends that postfeminism is a temporal construct of the late 1980s–early 1990s that replaced second-wave feminist activist politics with a neoliberal sensibility that discarded an "authentic" politically engaged movement focused on challenging patriarchal oppression in education, employment, law, reproductive rights for an individualist rhetoric devoid of politics.

Media studies scholars and cultural critics have continually circulated and engaged the term *postfeminism* especially in relation to the characters on the popular, zeitgeist defining series *Sex and the City* and *Ally McBeal*.[18] The pessimistic perspective criticizes the series for apolitical individualism, consumerism, and commodification understood as reducing the aspirations of second-wave feminism. Further, they are relegated to a benign consumer lifestyle with superficial allusions to empowerment, freedom, and choice unrelated to the second wave's radical collective activism and advocacy.

The use of second-wave feminism as the point of comparison is ironic since Black women, queer women, women of the Global South, and their intersections challenged the White, heterosexual, US centered middle-class biases of the second wave and generated more inclusive frameworks for feminism.[19] These interventions informed the contours of third-wave feminism in the 1990s, which included the embrace of "Girlie" culture, the Riot Grrrl zine and musical culture, as well as greater racial, sexual, and class consciousness. Nonetheless, many critics of postfeminism view the era and sensibility skeptically as another manifestation of a lifestyle-oriented feminism. As such second-wave feminism's practices and achievements remains the central anchor point for feminist critics of postfeminism.

The optimistic view understands postfeminism as a paradigm defined by greater choice, freedom, and self-fashioning indebted to the structural and political gains of second-wave feminism. Rather than discarding the past, postfeminist representations change the conversation by challenging rigid standards of how political commitments align with women's personal expression, including the embrace of femininity, sexual pleasure, and negotiated readings of problematic popular culture. As Adriaens and Van Bauwel note, postfeminism as a concept circulates mostly in scholarly discourse and is not necessarily central in activist spheres.[20]

Among more optimistic critics the "lifestyle" aspect of second-wave feminism epitomized by the "personal is the political" ethos is an important strand of feminist organizing. Drawing from a range of examples, including music, sartorial freedom, and alternative living arrangements, Hagelin and Silverman note how feminists of the late 1960s and 1970s understood "that cultural choices could project a powerful message about their feminist identity that was aligned with their politics." Some of the second wave's leaders' initial objections to consciousness-raising now seem dated and insensitive to the range of ways women wanted and needed to engage collectively to process their bodies and experiences.[21] Relatedly, third-wave feminism drew greater attention to the different diverse ways the category of "woman" could be understood, including more awareness of race, class, and gendered embodiment.[22] Some critical substrands within the postfeminist discourse are the distinct digital mobilizations of fourth-wave feminism; the role of postrecession financial and social precarity on the aesthetics of female centered television; the antiaspirational female antiheroine, informed by financial and social precarity; and the emergence of subgenres such as "popular feminism" and "celebrity feminism."[23]

*Broads, Sisters, Exes* employs the emergent feminisms approach to foster a nuanced perspective on how creatives integrate feminist elements in their productions. In television, emergent feminism surfaces in the way women creatives place multiple waves of feminism in conversation with each other and respond to the dynamic sociocultural contexts in their series. For example, because Millennials are digital natives, cell phones, texting, and references to social media sites pervade the programs I examine. By association they have significantly advanced the internet and social media as activist spaces. The notion of fourth-wave feminism captures how feminists are using digital spaces "to make visible marginalized voices and bodies, either through amplifying the stories of others or through drawing attention to their own experiences, which has opened up significant spaces for resistance to hegemonic femininities."[24] The tension between the rise of a digitally mediated "popular feminism" and the corresponding backlash of "popular misogyny" is an ongoing challenge that Millennial feminists navigate constantly, which informs my analysis of *Shrill* and *I May Destroy You*. Similarly, feminism might inform some of the themes a series explores such as inappropriate workplace behavior or women's experiences seeking abortions, but the narrative content of series is not confined to overtly topical themes or polemical tones. For example, on *Girls* the character Jessa's abortion appointment is darkly comic, whereas the character Annie's abortion is depicted plaintively on *Shrill*. Since the 2022 overturning of the *Roe* decision future series might depict reproductive access differently to mirror the renewed advocacy for women's reproductive rights.

The malleable nature of feminism itself speaks to the way numerous authors have enumerated the critical dead end of assessing cultural texts along a rigid political axis. Pender's discussion of *Buffy the Vampire Slayer* questions the logic of "the transgression/containment model" in which characters are "good" if they transgress dominant stereotypes and "bad" if "contained in cultural cliché," which artificially restricts ways of interpreting a series.[25] Beyond "ideological purity" lies a more fruitful opportunity to "harness the energy they bring to viewers so as to push the cultural conversation about women in more genuinely progressive directions." Indeed, boiling down every text "to its patriarchal capitalist white supremacist skeleton" is "rote" and ineffectual even if this feigns "as if revealing something new."[26] Differences in generation, economic access, and social location also color perceptions of what constitutes "authentic" or "legitimate" feminism.

Finally, we must place media and popular culture in context. While television is ubiquitous and powerful it is not the nexus of political organizing. Rather than burdening it with this responsibility it is more credible to examine its possibilities. Dow reminds us "we need to appreciate media for what it can do in giving us images of strong women; yet, at the same time, we need to maintain a very keen sense of the limitations of media logic."[27] Even then "strong" could be understood as too narrow for the ways it disallows vulnerability, struggle, and uncertainty as part of women's experiences and representations. I optimistically share Hagelin and Silverman's view that for many audiences, viewing contemporary women-centric series "may become inquisitive, engaged, and hailed within a community of like-minded others, eager to process and discuss the shows they see. This is no formula against complacency, but it does suggest that lifestyle feminism has a role to play in the larger struggle for emancipatory politics."[28]

To return to my earlier point: What is possible when examining women-centric series of the 2010s–2020s? Placing genealogies of feminist-oriented television series in conversation with contemporary discourse on the television form and industrial shifts in popular media allows us to further place these 2010–20 era series in their proper contexts.

## "Good" and "Complex" Postfeminist Era Television

We could accurately frame the series this book focuses on as emerging during the postfeminist era of television, which overlaps the emergence of several critical perspectives on the maturation of television as a form. These include the term "quality television," the notion of television's "cinematization," the process of television's "legitimation," and the theory of "complex television." These are separate concepts and I explore them briefly to establish the most useful framework for understanding the series this book examines. The backdrop of these shifts occurred as the audience for broadcast television declined as viewing options expanded, including video on demand and streaming services, thus they are also products of the postnetwork television era.[29] I explore this further in chapter 1, so this section addresses the association of television programs within the "quality television" paradigm.

Television scholars commonly associate "quality television" with media studies scholar Robert Thompson.[30] Integral to his analysis is its *lack* of a clear definition. Cardwell, however, argues that "quality television" is understood as a generic term more recognizable for our "observation and apprehension of textual qualities than on our immediate, subjective responses." These "quality" aesthetic markers include serious themes, high production values, naturalistic performances, accomplished actors, and a distinctive visual style and sound design. "Quality television" is also understood in media industries as shorthand for programming with demographic appeal to "the 'quality audience,' the educated, upscale, urbane demographic."[31]

The most common critique of the concept is its reinforcing of taste hierarchies. For example, Cardwell cites a British television critic who suspects the term is little more than a "middle brow" term attempting to distinguish certain commercial products from others.[32] Mittell also pinpoints its muddled implications noting the hierarchy implied and the lack of critical value "either as a textual category with analytic or evaluative precision or as a label for how television circulates culturally."[33] Both scholars also challenge the assumption that "quality" equals "good" given that many quality television series may have high production values but are experienced as "dull, conventional, or pretentious."[34] The broader issue they both point toward is a more transparent conversation about what actually makes television satisfying, resonant, or simply "good" for viewers, which is distinguishable from the "quality" genre.

A similar type of critical skepticism has met the term "cinematic." The notion of television's critical "legitimation" is tied to the hiring of filmmakers and screenwriters, the elevation of television showrunners as "auteurs," and the use of film techniques in television production, both of which imbue television with a new level of cachet by association.[35]

The cinematic argument has some notable limitations. Mills and Jaramillo note how it presumes that film and television conventions and norms are, or have ever been, "stable" categories, overlooks the different technical specifications of television and film such as picture resolution, glosses over ways the film industry has borrowed from television, such as editing techniques, only applies "cinematic" to television drama, and equates "cinematic" elements are with narrative "quality." These notions reinforce the hierarchy of television as "film's poor relation." The critical subtext of challenging the film and television hierarchy is the value of exploring television's distinctive qualities as a medium, such as the communal viewing experiences tied to television's liveness and the wide range of techniques (e.g., multiple-camera and single camera approaches to comedies) television series employ.[36] Numerous scholars have focused on television's unique aesthetics and developed useful concepts such as "spectacular television" and "women's indie television" that have expanded the range of critical tools for understanding television as a medium.[37]

If "quality," "legitimate," and "cinematic" are insufficient terms for framing the aesthetic value of the programs studied, "good" and "complex" offer useful alternatives. Two alternatives to the maturation discourse that illuminate my selection and framing of the series I examine are interrelated. First, the critical desire to articulate an aesthetics of television as a medium independent of "elevating" it through analogies to other forms (e.g., film). A critical step in articulating television's distinctive identity is to analyze and discuss programs that exemplify aspects of its potential. My readings attend to this concern in multiple ways by addressing the industrial and social contexts that produced them in concert with the aesthetic innovations they represent. Curating a list of exemplary television series to develop a book-length argument is a selective process by definition, and there is value in addressing the logic behind my selections. Simply put, on a descriptive level the series I explore share notable characteristics, and one of these characteristics is that these series are "good." They are watchable, compelling, relevant, and represent important values Cardwell and Mittell illuminate, which is the second element of the alternative maturation discourse.

This second dimension is a shift from the illusion of "objective" television criticism toward one where scholars and critics acknowledge the evaluative aspect of the programs they study. Mittell defines evaluation as, "the active process of engaging with aesthetic criteria, textual features, and cultural circulation."[38] In this mode scholars recognize their social location and biases and address what they believe makes a program "good" and worth examining with attention to form and content.

The most consistent standard scholars have articulated about "goodness" relates to what Cardwell refers to as stylistic integrity, notably, "a high level of synthesis and cohesion between stylistic choices and the programs' 'meanings.'" Camera movements, musical choices, and editing are examples of stylistic choices "coherent with the program as a whole and the moment in which they are contained." They contribute to the way viewers experience different programs' meanings by enabling "us to regard our lives slightly differently, especially in terms of the relationship (of whatever kind) between the physical and practical elements of life and the ideals and ideas not customarily visible but that are nevertheless determining."[39] Mittell unpacks the concept of "good" television through thoughtful readings of *The Wire* and *Breaking Bad*. Mirroring Cardwell's discussion of style and meaning he engages the series to "tease out qualities of complexity and each series manages to succeed in accomplishing its own ambitious aesthetic approach" rather than comparing them or trying to establish their universal value among television dramas.[40]

The emphasis on stylistic integrity and aesthetic coherence is central to the appeal and watchability of the series I examine. Though they may differ in subject each program is highly *stylized*, and their internal stylistic integrity imbues them with an unusually distinct and coherent voice aesthetically. The *collective* efforts of the creative staffs of television programs shapes their execution, which limits the utility of the "auteur" theory prevalent in film studies despite our predilection to privilege single authorship.[41] A more fitting approach is to recognize how many of the creators of the series cultivated a distinctive voice *prior* to working in television through independent films, YouTube videos, journalism, and/or other arenas of expression. The presence, rather than the dominance, of this strong authorial voice makes the series unique in tone and execution without diminishing the collaborative nature of television production.

The distinctive authorial voices of woman-identified creatives, in concert with their creative partners, of various genders, including Rachel Bloom and Aline Brosh McKenna (*Crazy Ex-Girlfriend*); Michela Coel (*I May Destroy You*); Lena Dunham and Jenni Konner (*Girls*); Ilana Glazer and Abbi Jacobson (*Broad City*); Issa Rae and Larry Wilmore, who identifies as a man (*Insecure*); have opened up television to a different kind of storytelling. Tracing these discernibly women informed grammars of early twenty-first-century television is key to this book's critical aspiration. Though I limit my scope to a set of programs with specific characteristics, including their focus on Millennial generation characters, the production and writing of Sharon Horgan (*Pulling*, 2006–9, BBC 3; *Catastrophe*, 2015–19, Channel 4; *This Way Up*, 2019, 2021, Channel 4) and Lena Waithe (*Master of None*, 2015, 2017, 2021, Netflix), and the performances of contemporary actresses Aya Cash (*You're the Worst*, 2014–19, FX and FXX), and Zazie Beetz (*Atlanta*, 2016–22, FX) are also strands of this women-centric "good and complex" television. Further, most of the series I discuss have been recognized by various professional academies and guilds, and television critics, marking them tacitly as "quality," but their value transcends these measures.[42] I am confident they have inspired other shows and authors to tell aesthetically coherent, women-centered stories that speak to the cultural moment both currently and, most likely, in the future.

Both the awareness of the range of emergent feminisms present in the series and their good and complex aesthetics allows us to delve into ways prior women-centric series—notably *Ally McBeal*, *Buffy the Vampire Slayer*, and *Sex and the City*—have shaped the terrain among a newer generation of series that emerged in the 2010s onward.

## Borrowing and Responding: Contemporary Responses to *Ally*, *Sex*, and *Buffy*

Building from prior references to "lifestyle feminism," let's return to the symbolic pillars of postfeminism *Ally McBeal* and *Sex and the City* because engaging them opens the door for my critical project. *Ally McBeal* and *Sex and the City* became major subjects for critical discourse from the late 1990s through the present. The White, upper-class, and individualist biases, and contradictory sexuality, of these series is one of the more consistent critical threads noted previously. Similarly, *Buffy the Vampire Slayer* is a popular topic of television studies scholarship relevant to my discussion.[43] Though it is less controversial among feminist media scholars than *Ally* and *Sex*, for reasons related to genre and narrative content, its stylization and relationship to feminist dynamics affirms its relevance for contemporary women-centric programming.[44]

Two notable aspects of these shows are particularly helpful for my analysis of 2010s–2020s era series. First, is their innovative use of music, fantasy, and surrealism, techniques that paved the way for many live action comedic series to push the form, including *Crazy Ex-Girlfriend* and *Broad City*. Second, is the discourse regarding how they depicted contemporary women's anxieties, including critiques of their lack of racial and sexual diversity. Whereas *Ally* and *Sex* focused on the shifting negotiations of adult women aspiring professionally, seeking fulfilling intimate lives, and developing a sense of self as topics worthy of weekly episodic exploration, *Buffy* focused more on female adolescence. Though many critics dismissed *Ally* and *Sex* as "distorted" versions of feminism, including their Whiteness, they are important touchstones for understanding the direction of more recent contemporary women-centric series.[45] *Buffy*'s challenges such as its lack of racially diverse and complex characters are also relevant here.

Stylistically, the synthesis of visual and aural techniques with traditional dialogue and "real time" action is an aspect of *Ally* and *Buffy* that illuminated the potential of telling women-centric stories within the form. Too often the formal aspects of women-centric programs are elided to emphasize their fidelity to certain feminist principles. This is an overlooked, though growing, site of analysis that might illuminate the aesthetic and cultural impact of these shows on the programs that followed.[46] The fusion of genre elements, creative interpolations of music, the way fantasy sequences complicate the tension between public and private affects, and narrative devices such as flashbacks and montages, are examples of formal elements that enhance our willingness to engage with serious topics within and beyond a text. For example, the narrative potential of the dramedy form pioneered by *Ally* and integral to the "cringe" tone of series such as *Fleabag*, *Girls*, and *Insecure*, the use of "feminine camp" in *Buffy*, the narrative role of fantasy in *Ally*, the layered ways humor enriches topical subjects in *Sex and the City*, and the ways music enhances the already "heightened reality" of programs like *Ally*, *Buffy*, and *Xena: Warrior Princess* (1995–2001, Syndicated) exemplify some of the important conversations about television aesthetics this study employs in its analysis.[47]

In terms of content, while many more contemporary shows borrow from the intimate, quotidian aspects of *Ally* and *Sex*, and tonal aspects of *Buffy*, we need to examine how contemporary women-centric shows have *responded to* and *challenged* some of their deficiencies or biases. For example, the multicultural casting and extensive character development of the women on Netflix's *Orange Is the New Black* depicts a remarkably broad range of experiences of many different kinds of women, including Asian American, Black, Latinx, queer, poor, middle-class, aged, and/or undocumented women's experiences. This includes narrative attention to their experiences inside and prior to imprisonment. HBO's *Insecure* and *I May Destroy You* center on African American and Black British characters, respectively. They are multicultural series, and while characters of multiple races are featured in well-developed secondary roles, the shows acknowledge *race* without making *racism* their center or educating White audiences about Blackness. *Girls* and *I May Destroy You* also challenge the sexually benign landscape depicted in many urban women-centric shows. *Girls*' early seasons often depicted consensual heterosexual sexual encounters between lead character Hannah Horvath and her boyfriend Adam Sackler that were uncomfortable, aggressive, and ambiguous in intent. *I May* places rape, sexual violence, and trauma at its center throughout the entire series and presents sexual violence, and associated traumas, as ongoing challenges for women, and queer men.

The creatives behind women-centric series are aware of their "new woman" television predecessors and the "postfeminist" sensibilities that inform *Ally*, *Sex*, and *Buffy*. They have, however, updated the formal elements and content of these series to meet the needs of today. Similarly, they are aware of both continuing feminist activist issues that span the different "waves" and emerging ones.

Many showrunners and creative personnel identify as feminists through their beliefs and actions. For example, Nash and Grant describe Lena Dunham's self-identification as a feminist writer, activist work in reproductive rights, and leading of an all-female writing team, to illustrate feminism's direct impact on showrunners.[48] Gerhard's notion about how television series "shadowbox" with various aspects of feminism is apropos as it captures how feminism can inform a program in various ways even if it is not a central storyline.[49] As new variations of feminism emerge they clearly strive to converse with the past and adapt to contemporary sensibilities. This is especially important for understanding the respectful yet critical relationship of third-wave feminism to second-wave feminism. Feminist principles might inform the practices of cultural production in terms of writers, producers, casting agents, music supervisors, and other roles. Even if creative personnel advocate for feminism in their lives this does not mean feminism is always the most dominant or salient creative force even if it informs, infuses, and inflects programs. For example, several of the Latina identified actresses cast on *Orange Is the New Black* challenged stereotypical depictions, which led to changes in how characters were written and developed.[50]

Rather than translating feminist elements in literal or didactic modes, or in tokenizing fashion, contemporary showrunners have advanced the more serialized nature of today's "complex television" by integrating the quotidian aspects of female-identified people into their series. Most of these series are "dramedies" whose showrunners integrate feminism in a variety of ways.

For example, *Girls* constantly pushes boundaries in depicting young (mostly White) women's navigations of contemporary sexual politics, including the way men "gaslight" women sexually, and does so by employing subtle, "unspectacular" techniques that do not draw attention to their formal elements. In "American Bitch" (6.3), *Girls* employs Hannah's professional status as an emerging writer to address the way so-called cancel culture intersects with the #MeToo movement. The unusually tense, haunting, and disturbing tone garnered considerable attention for its topicality and its pivot from the show's usually casual tone.[51] Comparatively, *Crazy Ex-Girlfriend* uses music, choreography, and an ironic comic sensibility to capture the stigma of mental illness for women throughout its four-year run. While mental illness is a serious concern with unique impacts on women's sense of self-worth and productivity and how others perceive them (see: the show's title), the show uses a range of tools such as humor and the inherent surrealism of musicals rather than addressing it in an earnest or stentorian fashion. The show's approach to a "topical" concern is characteristic rather than an isolated instance.

Even beyond overt references many women-centric series of the first decade of the twenty-first century evoke the socioeconomic context of the era. For example, numerous scholars have tied shows like Issa Rae's web series *The Misadventures of Awkward Black Girl*, *Girls*, and *Broad City* to the post-2008 recession. Notably, they have described how the characters' attitudes about the dashed promise of financial stability and romantic fulfillment constitute a discernibly "precarious" existence and anti-aspirationalism significantly different from the ambitious characters of "new women" series like *The Mary Tyler Moore Show*.[52]

Instead of approaching feminist concerns in traditionally "serious" genres, such as documentary, or employing an isolated "topical" approach, the contemporary shows have channeled their energies through more experimental approaches. By blending drama with comedy, integrating animation, music, and choreography, employing digital technologies, and drawing from independent film, contemporary women-centric series incorporate a more layered form of comedy beyond the formulaic nature of the traditional network sitcom with its predictable rhythms, an A and B storyline, and laugh track. The contemporary shows are not necessarily catalysts for policy, legislation, or social movement actions, even when the creative team's members identify as activists. The forms they use, however, deftly depict elements uniquely resonant with different women's experiences.

## Negotiated Readings

*Broads, Sisters, Exes* is composed of close textual readings of a select group of television series I label as "sisters." I use the term in quotation marks because each show is executive produced or run by women-led creative teams and share a narrative focus on women-centered characters and storylines. It simultaneously recognizes the limits of an imagined universal womanhood or sisterhood. As Kendall argues, "A one-size-fits all approach to feminism is damaging, because it alienates the very people it is supposed to serve, without ever managing to support them. For women of color, the expectation that we prioritize gender over race, that we treat patriarchy as something that gives all men the same power, leaves many of us feeling isolated."[53] Relatedly, many media studies scholars have noted how liberal White feminist-identified creatives often lack self-awareness about racial nuance. Even when showrunners create "well-meaning White lady" characters, we might find "white women trying to be inclusive and antiracist but falling short by overemphasizing their own emotional reactions to other people's suffering or by asking for people of color to educate and support them on their journey to understand inequality and advocate for change."[54] The visibility of "straight, white, cis-gender, able-bodied, conventionally pretty women" has also raised concerns about "the limited version of feminism that attains mainstream mediated visibility."[55]

For this study, recognizing the complexity of women's experiences is integral to examining women-authored and women-centered works because woman is always an intersectional and dynamic category. Women embody their identities in disparate ways that necessitate nuanced understandings of the diverse stories each series tells and the varied approaches their creative teams employ. The overlaps and divergences among the series are not merely benign paradoxes. They offer a unique opportunity to think about women's authorship complexly. The oscillations between how White/women of color, straight/queer women, cisgender/gender variant women, and American/British women tell stories on television pushes us to the limits and possibilities of identities in new and interesting ways.

The book's analysis adapts Johnson's "negotiated reading" approach, which acknowledges "the kinds of pleasure available to women in the current media culture includes the pleasures of oppositional reading as well as the pleasures of seeing feminist concepts dramatized on television."[56] Many of the creative teams behind acclaimed, contemporary women-centric series of the 2010–2020s are keenly aware of issues affecting women's lives based on their public affiliations, statements, and/or commitments. As writers, producers, and/or directors they have found creative ways to translate aspects of feminist thought and practice into their art, including the composition of their creative and production staffs, and program content. Examining how their aesthetic and creative choices allowed them to tell new stories in innovative ways is thus central to my focus.

The aesthetics of the "good" and "complex" series employ different registers of spectacle ranging from techniques borrowed from the "filmic spectacle" of classic Hollywood musicals (e.g., *Crazy Ex-Girlfriend*) to the "unspectacular" style (e.g., *Girls*) informed by US indie films. In between these poles are numerous elements, including animation, aural layering, integration of social media, and metaconscious aspects, which inform the narrative approach. My critical emphasis on the aesthetics of the series illuminates the nature and range of storytelling choices in shows that "are clearly pro-woman and negotiate feminist ideas" rather than positioning them as the *exclusive* province of woman identified creatives.[57]

The relationship of pleasure and power allows us to pay intricate attention to how television series employ a range of formal and aesthetic tools to illuminate, challenge, interrogate, and sometimes reinforce, a range of social arrangements. The shifting nature of the medium itself, including shifts in how it can be accessed creatively and who has access to create programming, also signifies important aspects of social dynamics.

This is a comparative study that originated with an analysis of *Crazy Ex-Girlfriend*. Best described as a musical dramedy with original music and choreography, a multicultural cast, and topical narrative threads it debuted in the mid-'00s to great acclaim. Though it is not unique in defying genre and experimenting with formal innovations it is arguably the most ambitious and metaconscious of the series studied in drawing from musical theater, Hollywood film musicals, romantic comedies, commercial music videos, YouTube videos, and various popular music genres to tell its four-season story. Integral to these stories is a highly cultivated metaconsciousness or hyperconsciousness rife with self-referential media allusions, pastiche, and parody.[58] Thematically, *Crazy Ex-Girlfriend*'s storylines address a wide range of contemporary social navigations, including contemporary iterations of feminism, racial and economic privilege, sexual diversity, mental health stigmas, and the impact of social media, among others. The ambitious synthesis of audiovisual style and topicality intrigued me and helped me expand beyond the series to other innovative women-centric programs.

An important aspect of *Crazy Ex-Girlfriend* is the way it strategically decentered its White, straight, cisgender protagonist, Rebecca, and made room for its supporting characters, including two women of color, Heather (Vella Lovell) and Vanessa (Gabrielle Ruiz). Whereas *Ally*, *Buffy*, and *Sex* centered on White straight female subjectivity with rare exception, newer shows often acknowledge and decenter White normativity by shifting the focus from their White leads to tell stories of overlooked women more fully. *Orange Is the New Black* increasingly decentered its White lead Piper Chapman (Taylor Schilling) in the second of its seven seasons. For example, the character Susan "Crazy Eyes" Warren (Uzo Aduba), an African American queer woman with developmental and mental health struggles and a complex backstory conveyed through flashbacks, is arguably more complex and iconic than Piper. Similarly, the complex storyline of a Black woman transgender inmate, Sophia Burset (Laverne Cox), spurred a national conversation about gender identity.[59] On *Shrill*, lead character Annie Easton's (Aidy Bryant) best friend Fran (Lolly Adefope) is a lesbian of Nigerian descent who has a professional, intimate, and family life, and the series gives her substantive storylines, including an episode focused on her family. Similarly, *Crazy Ex-Girlfriend* slyly acknowledges Rebecca's obliviousness to her socioeconomic privileges with characters and situations that often confront her into addressing her privilege, a key theme of its final season.

Just as many of the series perform this critical work internally, the chapters similarly pivot to illuminate themes beyond the White, middle-class normative lens that dominates studies of postfeminist-era series. What interests me is not simply "diversity" but rather how shows are holding those with dominant identities accountable for the social space they occupy as well as how series led by and focused on women of color tell stories cognizant of White dominance but not limited to reacting to Whiteness. For example, *Insecure*'s showrunner, Issa Rae, has intentionally created space for Black awkwardness, quirkiness, and ordinariness.[60] Though *Jane the Virgin*'s showrunner Jennie Snyder Urman is a White woman, the series explores a gamut of concerns particular to the multigenerational Venezuelan American female family, including sexual mores, familial expectations, and spirituality, in a manner that acknowledges racism and xenophobia without limiting its focus to them. The "good" and "complex" principle linking the series entails more incisive attention to the form and the scope of representing women.

## The Study's Parameters

*Broads, Sisters, Exes* examines the formal, narrative, and thematic qualities of nine "good" and "complex" women-centric dramedies that aired on US television and streaming services from 2012 to 2020. The dramedies studied tell the stories of women characters primarily and were led or co-led creatively by women in showrunner and/or executive producer roles. Additionally, many of these creatives regularly advocate for greater industry representation for minoritized people in television, including hiring women in multiple creative roles.

The study is limited to series written primarily in English and focuses on seven series produced in the United States; it also includes two joint productions between the BBC and US-based media companies. The book's inclusion of two iconic British series informs my discussion of the British broadcast industry's gradual shift from public ownership to more privatized structures and the transnational nature of contemporary television in chapter 1. Finally, the series differ in key details such as plots, characters, and locations, but are unified by a discernible feminist sensibility transmitted through innovative approaches to storytelling that have expanded the vocabulary of contemporary television. It's worth noting that several Generation X showrunners, including Tina Fey, Shonda Rhimes, and Amy Sherman-Palladino, played a significant role in the '00s, making women more legible as showrunners to the industry and viewing public and ushering feminist elements into comedic and dramedic characters, work that Press describes masterfully in her 2018 study of women creatives.[61]

Given these parameters there are numerous series I do not include. These exclusions are based on the era in which characters are living (e.g., *The Marvelous Mrs. Maisel*), a generational focus beyond Millennials (e.g., *One Mississippi*, *Transparent*, *Younger*), and/or conventional genre aesthetics (e.g., *The Mindy Project*). Comedian Awkwafina's *Awkwafina Is Nora from Queens*, which premiered on Comedy Central in

2020, reflects the urban, coming-of-age sensibilities evident in several of the nine series featured, though its focus on an Asian American lead character is unique. Stylistically and thematically it is arguably more exemplary in execution than innovative compared to the half-hour series that preceded it such as *Girls*, *Broad City*, and *Insecure*. As a series that is still airing, as of this writing, its narrative arc and ultimate influence remain open-ended.

Several series feature compelling Millennial generation women in lead or supporting roles, including *Atlanta*, *Master of None*, *Shameless*, and *You're the Worst*, yet do not tell primarily women-centered stories and are led creatively by man-identified showrunners. Additionally, several women-centered comedic series, notably Amy Schumer's *Inside Amy Schumer*, and Robin Thiede's *Black Lady Sketch Show*, are iconic examples of Millennial women's innovative approaches to comedy. As sketch comedy series, however, their structure falls outside of the character development and serialized storylines central to the series this book examines. Throughout the book I note more recent post-2020 series discernibly influenced by the series I address, including *Everything's Trash*, *Harlem*, *Single Drunk Female* (2022–23, Freeform), and *Somebody Somewhere* (2022–present, HBO), but these fall outside of the 2012–20 period.

*Broads, Sisters, Exes* is composed of chapters centered on a series of close readings of key episodes from the series brought together based on notable shared qualities in their storytelling. These include chapters focused on television series linked by the uses of the following: US "indie" film aesthetics, genre homages, musical pastiche, surreal visual effects, and different orders of time such as flashbacks and the breaking of the fourth wall.

Though my study situates the series in historical contexts of women in comedy, which includes critical attention to the changing nature of the television industry, my study is not a chronological history of women in contemporary television. Nor does it intend to serve as the definitive history of each individual series as such a project exceeds the critical scope of this study. Several series have already generated books and edited collections, and many have garnered critical attention among scholars of feminism and media studies, and beyond, which hopefully illustrates the critical relevance of these series for a variety of scholars.

By definition I offer capsule histories of each series emphasizing how their genesis and development informs their aesthetic. Structurally, my analyses focus more on depth than breadth by emphasizing key formal, thematic, and narrative characteristics that define each show. The chapters typically focus on a key episode and illustrate how it represents the formal approach of the series. Because most series establish their formal and thematic blueprints in their debut seasons, I tend to focus my analysis on a specific episode and/or notable episodic moments from the earlier seasons, with exceptions. Because many "quality" or "prestige" series developed modest audiences through critical acclaim, word-of-mouth, and industry buzz their inaugural seasons are pivotal to their ability to build an audience and endurance beyond one season.

The primary exception is the BBC One and HBO coproduction *I May Destroy You*, which aired for a single season on HBO and is composed of twelve episodes. British series tend to have abbreviated seasons compared to US counterparts. Similarly, the BBC and Amazon Prime series *Fleabag*, also analyzed in the book, is a two-season series composed of twelve episodes total. Given these production contexts and parallels, as well as its myriad innovations, I decided to include *I May Destroy You*.

## Chapter Descriptions

The next chapter, "Gains from 'Losses': Mining the Monoculture for New Narrative Possibilities," chronicles how the US television industry's shift from the network to the "postnetwork" era parallels its increasing focus on niche over mass audiences. I link this to changes in the interplay between British and American television programming. The postnetwork shift, alongside technological developments such as user-generated content sites like YouTube, engendered more opportunities for burgeoning creatives. This was less a political shift than the industry's response to a market more focused on demographic resonance and media buzz than traditional metrics like ratings. The transition from web series to network, cable, and/or streaming series was not a linear process for the newer showrunners, but the period depicted represented a discernible pivot for different creative voices. Many of the issues the Screen Actors Guild–American Federation of Television and Radio Artists (SAG-AFTRA) and Writers Guild of America (WGA) strikes of 2023 raise about proper compensation and the use of technological tools such as Artificial Intelligence (AI) add complexity to how we understand the dynamics of the postnetwork era.[62]

Chapter 2, "Low-Key like an Indie Film," explores the way "good" and "complex" series often adapt aesthetic aspects borrowed from the "unspectacular" production style and narrative approach of 1989–2010 "indie" cinema. These include their use of "blank style" in camera, framing, and editing, emphasis on character development over plot, and focus on emotional spectacle in mundane settings and situations. The chapter's episodic analysis places *Girls*, *Shrill*, and *Insecure* in conversation with Ford's 2019 analysis of the women-centric dramedy genre. I explore the stylistic and thematic innovations of *Girls*, which debuted the earliest among the series and created a new space for urban postbaccalaureate women's negotiations of emerging adulthood in a serialized comedic form. The reading emphasizes its deft use of dialogue and signature visual techniques to depict characters' transitions into adulthood. My discussion of *Shrill* centers on the way it uses the indie template *Girls* established to bridge personal and political issues. Notably, its approach to interracial friendship dynamic, fat stigma, and the polarized nature of media stretches the women-centric dramedy from its usual insularity toward greater engagement with larger social issues in an intimate manner. The concluding analysis of *Insecure* expands on Ford's original argument by exploring how the Whiteness of the "indie" cinema world, and the series it has inspired, necessitates several significant critical interventions by the showrunners and creative team behind *Insecure*. The series centers Black Millennial women's subjectivity in its dialogue, setting, music, and themes, and subtly, and humorously, acknowledges the quotidian specter of racial microaggressions.

Chapter 3, "Got to Be (Sur)Real: 'Remixing' Gender through Genre," explores how three "good" and "complex" series employ a wide range of metaconscious and surreal techniques to center Millennial women and simultaneously challenge the gendered aspects of genres. I explore how *Crazy Ex-Girlfriend* synthesizes elements of musical theater, romantic comedy, popular music song structures, and popular music videos to challenge tropes of these genres. I trace the ways *Broad City*'s highly stylized fusion of the "stoner comedy" and "women's buddy comedy" genres are subverted through its play with film tropes, hip-hop iconography, and surreal aural and visual distortions, and its central duo's personae update the "unruly" woman personae. The narrative tensions between highly gendered cultural traditions emphasizing family and faith, and contemporary opportunities for women to exercise personal and professional autonomy are central to *Jane the Virgin*. I explore how these themes inform its knowing blend of melodramatic serialized forms, notably soap operas and telenovelas, with the intricate aesthetic awareness of contemporary complex television. Central to this chapter are the artful ways each series deconstructs and subverts genre elements to illuminate a broader range of possibilities for women's relationality, especially in areas of friendship, intimate relationships, family, and individual development.

Chapter 4: "All in the Timing: Temporal Play and Women's Hidden Subjectivities," examines how *Fleabag*, *I May Destroy You*, and *Orange Is the New Black* actively "play" with traditional narrative temporality to tell stories that defy conventions of female character archetypes and challenge genre conventions. *Fleabag*'s breaking of the fourth wall and reliance on flashbacks told from the perspective of its titular lead offer bold alternatives to the tropes of "likability" and conventions of women's friendships common to comedies centered on women. *I May Destroy You*'s interspersing of flashbacks, social media time, and flash sideways constitute a radical reinvention of how the trauma of sexual assault is depicted on television. The series narrative emphasis on the pervasiveness of different forms of sexual trauma through the experiences of Black British Millennials, including two women and one queer man, expands the scope of stories told within the Millennial television paradigm. Finally, the chapter capitalizes on the lyric refrain of *OITNB*'s theme song "You've Got Time" by exploring how it centers flashbacks into its narrative architecture. Over seven seasons it transitioned from its initial focus on its White upper-middle-class protagonist to tell the story of less visible women. I trace the elevation of Tasha "Taystee" Washington, a Black inmate of the Millennial generation whose story depicts many signposts of systemic racism and economic struggle, from a supporting character to one of its most complex and important characters. These three series illustrate how the use of temporal play, an element seen in several other series in the study, generates unique opportunities for narrative richness and character development.

"Coda: Pivots, Influences, Challenges, and Possibilities" concludes the study by assessing how the creative pivots the book outlines have shaped more recent women-centric television creators and aesthetics. Many of the narrative themes and aesthetic approaches the 2012–20 "good" and "complex" series pioneered have coalesced into a rich menu of options for writers, producers, and directors seeking to tell engaging stories about women. Though many of the series discussed in the current study feature queer women and conclude with storylines beyond the heteronormative family structures, I discuss the increasing prominence of trans, gender nonconforming, and nonbinary voices among television's storytellers and performers.

The Coda acknowledges these gains as well as the enduring challenges of deeply ingrained racial and gender biases, among others, in the US and UK television and film industries that inhibit access to resources for people of color whose racial and ethnic identities coexist with various categories of gender, ability, sexuality, and nationality. These systemic biases have inspired awareness campaigns and advocacy for greater diversity and more authentic inclusion of underrepresented voices especially women and people of color. Many of these efforts have resulted in more overt efforts for inclusion and accountability by media organizations and broadcasters, policy changes within professional academies, and the proliferation of talent development programs. The overlap of these efforts with post-2020 political backlashes against progressivism and renewed advocacy for greater compensation by actors and writers struggling with the inequitable economics of the "postnetwork" era media industry highlights the unique opening of 2012–20 and the need for ongoing vigilance for gender and racial equity.

# 1

# Gains from "Losses"

## *Mining the Monoculture for New Narrative Possibilities*

The "good" and "complex" series I discuss in the following chapters would not exist without the industry's dual recognition that certain niche audiences exist to consume shows *and* its interest in them being sufficiently appealing to be profitable or viable financially. Structurally, three series originate from streaming services (*Fleabag*, *Orange Is the New Black*, *Shrill*), three from premium cable channels (*Girls*, *I May Destroy You*, *Insecure*), two from linear broadcast television networks (*Crazy Ex-Girlfriend*, *Jane the Virgin*), and one (*Broad City*) from basic cable. These formats have different economic models. Further, while some of the showrunners were discovered through experience in independent film (Lena Dunham), and web series (Rachel Bloom, Ilana Glazer and Abbi Jacobson, Issa Rae), others were adapted from existing literature (*Orange Is the New Black* and *Shrill*) or television series (*Jane the Virgin*) by established showrunners.

The conventional approach to cultural studies focuses on ideological elements often with limited consideration of television's aesthetics. Additionally, cultural studies scholars have long drawn on methods based in the "mass media" era when fewer media choices meant popular texts had a broad reach measurable by ratings, thus potential ideological impacts. As Lotz reminds us the technological diversification of how and when we view television content, and the long-held reluctance of streaming services to share audience data necessitates different approaches to assessing impact and cultural relevance.[1] Industrial changes, including the newfound profitability of "niche" audiences, altered the aesthetic possibilities of television, including what stories are told and who gets to tell them. Ideological strands related to social identity are integral, after all this is a book about women and their intersections with various social categories of experience, and yet my focus is necessarily broader because the content of their stories is inseparable from their aesthetic composition.

Women comprise approximately half of the US population, and yet popular culture focused on and/or directed toward women is frequently perceived as "niche." What was once a marginalizing notion, however, has gradually destabilized the notion of mainstream or mass culture and expanded access for a wider range of creatives. The transition of US and British media industries from focusing on the "mass audience" toward appeals to "niche" audiences is well captured by Chris Anderson's "long tail" theory. He carefully notes, "This shift from the generic to the specific doesn't mean the end of the existing power structures or a wholesale shift to an all-amateur, laptop culture. Instead it's simply a rebalancing of the equation, an evolution from an 'Or' era of hits or niches (mainstream culture vs. subcultures) to an 'And' era. . . . Mass culture will not fall, it will simply get less mass. And niche culture will get less obscure."[2]

Despite the creative possibilities niche culture has unearthed, critical discourse about the decline of a unifying monoculture in the United States has persisted. Scholars such as Robert Putnam have raised broad concerns about the decline of civic engagement and communal values in the United States and tied these trends to declining trust in civic institutions, technological changes, and various social movements.[3] Several media critics, such as Alain Sylvain, have linked it strongly to popular culture and noted that society's reliance on popular culture has traditionally made it an important source of shared identification, and the increased fragmentation has polarized the nation into echo chambers.[4]

The notion of a cultural decline coincides with the increasing visibility of women, people of color, and other minoritized communities in popular media in the United Kingdom and the United States. I find the decline rhetoric unconvincing for three reasons. First, it ignores the constructed nature of the so-called monoculture. Second, it overlooks deeply entrenched social divisions and perceptions that preceded the digital era, particularly the digitally informed postnetwork era of television I'm addressing. Third, and most relevant to *Broads, Sisters, Exes*, it fails to offer a critical perspective on how the nichification of popular culture has opened doors for creatives, often from historically minoritized populations, to offer more innovative original work that resonates with previously overlooked audiences. These observations shape chapter 1's focus on the industrial and cultural factors that made the series I discuss viable.

The rise of innovative and inclusive programs is not a simple triumph of do-it-yourself (DIY) independent culture over a bland corporate monoculture. Creatives seeking outlets enter into an industry highly strategic about the nature of its audience, what it's willing to invest in and engage with, and always seeking models for profit. Quality and innovation can be enabled but are not inevitable.

## Deconstructing Common Culture (and Meditations on the New Monoculture)

Anderson's optimism must be understood as an outgrowth of his cleareyed understanding of the constructed aspect of the monoculture. As he notes, "What we thought was the rising tide of common culture turned out to be less about the triumph of Hollywood talent and more to do with the shepherding effect of broadcast distribution." Despite the nostalgia for the loss of a monoculture, a closer look reveals, "It wasn't that everyone wanted to watch primetime *Seinfeld*, but that's what was on, and it became universal by default." By recognizing how linear broadcast network's media dominance contributed to the artificial perception of cultural unity we are also primed to acknowledge the needs of audiences *underserved* by mass media, which could only serve so many interests.[5]

Audiences interested in more sophisticated television have arguably *existed* for decades, but industrial forces have limited their access. For example, Lotz has explained how independent producers were only able to produce shows for the big three broadcast networks through legislation from the 1970s, which broke up networks' monopoly on production and syndication. As a result, television matured through the more topical and culturally relevant productions of independents, notably Norman Lear's Tandem Productions and MTM Enterprises.[6]

In the decades after this opening, cable channels pushed television's creative boundaries. The combination of increased cable subscriptions, the development of convenience technologies, the rise of streaming services, and the mobility afforded to viewers through multiple devices have redefined the nature of television and forced broadcast networks to adapt. They had to figure out how to embrace niche tastes and the prized content these niches favor and still remain profitable. Their ability to do so is best interpreted as strategic, not necessarily an altruistic, ideological, or political pivot. Prized content is content audiences are willing to pay for so the content on basic and premium cable, and subscription services, has to distinguish itself from network content by definition to justify itself. As such network content has to offer viewers something extraordinary to compete.

Broadcast television's embrace of demographics was part and parcel of its experiment with "Quality TV" in the 1980s, which entailed responding to more competition by altering "the network business, from changes of ownership to techniques of audience measurement. Many of these developments furthered the movements toward niche audience targeting and programming with demographically specific appeals." Examples of this pivot toward more sophisticated audience tastes from the 1980s and 1990s include *Hill Street Blues*, *thirtysomething*, and *Twin Peaks*. This wave was arguably an exception to typical broadcast fare, not necessarily a widespread practice.[7]

Comparatively, US cable channels were already embracing "quality" since it was specialized by definition. By the 1990s and '00s cable stations were challenging broadcast network conventions in various ways. Many began debuting shows throughout the year rather than maintaining the September to May schedule and establishing select signature airtimes for their original primetime series, such as HBO and AMC's emphasis on Sunday nights for *Sex and the City* and *Mad Men*. They also gave showrunners greater creative freedom to experiment with different show lengths beyond lengths informed by advertiser supported commercial slots. Cable stations also re-aired episodes multiple times during the week to build interest rather than waiting to broadcast reruns during the summer and standardized shorter, often

ten-to-thirteen-episode seasons. Creatively speaking these structural choices were better able to attract creative talent from the film industry, which imbued cable programs with cachet and generated critical buzz for their programs. This environment also fostered more experimental and specialized shows that could take risks differently than advertiser supported television.[8]

These examples illustrate the artificiality of television's monoculture as an outgrowth of broadcast network industrial practices. One that increasingly fell out of favor as cable channels offered consumers and creatives more alternatives. The rise of convenience technologies that gave consumers more options for when they watched television content, the increased consumer usage of mobile devices (e.g., smart phones), and the techniques of streaming services, notably partial and/or full season "drops" for original series, disrupted television's norms. Viewers witnessed a veritable deconstruction of the physical and creative properties of television as did current and potential creatives. These gradual shifts, which migrated from cable to broadcast networks, promised new possibilities. For emerging writers and performers, the launch of new creative outlets, such as YouTube in June 2005, generated new opportunities.

The subtext of this wellspring of opportunity returns us to this question of who has traditionally had access to participate in television's creative class and what kind of stories have proliferated. Implicit to the perceived promise of niches is an unnamed reality that content created by and depicting minoritized populations, across a variety of social identities, including ability, class, gender, race, and sexual orientation, is one of television's historic deficits. This reality includes biases present in broadcast *and* cable television.

## Acknowledging Predigital Social Biases in Television

This brings me to my second point regarding the ways the faux nostalgia for the monoculture overlooks issues of underrepresentation and exclusion of historically marginalized voices rooted in popular media designated as "mainstream." Just as celebrations of pride respond to histories of shame, critical attention to diversity in media representation must acknowledge and attend to legacies of systemic invisibility and exclusion.

In the television industry women's authorship remains novel based on who has access to create series for broadcast networks, cable channels, and streaming services, and, more often than not, the nuances of the storytelling itself.[9] There are discernible combinations of themes, characterization, and storytelling devices evident in these series that was less possible and less visible in an earlier era.

In a poignant appreciation of *Sex and the City*'s innovations, television critic Emily Nussbaum addresses critical biases against the series, compared to the effusive praise offered to *The Sopranos* and *Breaking Bad*, noting "High feminine instead of fetishistically masculine, glittery, rather than gritty, and daring in its conception of character, *Sex and the City* was a brilliant and, in certain ways, radical show. It also originated the unacknowledged first female anti-hero on television: ladies and gentlemen, Carrie Bradshaw." She also questions the broader devaluing of feminine culture, especially "the assumption that anything stylized (or formulaic, or pleasurable, or funny, or feminine, or explicitly about sex rather than violence, or made collaboratively) must be inferior."[10] Levy similarly lauds the series *Girls* as bold for "its foregrounding of marginalized and trivialized issues in women's lives insisting that the 'feelings of women' matter." Despite clear advances for women in media numerous critics, such as Levine, note the persistent dismissals of feminine popular culture in general as "trifling."[11]

The narrow perception of women characters and women-centric storylines is rooted in the history I outline in the introduction. As noted, since the 1970s television has steadily expanded the roles of women beyond the domestic sphere, inflected characters with activist perspectives, and included more racially diverse characters. Women were rarely producers, directors, or writers of television programs, however, even if these series opened up more opportunities for performers. The growing awareness of women as a consumer demographic informed early 1980s series such as *Cagney & Lacey* and *The Scarecrow and Mrs. King*, and the formation of the Lifetime Channel.[12] The 1980s also witnessed acclaimed series centered on women characters such as *Kate & Allie*, *The Golden Girls*, *Designing Women*, *Murphy Brown*, *The Days and Nights of Molly Dodd*, and *Roseanne*, which laid the groundwork for 1990s era debuts, including *Ellen*, *Grace under Fire*, and *Thea*.

This expansion of programs did not directly parallel the opportunities for women-identified producers, directors, and writers. Most of these series were led by creative teams dominated by men. Even important late 1990s predecessors to this book's "good" and "complex" series, *Ally*, *Sex*, and *Buffy*, were created by men-identified showrunners, though some employed primarily women writers. My intention is not to discount the possibility that men could write credible authentic women characters, especially since many scripts are collaborations. Rather I am asking why women-identified creatives lacked access, and I am lamenting all the potential storylines, themes, characters, and narrative possibilities that went unrealized by exclusionary practices.

While many astute observers of media trends could intuit that women are underrepresented as characters and creators, *Inclusion or Invisibility? Comprehensive Annenberg Report on Diversity in Entertainment* (CARD) of 2016 quantified key structural patterns related to gender, race, and sexuality in the film, television, and streaming industries. The report's analysis, which included 109 feature films and 305 scripted series released between August 2014 to September 2015, noted four key data points: First, less than 40 percent of all speaking characters on scripted series were girls and women, 36.4 percent were women on broadcast networks, 37.3 percent on cable channels, and 38.1 percent on streaming series. Second, women were significantly underrepresented as directors of scripted series: 17.1 percent were women on broadcast networks, 15.1 percent on cable channels, and 11.8 percent on streaming series. Third, women were significantly underrepresented as writers of scripted series: 31.6 percent were women on broadcast networks, 28.5 percent on cable channels, and 25.2 percent on streaming series. Finally, almost a quarter of 487 show creators were women (22.6 percent) and 77.4 percent were men. On the broadcast networks, 22 percent were women; on the cable channels women were 22.3 percent; and on streaming series women were 25 percent. The report found similar patterns of exclusion from speaking parts and director's roles from racially underrepresented groups.

The scope of this unique and groundbreaking report is useful for illustrating how gender and racial exclusions operate systemically in terms of television representation and the creative class. At the time these data were collected, women constituted 50.8 percent of the US population and ethnic minorities 37.9 percent, so women and racial minorities are not represented proportionally onscreen or behind the camera.[13]

These data were collected during the midpoint between the 2012–20 era I study, when half the shows I examine were airing, and likely represents an *improvement* over earlier patterns in gender and racial representation. More recent industry studies I discuss in the coda indicate persistent underrepresentation as an ongoing challenge.

One of the main creative opportunities for emerging creatives was the rise of "open TV" in the first decade of the twenty-first century. Online distribution platforms, such as YouTube, were integral to how several showrunners developed their aesthetic, built audiences, and were able to secure production deals. The rise of "open TV" has also changed the nature of "legacy TV" by serving as a relatively affordable way for emerging producers to create. As Christian notes, "open or networked television distribution occurs via Internet or web protocols. It is digital, on-demand, and peer-to-peer, meaning any participant in the web—a producer, a fan, a sponsor—can directly connect to another at any time, eliminating the need for legacy network executives."[14] Open TV's growth stems from technological and industrial shifts ranging from more affordable production equipment to greater access broadband, among others. As such open TV has incubated the talents of emerging independent producers who felt excluded from or underrepresented on legacy TV. The result was a new generation of indie producers who "experiment with genres, forms, and platforms; create work samples to raise their industry status; or work to build an enduring business for audiences underserved by market-driven narrowcasting."[15] Several of the showrunners I discuss have roots in open TV.

Prior to her breakthrough series *Misadventures of Awkward Black Girl*, which premiered on YouTube in 2011, Issa Rae produced the web series *The Fly Guys* and *Dorm Diaries*.[16] *Misadventures*, however, made a far greater impact. As Rae has explained, open TV platforms were the only venues that would allow her to tell the stories she sought to tell with *Misadventures*, "I don't think the mainstream media understands people of color are multidimensional. For some reason, there's an idea that only white people are relatable. I don't think it's necessarily racist. But it's odd, because the people who watch the most television are black women, so we should be represented in more ways."[17] The resonance of *Misadventures* led to national profiles of Rae and caught the attention of other Black performers and creatives, who mentored Rae and contributed to her funding efforts.[18] She parlayed her success as an open TV producer into a production deal with ABC. Though they declined to produce her proposed series in 2013 she signed a two-year first look production deal with HBO, which led to *Insecure*, which premiered in 2016.[19]

Abbi Jacobson and Ilana Glazer, the creators and stars of *Broad City*, also have open TV roots. They met in a New York–based improv practice group in 2007 and collaborated on writing video sketches that blended realism and absurdism. Gradually, they translated these into a television series format with a regular release schedule via the web series *Broad City* of 2010. The series unique point of view and popularity culminated in a production deal with FX. After the network passed on the series it was picked up by Comedy Central, which had strategically pivoted toward courting more young women viewers, and premiered in 2014.[20] Rather than simply re-creating the web series directly Glazer has noted how they refined it to the contours of television, which emphasize accessibility and familiarity.[21] *Broad City* aired on Comedy Central from 2014 to 2019 to critical acclaim and industry recognition.[22]

Considering these examples, the cultural climate for women in internet culture is essential to this discussion. Beyond the initial internet content that launched their careers many women creatives are highly public figures with a prominent social media presence. For example, Dunham capitalized on the notoriety of *Girls* to discuss her identity as a feminist in multiple forums and copublished the online feminist newsletter *Lenny Letter* from 2015 to 2018.[23] The blurring between their public identities and the content of their shows is important because the internet has gradually eroded the previous firmness of the partition between media personnel and their audiences. The implications for women have been complex.

Banet-Weiser links the rise of "popular feminism" with the parallel growth of "popular misogyny" and places them both within the new "economy of visibility" rooted in media technologies. In this new economy "feminism manifests in discourses and practices that are circulated in popular and commercial media, such as digital spaces like blogs, Instagram, and Twitter, as well as broadcast media. As such, these discourses have an accessibility that is not confined to academic enclaves or niche groups."[24] The rise of internet technology in the mid-1990s and its refinement in "Web 2.0" inspired many commentators to ruminate on how it might foster greater inclusion for everyday people. From a fan culture perspective, the notion that "we have the ability to be more strongly tied to just as many if not more people with a shared affinity for niche culture"[25] is well supported by the ways television networks and streaming services have become more strategic in their promotional strategies through savvy fan engagements as well as the creation of extratextual and/or paratextual content.[26]

A more worrisome trend undergirding these democratic possibilities, however, is the tension between the expansion of expressive outlets, notably social media platforms, and the proliferation of historic prejudices. When we consider the largely unregulated nature of the internet and how the anonymity of internet communication decreases social accountability it's even clearer how blogs and other opinion sites created spaces for preexisting and new antisocial perspectives to manifest. In a parallel to how media technologies have popularized certain versions of feminism, Banet-Weiser reminds us how the technological affordances of social media have authorized popular misogynistic expressions in a similar manner as popular feminism, noting "the audience is wider, the circulation happens on many interconnected networks with relative ease, and the broader cultural political context, symbolized by the election of Trump, as well as other extreme-right successes around the world, endorses an aggressive, defensive popular misogyny." Some prominent manifestations of misogyny are the mediated responses to popular feminism, implicating it as a threat to patriarchy, masculinity, and White racial domination accompanied by threats of violence toward self-identified feminists on social media.[27] Similarly, Smith addresses trolling toward fat acceptance and body diversity advocates by noting, "Thus, it is no surprise that the most vicious trolls are men carrying out a societal expectation to disassociate from their humanity with no consideration for context or the humanity involved in the particular subject matter. Not surprisingly, being female is a major characteristic of troll victims."[28]

The overlapping of media forms requires us to consider how the television figures I discuss reflect the imprint of misogynist and racist media culture in their creative work. For example, in her memoir *Shrill* Lindy West chronicles the misogynist responses she received online after debating comedian Jim Gaffigan about the boundaries of comedy, particularly so-called rape jokes on the television series *Totally Biased*.[29]

*Shrill*, which serves as the basis of the original Hulu television series, adapts some of West's experiences onscreen through the character Annie Easton. One of its most compelling narrative arcs from season one through the beginning of season two depicts the persistent nature of misogynistic internet trolls who object to Annie's forthright essay on fatness in the fictional publication the *Weekly Thorn*.

Similarly, the renewed visibility of activist Tara Burke's original hashtag, #MeToo, in 2017, inspired national and global conversations and some palpable actions geared toward increased corporate and social accountability for sexual assault, discrimination, and harassment.[30] This remains an ongoing struggle that television writers have integrated into their work. Showrunner and actress Michaela Coel's series *I May Destroy You* chronicles the lead character Arabella's, and her friends', navigations of various forms of sexual assault and abuse while navigating their lives in the urban environment of London. At the end of episode five (". . . It Just Came Up") she experiences immediate social media buzz after publicly exposing one of her sexual abusers. By episode nine ("Social Media Is a Great Way to Connect") we witness the collision of amplified internet fame—at the beginning of the series we learn that Arabella is a minor internet star whose first book was an outgrowth of her viral Twitter posts—*and* popular misogyny. Suddenly, her screenshots shift tonally from affirmations to toxic misogyny.

The creative promise endemic to the television industry's pivots from mass media to "masses of niches" is connected intricately to the ways broadcast networks adapted to the threats and innovations of cable, and later, streaming services. Even though these shifts opened doors for new voices who could serve the interests of niche audiences the root of these overlooked niches is a narrowly constructed notion of who constituted the "mainstream." The lack of gender and racial equity, as documented in the CARD report, continues to haunt the broadcast industry even as it welcomes new voices. Although the internet has provided a variety of ways for emerging artists, especially those from minoritized groups, to gain access to the industry, this access has entailed frequent reminders for women, people of color, and other minoritized communities that their "mainstream" status is tenuous and conditional upon their ability to tolerate and navigate toxic internet culture.[31] Thus, the opening up of media industries requires us to consider how women-identified creatives have contended with restrictive forces, in terms of who is traditionally represented on "mainstream" television and who gets to helm such stories, to fully understand the innovations of their stories and approaches to storytelling.

## How the Nichification of Popular Culture Opened Doors

In the late 1980s and 1990s established comedians like Roseanne Barr, Brett Butler, Margaret Cho, Ellen DeGeneres, Jerry Seinfeld, Sinbad, and Thea Vidale had enough momentum to convince major broadcast networks to develop series around their personae. Generally, the women-centric shows within this group adapted aspects of their stand-up personae into the familiar roles of mothers (married or single), or single career women looking for love. Though women were underrepresented on television when their series aired, they, as comedians and actresses, were relatively "safe risks" with discernible industry track records. Though the series varied greatly in ratings, critical perceptions, longevity, and influence, they represented a commercial archetype that endured well into the first decade of the twenty-first century. For example, sitcoms starring comedians Wanda Sykes and Cristela Alonzo are more recent examples of original comedienne-centered multicamera sitcoms of the first decade of the twenty-first century filmed in front of live audiences.[32]

As the television industry transitioned into the postnetwork era the traditional routes of "discovering" new talent have taken some radical departures. One can imagine an established independent production company such as Carsey-Werner-Mandabach Productions confidently pitching *Roseanne* and *Grace under Fire* to ABC, based on their commercial success with *The Cosby Show* and *A Different World*. Comparatively, the notion of women-identified "unknown" (e.g., "niche") talents, pitching unorthodox storylines that they would write, direct, produce, and/or star in represents a newer ecology of television.

While television's lack of gender balance in the 1980s to the first decade of the twenty-first century suggests that making shows centered on women was often a challenge for producers/showrunners, the generic orientation of these shows, mostly focused on domestic matters or the pursuit of love, made them palatable creatively. Comparatively, the media industry's shift toward a mass of niches might partially explain the viability of the following three television show "pitches": Series #1: a 30-minute comedy shot in the intimate style of an indie film focused on the professional struggles, awkward intimate lives, and complex friendships of four 20-something White women, including three postbaccalaureates and an NYU student, living in New York. Series #2: a dramedy—with varying episode lengths—about a wealthy young White woman sentenced to a short prison term because of a minor drug offense who is surrounded by multicultural ensemble of prison mates from all walks of life, including a Black trans woman of color, an "undocumented" Latina, women who struggle with various forms of mental illness, and queer women. Critiques of the Prison Industrial Complex (PIC), sexual exploitation by male prison guards, and the potential for riots are recurring themes. Series #3: a dark comedy centered on a promising young Black British woman Millennial writer whose sexual assault haunts her as she and her friends, who navigate their own sexual traumas, try to survive financially and socially in contemporary London.

These capsule summaries of *Girls*, *Orange Is the New Black*, and *I May Destroy You*, obviously flatten out many of the details and nuances of how these shows were conceived. My point is that none resembles the kind of fare people refer to when they lament the decline of the "monoculture." If we can agree that shows about women are minoritized on television, unpacking this further reveals the types of women not present, including women of color, women who are overweight, queer women, women who have been traumatized, women who struggle with mental illness, trans women, women who get high, women who have bad sex, and various combinations of these characteristics. There might be one or two representations of these categories during the broadcast era, but these women were exceptions. The range of women's experiences has emerged more fully through post-network-era programming. The "good" and "complex" shows are not generic; many of them blur or expand the boundaries of television genres, employ aesthetic techniques from various mediums, center on characters we have rarely seen on television, and raise questions about the very nature of "mainstream." When we speak of a loss of common culture, whose culture are we really referring to? The absences I have listed would suggest the presumed "niche" of women's programming is far more diverse and expansive than the "niche" label implies.

The "good" and "complex" series decenter the ratings-driven focus of the mass media era and reflect not only the rise of niche interests and audiences but an expanded understanding of what makes programs culturally relevant. Four elements—*demographic resonance*, *critical relevance*, which is tied to *innovative content, themes, and/or aesthetic choices*, and the prominent role of *multidimensional engagement points*, including social media, fan communities, streaming based syndication, online retail opportunities, and unique audience engagement opportunities such as live performance—indicate how the "good" and "complex" series expand our conception of the presumed vastness of broadcast era "monocultural" programs and the presumed "limitations" of niche culture. I discuss the relationship of the CW's *Crazy Ex-Girlfriend* to explore these four elements.

## Monoculture vs. Niche Case Study: *Crazy Ex-Girlfriend*

The nine series I explore are unique in many aspects. When viewed comparatively we see the ways they push us to think about television in new ways beyond "monocultural" conventions. I focus on *Crazy Ex-Girlfriend* (referred to hereafter as *CXG*) to illustrate how it represents the four elements. Further, it has the broadest mix of genres, and the tensions between its low ratings and endurance was a common trope of many critical commentaries on the series.

A little over a year after completing her undergraduate degree in drama at New York University's Tisch School of Drama, actress, comedian, and writer Rachel Bloom became an "internet sensation" through the premiere of her unlikely YouTube video: "Fuck Me Ray Bradbury." Perfectly curated for YouTube the video knowingly recreated the coy, thinly veiled erotic iconography from Britney Spears's 1999 teen pop hit ". . . Hit Me Baby One More Time" video from the costumes to the choreography. Musically, "Fuck Me" was a catchy punk-inflected rock song, centered on a raunchy, tongue-in-cheek lyric come-on to the famed sci-fi writer delivered with the belting power of a pop diva and the wit of a skilled comedian.[33] Though Bloom had gained experience as a member of her college comedy troupe, as a performer in the Upright Citizens Brigade Theatre, and in various industry roles, the video solidified her as a promising new authorial voice.

Four years later she and writer Aline Brosh McKenna (*Devil Wears Prada*), and director Marc Webb (*The Amazing Spider Man, 500 Days of Summer*) filmed *CXG*'s pilot for Showtime.

Bloom's YouTube channel racheldoesstuff transfixed McKenna who noted, "I watched all of them. I was bewitched," she says. "In every video, there's a moment of painful introspection; the characters realize the direness of their predicament, then shake it off." Showtime ultimately declined the series, and it was reconfigured for broadcast and aired on the CW for four seasons.[34] A decade earlier Bloom's rise would have been inconceivable, literally: YouTube did not exist in 2004. Though there were multiple steps between Bloom's auspicious video and co-creating *CXG* with Brosh McKenna, the fact that video stardom is a viable pathway is integral to her story, as it is for creatives like Ilana Glazer and Abbi Jacobson, and Issa Rae. What changed?

### *Demographic Resonance*

Though *CXG*'s ratings were low among network shows its niche orientation allowed it to endure for four seasons. The CW network targets female viewers eighteen to thirty-four primarily; a niche that sustained the show.[35] As such, *CXG*'s survival exemplifies the "post-network" era where the television audience is "more accurately understood as a collection of niche audiences."[36]

Based on these shifts several writers have suggested a new monoculture emerging that operates on a lower scale than shows of the past, based more on discourse and resonance than ratings. Yao ties the survival of postnetwork streaming series to changing economics, noting subscription services "don't need monocultural hits to function. Instead they just need to make sure that they make targeted content that can be delivered to the right audiences. Monocultural hits engage a large population at once, which offsets its costly production, but niche shows drive engagement just the same, albeit on a smaller scale, and they are much easier to come by."[37]

Though *CXG* is a CW series, the network's parent companies CBS and Warner Bros. made a streaming pact with Netflix in 2016 giving the series a different life by making it constantly available and thus able to attract new fans in between seasons.[38] While no quantitative data clarify this explicitly, the notion that a *low-rated* broadcast series would attract an audience sufficiently large to justify the expense of syndicating is noteworthy given the traditional broadcast mandate of five seasons (approximately 100 episodes) for syndication.[39]

Implicit to some of the critiques of the declining monoculture of the past are concerns that more aggressively marketed programs and the influence of gatekeepers could still flatten out taste culture. Because critical tastes are often progressive in their search for underrepresented voices they are specialized and do not always reflect those of the majority of the public. In women-centric shows this progressive critical bias is an *asset* that benefits shows with minoritized content.

### *Critical Relevance and Innovations*

Despite low viewership critics regarded season one of the series very positively, which grew as the series continued. Several writers cited season one's music and staging as innovative and representative of emerging television trends.[40] *CXG*'s innovations also generated considerable interest in its showrunners and actors.[41] A deliberate formalism infused with women's perspectives on intimate relationships informed *CXG*'s development from the very beginning. According to Bloom, "We really pitched it like a 52-hour movie and it always felt right. The story was always in four phases. It was always about denial, admitting you're in love, rebelling against that love somehow and finding this dark night of the soul and coming out of it and starting from scratch."[42]

Critical appreciation from critics and journalists, combined with the ways passionate fans employ a series of networks to communicate their interests, are defining the nature of cultural relevance. Lotz recognizes that though "21st-century television texts—distributed by Internet and other technologies—may rarely reach a 'mass' audience, these texts still do ideological work and can be profoundly important to those who view them."[43]

Comparing the different discourse around the finales of HBO's acclaimed *Game of Thrones* and CBS's ratings hit *Big Bang Theory*, Yao noted, "a TV show doesn't become a 'monocultural hit' just by virtue of having a large viewership; it has to drive our conversation by being a common topic that unites people. In other words, it has to become a shared cultural experience."[44] Chayka compares the discourse surrounding HBO's *Succession* and the more popular NBC series *This Is Us* to make a similar point about the cache of buzz and acclaim.[45] *CXG* benefited from its success with its target demographic and critical attention.

I expound on its innovations in greater detail in chapter 3, but I address one aesthetic and distributive aspect briefly to illuminate the scope of its innovations. In the case of *CXG*, YouTube was not just part of Bloom's origin story as a writer and performer but integral to the series' aesthetic. In a parallel to MTV's influence on 1980s era films (e.g., *Flashdance*) and television series (e.g., *Miami Vice*), YouTube influenced the content and composition of television series. *CXG*'s 150+ original songs are central to its appeal, and YouTube provides an accessible platform for the series to appeal to viewers looking to revisit a favorite song and for interested viewers to get a taste of the series. Notably, its signature songs are filmed and recorded like music videos in their editing and timing, making them easily translatable to YouTube where they can be viewed infinitely without exposition. Newman notes, "The raunchy and hilarious novelty of these shareable numbers" of *CXG* are "made for YouTube as much as for airing on the CW."[46]

These creative choices make the YouTube informed filming style integral to the creative and distributive aspects of the series. "Shareability" perfectly describes the relationship between postnetwork consumption modes, which viewers access on mobile devices, and the digestible nature of content. One of the consequences of convenience technologies and broadband delivered programs is an increase in the deliberateness of how viewers use television. Associated with this are adjustments in how programs are created and distributed.[47] *CXG*'s approach also speaks to Lotz's observation that post-network-era programs continue to do "cultural work long after they are 'dropped' into the library and the first wave of viewers encounter them."[48] Though *CXG* originated on a broadcast network the ubiquity of its music videos on YouTube and its syndication on Netflix, as well as the purchasable episodes on various platforms, reflects the dynamic nature of how we understand television content in the postnetwork era.

### *Multidimensional Engagement Points*

We should also consider the varied ways viewers, consumers, and fans can access *CXG*. They exemplify the changing nature of television in terms of temporality, access, and fan engagement. After premiering on the CW, *CXG*'s first episode could be viewed (with commercials) on the CW's website, and song clips could be accessed on YouTube. Consumers could also purchase individual episodes on sites such as Amazon Prime and iTunes and entire seasons on DVD. As a musical series the soundtracks for each season were released for streaming and purchasing; Bloom actively promoted the series and engaged with fans on social media sites; and its fans created their own communities, including fan groups, discussion forums, and *CXG* inspired merchandise. CBS and Warner Bros. further increased access to the series via a streaming pact to rebroadcast multiple CW series, including *CXG* and *Jane the Virgin*, to Netflix. Additional avenues for fan engagement included the cast recreating key musical scenes from the series in a concert series, and televised cast reunions.[49]

Examined collectively current and potential viewers can access *CXG*, including various aspects of its content, in multiple ways. Viewers have never been limited to accessing the series during its first run or during summer reruns as they would have for most broadcast series during the broadcast and multichannels transition era. Though the series ended its first run in 2019 the ability to view videos online, purchase merchandise, participate in fan communities, follow the cast on social media, attend concerts, read Bloom's 2020 memoir, and so on reflect the "long tail" theory.[50] Though it is unlikely a show with *CXG*'s low viewership would have lasted beyond one to two seasons in a previous era, in the postnetwork era the series could transcend its alleged niche appeal by virtue of the more wide-ranging access options. The result is an open-ended text that can be discovered and rediscovered, continuously imbuing it with a more expansive popularity unique to the postnetwork era. In addition to critical acclaim it has also garnered attention from media studies scholars, which further distinguishes it from other series in an era defined by an abundance of television content.[51]

As a musical with a strong comedic dimension *CXG* is unique among the series that lends itself to certain elements such as music videos. What's key is the fact that the impact of contemporary series is less about big ratings. Consider, for example, that streaming services have generally resisted sharing ratings information. Yet the lack of data did not prevent a series like *Orange Is the New Black* from instantly inspiring attention from scholars and cultural critics beyond initial program reviews.[52]

Similarly, the unexpected disruption of the COVID-19 pandemic led to a resurgence of interest in HBO's *Girls*.[53] Its availability on HBO Go (later HBO Max and now Max) enabled this rediscovery to occur. Many of the series would appear "niche" in the network era, but changes in the industry and the creative innovations of these series, and others, has changed the discourse on what television matters and why.

Reynolds offers a measured, pertinent assessment of the alleged decline of the monoculture in the 2010s noting, "the slow collapse of a centralizing and synchronized common culture has opened up the space for a profusion of micro-scenes, each running its own timeline. In this flourishing post-geographical world of 'local' cultures not tied to location, small is bountiful and significance doesn't need to be universal to matter."[54] The following chapters examine the formal and thematic innovations of nine "good" and "complex" series. Each one focuses primarily on one of three overarching themes, including the influence of US indie film aesthetics on three series, the synthesis of surreal techniques on three series, and the narrative use of different "orders of time" on three series. The chapters note the interplay of these elements within shows as well. Collectively these techniques illuminate a diverse range of contemporary women-centric subjectivities. The chapters complement each other thematically and can be read in any order. The coda further reflects on themes drawn from the three core chapters and future implications.

# 2

# LOW-KEY LIKE AN "INDIE FILM"

Anyone who has seen *Passion Fish* (1992), *Walking and Talking* (1996), *High Art* (1998), *All the Real Girls* (2003), and *Medicine for Melancholy* (2008) might find it easier to recall the characters, their relationships, or the way the films made them feel than what *happened* plot-wise. Though they were each made by independently oriented directors of different cultural backgrounds, genders, and ages, the films share a discernible emphasis on character development and tone over plot and action. These films often move at a languid pace where their narrative destination is often far less important than the emotional and psychological journeys their characters experience. These characteristics define them against mainstream Hollywood studio films of their vintage and inform their discernibility as "independent."

Many viewers might recognize similar qualities in contemporary television series such as *Girls*, *Insecure*, and *Shrill*, women-centric series focused more on small moments and quiet revelations than spectacular events. Stylistically, they reflect the convergence of film and television that Ford defines as the women-centric dramedy.[1] These series, and others such as *Better Things* (2016–22, FX) and *One Mississippi* (2015–17, Amazon), "perform and articulate their feminist sensibility through low-key styles of filmmaking that emphasize emotional spectacle" as opposed to the more spectacular cinematization associated with male-focused "quality television" series.[2] Ford's framing provides an essential critical intervention that illustrates the relationship between indie films and television production and offers a feminist-based rendering that acknowledges the range of styles and content capable of transmitting ideas about women. Additionally, she contrasts the "unspectacular" approach with other forms that might be perceived as more powerful such as the "filmic spectacle" of the musical series *Crazy Ex-Girlfriend* and the "speechifying form of spectacle" in series such as *Parks and Recreation*, *Scandal* (2012–18, ABC), and *The Marvelous Mrs. Maisel* (2017–23, Amazon Prime Video).[3] She opens the door for rethinking how we conceptualize what forms can present a woman-centered perspective affectively.

As television genealogies of 1970s–1990s women's comedies have revealed, previous generations of women-centered series addressed women's issues, such as reproductive rights, workplace harassment, and sexual violence, in overt tones. Comparatively, many Millennial generation creatives are more inspired by US indie films than traditional sitcoms and depict elements of sociopolitical concerns in more muted tones. Further they have expanded women's issues to include the uncertain territory of how to show up in familial, platonic, and romantic relationships young women navigate especially in an era of greater educational access, technological advancement, and personal choice about sexuality and family.

*Girls*, *Shrill*, and *Insecure* exemplify an innovative approach to storytelling where the intimacy of the writing, filming, and acting parallel the intimate nature of their themes. The intimacy of the serialized format is uniquely well-suited to the intricate, character-driven stories a subset of "good" and "complex" television creatives seek to tell about their women characters. This understated aesthetic approach reflects "the continuing influence of the third wave, with its focus on micropolitics and challenging sexism and misogyny insofar as they appear in everyday rhetoric, advertising, film, television, literature, and the media."[4] Notably, the everyday textures of sexism, and misogyny, as well as racism and homophobia, infuse the series differently, which gives each show a distinctive character.

As valuable as the women-centric dramedy framework is for my analysis I place it in conversation with other critical contexts to assess the distinct aesthetics of the three series. *Girls* is the earliest series the book discusses and the most groundbreaking. From the narcissistic behavior of its "flawed" lead Hannah Horvath to its dampened, unspectacular tone the series has an experimental quality that mirrors the instability and discovery endemic to the various aspects of emerging adulthood its depiction of characters experience. *Girls'* intricate narrative structure effectively immerses viewers in the culturally insular and often absurd lives of White Millennial hipster characters living in Brooklyn. While various critics have rightfully cited its cultural blind spots, I emphasize how it creates an internal language through dialogue and signature filming techniques to dramatize the tense transition of postbaccalaureate adulthood.[5]

*Shrill*, a comedic adaptation of author Lindy West's essay collection, centers on Annie Easton, a White Millennial woman aspiring to a career as a writer, who makes many mistakes in her career and relationships much like *Girls*. Whereas *Girls* centers its stories on personal revelations that help its characters grow up, and treats social realities as clandestine, the intimate relationships of characters on *Shrill* frequently place them in direct and indirect situations inflected by social issues. Throughout its three seasons the central role of friendship for Millennial women, the ongoing impact of body politics on women's sense of self-worth, and tensions between the lived experiences of Black people and White liberalism, are connective threads that help it balance aspects of the personal with the political.

*Insecure*, which focuses on Black Millennials based in Los Angeles, stars a "flawed" Millennial lead character, Issa, who, like Hannah and Annie, refuses to serve as a role model for women. Unlike them she also refuses to compromise her awkwardness, insecurities, and quirkiness in service of the racial respectability trope. Because Black creatives have struggled to secure support for their creative projects or complex representation the series is significant for both broadening the range of Black, college educated urbanite characters on television, and incubating a new generation of Black women creative talent in writing and directing, behind the camera.

Before analyzing the individual series, I define some of the more salient distinctions between "indie" and mainstream cinema, including aesthetic elements understood as "smart," which further distinguish indie films.[6] Next, I reconceptualize the "smart" elements embedded in Ford's argument by reflecting on the often overlooked racial dynamics of women-centered shows and opening up a critical space for understanding how the racial politics of the entertainment industry frequently requires Black creatives to tell overlooked stories *and* create opportunities for writers and directors of color.

## Post 1989: Defining "Indie" Filmmaking and the "Smart" Sensibility

Independent film refers to "production, distribution, and exhibition outside of the Hollywood studios and mainstream theater chains" in the American film industry and oppositional techniques associated with a specific place.[7] For example, the "New American Cinema of Jonas Mekas, John Cassavetes, and Shirley Clarke; the New Hollywood Cinema of Francis Ford Coppola, Robert Altman, and Martin Scorsese; the French New Wave; and the New German Cinema" exemplify the creative cohorts evoked by the term "independent."[8]

Though independent films earn this distinction via material conditions and aesthetic elements outside of the mainstream Hollywood system, the inaugural Sundance film festival, especially responses to Steven Soderbergh's *sex, lies, and videotape* (1989), are a key turning point in perceptions of the genre.[9] Newman distinguishes independent from the term "indie" by locating indie in the 1989–2011 Sundance-Miramax era tied to Sundance and the commercial reign of the prominent "mini-major" subsidiary Miramax Studios from the 1990s to 2010s.[10] Though independent films differed from the mainstream commercial cinema of their era, the other distinction of "indie" films, besides chronology, is commercial and rhetorical, notably, they "achieved a level of cultural circulation far greater than in earlier eras, making independence into a brand, a familiar idea that evokes in consumers a range of emotional and symbolic associations."[11] Integral to this circulation is the relative accessibility of "indie" films. As Levy notes, the American films comprising this era do not conform to typical notions of avant-garde, experimental, or underground films since "with few exceptions, there is not much edge, formal experimentation, or serious challenge to the dominant culture."[12]

The legibility of films as "indie," "comes into being in comparison to other categories of cinema contemporaneous to it, such as Hollywood blockbusters and prestige pictures, foreign imports, and avant-garde works. . . . It is itself a form of niche media, a reaction against conglomerate gigantism and at the very same times, considering its mini-major producers-distributors, a symptom of it."[13] The wide field of "indies" includes films as varied as *Welcome to the Dollhouse* (1995), *Eve's Bayou* (1997), *Ghost World* (2001), and *Lost in Translation* (2003).

One aesthetic unifier of many of these films is the use of a "smart" sensibility. Though Sconce outlines specific techniques such as "blank style"—the use of long shots, static composition, and sparse cutting, which center character and dialogue over spectacle and give films an observational quality for audiences—the bigger import of smart cinema is its "symbolic opposition to the imaginary mass-cult monster of mainstream, commercial, Hollywood cinema."[14] Though "smart cinema" is not inherently "indie," the sensibility frequently *informs* such films and speaks to the broader movement against what is perceived as mainstream and conventional. In television production it's worth reiterating my argument in chapter 1 that premium cable channels, subscription-based streaming services, and even basic cable, have pushed the boundaries established originally by network television. The range of formal and thematic innovations of these formats, including more serialized narration, techniques adapted from film, and greater freedom to integrate more explicit language and sexuality, speak to a similar tension between innovative and more traditional television. Relatedly, just as independent, and later "indie" film, pushed the creative boundaries of mainstream cinema, networked television has arguably embraced some of the innovations modeled by the "indie" inspired television comprising this chapter.

## Conceptualizing Blackness in "Indie" Television Comedy

As noted, Ford provides an essential framework for analyzing the ways contemporary series evoke the women-centric indie films by Nicole Holofcener, Rebecca Miller, Greta Gerwig, and Jason Reitman.[15] I would add that in order to analyze the series *Insecure*, an exemplar of *Black* women-centric indie television, as well as the series it has inspired (e.g., *Everything's Trash*, *Harlem*, *Run the World*), another set of critical considerations must come into view. Ford's concept derives primarily from drawing parallels between television series focused primarily, or exclusively, on White women characters, and a discussion of women-centric indie films also focused on White women. What her analysis reveals tacitly is the lack of racial and ethnic diversity in the indie filmmaking world of women-identified directors, and the lack of racial diversity among contemporary women-centric television circa 2019 when her essay was published originally.

Levy's discussion of American independent cinema acknowledges the overlooked work of Black women "who have offered critical alternatives to the stereotypical portrayals of black women in Hollywood movies."[16] At the time of its publication few Black women directors had films commercially released, and this remains painfully true. Levy's survey discusses the work of Julie Dash (*Daughters of the Dust*), Leslie Harris (*Just Another Girl on the I.R.T.*), Darnell Martin (*I Like It Like That*), and Kasi Lemmons (*Eve's Bayou*), a remarkably slim list. More recently, Baker's book-length study discusses the work of Kathleen Collins (*Losing Ground*), Dash, and Lemmons, and adds Ava DuVernay (*Middle of Nowhere*), Tanya Hamilton (*Night Catches Us*), Gina Prince-Blythewood (*Love & Basketball*), and Dee Rees (*Pariah*) to the list. *All* of these filmmakers are independent and consistently discuss the arduous process of securing funding and distribution for their films, which informs Baker's observation that "their careers reflect the core element of the womanist artistic standpoint: they assert their identities as Black women, rebel against the dominant narratives and marginalization of Black women in film, and prioritize their creative vision over commercial success."[17] The constant resistance they faced, including the presumption their films lacked broad appeal and were too "ethnic," speaks to a different creative reality than their White women counterparts. Notably, Black filmmakers, of all genders, have struggled to gain opportunities to author films in Hollywood and have had to work to challenge a century of stereotypical, one-dimensional portrayals of Black people.

This lack of access and combating of stereotypes applies to television insofar as Black showrunners are also underrepresented, as are series focusing on Black characters. A brief analysis of representations of Black women leads in US television comedy offers the most relevant way to illustrate why this deficit complicates the notion of a "deracialized" woman in the women's indie television formulation. Prior to *Insecure*'s debut on HBO in 2016, American television had rarely focused on a single Black woman as the lead character in a sitcom. I distinguish this from Black women who served as the default leads in family-centered ensemble series such as Esther Rolle in *Good Times* (1974–79), Anna Maria Horsford in *Amen* (1986–91), Tina Lifford in *South Central* (1993–94), and Tracee Ellis Ross in *Black-ish* (2014–22). Similarly, this differs from women-centric ensembles such as *Living Single* and *Girlfriends*.

Television's first sitcom focused on a single Black female lead was *Beulah* (1950–53), who was a domestic worker for a White family. The series was adapted from a radio series and was highly controversial for its stereotypical depiction of Beulah as a modern Mammy devoid of an intimate life beyond serving the needs of her employers. This was followed by *Julia* (1968–71); *Gimme a Break!* (1981–87); the short-lived *227* spin-off *Jackée* (1989); *Thea* (1993–94) starring comedienne Thea Vidale; Tina Lifford in *South Central*; *Wanda at Large* (2003) starring Wanda Sykes; and *Whoopi* (2003–4) starring Whoopi Goldberg. That several series in this vein have followed *Insecure* is unique.

*Insecure* is the first US sitcom to depict the experiences of Black Millennial women, and it is also one of the few US sitcoms created, written, produced, and starring a Black woman of *any* generation. Rae, who began her televisual work as a web producer, co-created the show initially with veteran writer Larry Wilmore.[18] *Insecure*'s five-season run also makes it one of the few series focused on a single Black woman to last beyond a single season. Though it is singular in many respects and differs from Black women-centric series that followed such as *Twenties* (2020–22), *Run the World* (2021–present), *Harlem* (2022–present), *Everything's Trash* (2022–23), and the Rae-produced *Rap Sh!t* (2022–present), its style, tone, and diversity have made space for a wide range of representations.

The issue *Insecure* raises in Ford's concept of "women's indie television" is the following: If "indie" cinema signifies a resistance to mainstream conventions symbolically and aesthetically, part of what's being resisted in many works by Black creatives is the lack of representation, structurally, and a lack of *complex* representations of Blacks. Further, if we apply the lens of "smart" cinema as a relevant shorthand for how many indie films distinguish themselves from the mainstream, we must consider it in racialized terms as well. In Sconce's original formulation critiques of White middle-class identity *by White filmmakers*, who presumably have an inside view, is one of the key targets of smart cinema. As such a filmmaker of *any* racial or ethnic background could employ most or all of the techniques he outlines.

While his argument does not explicitly preclude non-White filmmakers from making the White middle-class critiques, his essay is ambiguous on this issue; no Black filmmakers are included among the films he references. Rather than separating Black creatives from "smart" productions, or at least this specific element of such productions, I want to draw attention to two adaptations that racialize it differently and focus on "smart(er)" cinema and television. One, "smart(er)" Black productions can depict the ways racism, in covert and overt forms, inflects the experiences of characters without making racism their narrative center. Second, perhaps what makes some Black productions "smart(er)" than more conventional representations of Blackness is their ability to offer a wider, richer, and more authentic range of characters and situations than mainstream Hollywood. In my close reading of *Insecure* I delve into this more deeply by exploring the importance of representations of Black bohemian characters in film as well as the ways its juxtaposition of a multicultural Los Angeles with its deft responses to White microaggressions subtly critiques White cultural dominance within its narrative world and television in general.

As romantic comedies, the focus of *Love Jones* (1997), *Hav Plenty* (1997), and *Medicine for Melancholy* (2008) on Black urban heterosexual couples differs narratively from *Insecure*'s focus on lead character Issa (Issa Rae) and her best friend Molly (Yvonne Orji), two Black women trying to navigate their professional, romantic, and family relationships.[19] Whereas *Jones* and *Medicine* provide relatively equal time to both individual leads, *Hav Plenty* emphasizes its single heterosexual Black man's effort to acknowledge his unrequited desire. What connects them to *Insecure* is the relatively narrow focus on the intimate lives of college educated young professionals, or, in some instances, aspiring professionals, who are from discernibly Black middle-class backgrounds. This population's stories rarely get told in mainstream television and film, and *Insecure* locates promising narrative possibilities within this theme.

The other link is the relatively nebulous universe of Black filmmakers. Just as many women's indie series employ woman-identified directors from the indie film world, *Insecure* mines the talents of Black directors, especially Black women. As Rae noted in 2016, *Insecure* is "a mini boot camp for up-and-coming, diverse writers and showrunners."[20] Of its forty-four episodes, twenty-four were directed by Black women. Twelve episodes were directed by Black women who directed at least two episodes, including Melina Matsoukas (eight episodes), Stella Meghie (two episodes), and actress/producer/director Kerry Washington (two episodes). The remaining twelve are single episodes directed by a broad range of Black women, including directors from Britain (Cecile Emeke) and South Africa

(Liesl Tommy); those with primarily independent film backgrounds (Tina Mabry); those who are highly seasoned in television (Debbie Allen, Marta Cunningham, and Millicent Shelton); and actresses, including Regina King and *Insecure*'s own supporting actress Natasha Rothwell.[21]

Understanding these historical contexts related to Black film and television production, in terms of access, themes, and labor, is crucial for establishing's *Insecure*'s pioneering role historically. It also illustrates what greater diversity could foster in contemporary television if more women are granted creative opportunities. The importance of multicultural casting and diversity behind the camera also informs my reading of *Shrill*. Though it stars a White lead its main supporting characters are well-developed, consciously Black-identified characters. The series also has a culturally diverse creative team, which is also out of the ordinary for many White-dominated women-centric dramedies.

## *Girls*: Serializing Emerging Adulthood

*Girls*' innovation lies in the way it fuses indie film elements, such as its focus on dialogue, emotion, and tone over plot, with seriality. Though numerous series were shifting from episodic to serialized structures in the first decade of the twenty-first century, *Girls* was one of the first comedies to embrace the potential of the form to tell stories largely about Millennials experiencing emerging adulthood who also interact with people peripheral to this life stage. As a result, its humor derives more from awkward, absurd situations, generational schisms, and character quirks than sight gags or punchlines and registers in dampened rhythms, which gives its humorous moments a subtler punch than traditional sitcoms. My analysis addresses the series' comedically inflected dramatizing of emerging adulthood through its pointed dialogue, nuanced visual language, and purposeful use of seriality to develop characters and engage audiences.

### *Millennials and Emerging Adulthood*

When a new generation of television series emerged in the 2010s featuring women characters in their twenties struggling to find stable jobs and relationships, the characters were viewed as symbols of an indulgent, entitled generation, Millennials. *Time*'s 2013 cover story on Millennials,

"The Me Me Generation," amplified this perception. Though the article actually presented a more complex story about Millennials it has taken time for public perceptions to shift from reacting to the unfamiliar to understanding generational nuances.[22]

Despite popular culture stereotypes of Millennials as "lazy" and entitled, characters of *Girls* teem with desire and ambition. Hannah (Lena Dunham) aspires to be a serious writer, Marnie (Allison Williams) wants respect in New York's contemporary art scene, and Adam (Adam Driver) is an aspiring actor. While characters' sense of meaning is informed by professional goals they are defined by a much wider range of personal concerns. The show's seeming focus on the "micro" parallels indie films focused more on character development than plot. The lives of *Girls*' Millennials reflect relatable circumstances (e.g., student loan debt, low-paying jobs) but eschew the generic caricatures popular culture attributes to their generation. Numerous scholars have covered the precarity of the post-2008 economic landscape and the way it dashed relational and economic expectations for a new generation. While this is a relevant backdrop for *Girls* my focus is more on the formal textures the series employs to illuminate the postbaccalaureate landscape for Millennial women.[23]

A useful framework for understanding the exploratory, dialogue-centered approach and meandering pace is the notion of emerging adulthood as a life stage between adolescence and young adulthood typically spanning from eighteen to twenty-nine. Because certain paradigm shifts, including increased access to postsecondary education and older ages of marriage, are enduring trends, emerging adulthood is understood as a permanent life stage rather than a generational phenomenon. On *Girls* we routinely see dramatized depictions of many core elements of emerging adulthood. Because we encounter its core characters only a few years after college the experimental and often undulating rhythms of the series captures some of this liminality.

Hannah, for example, embodies many of the tensions of emerging adulthood. Though her behavior as a character stood out initially as off-putting, placing her character in conversation reveals many traits endemic to the life stage. She is trying to figure out the nature of her relationships with her parents, what kind of writer she wants to be, and what she desires in a romantic partner (*identity exploration*). In the process she holds multiple odd jobs, has a rotating group of multiple roommates, frequently strains the patience of her close friends, and endures a tense, unstable relationship with her boyfriend, Adam, in the first half of the series (*instability*).

Her self-involvement is a constant source of dialogue for parents, friends, and lovers who feel exploited or frustrated by her inability to empathize. Though this aspect of the life stage reflects a unique time where many young adults have more opportunities for personal development, her persistent introspection can easily spill into self-indulgence (*self-focused behavior*). Hannah often tries to express her authentic feelings respectfully with prospective employers, supervisors, friends, and strangers, but her behavior often feels inappropriate, and she can be slow to realize the impact of her actions. For example, during an interview she establishes rapport with her interviewer then makes a crass joke about rape. When she tries to host dinner parties her efforts to create "sophisticated" spaces often end in disaster because she is oblivious to conflicts between participants. This *in-betweenness* speaks to the awkwardness of trying to behave "maturely" but feeling unsure of the right approach. Despite interpersonal and financial challenges, the center of Hannah's persona is her aspiration to become a successful published author (*optimistic sense of possibilities*). Her faith in her talents drives her persistence.

One of *Girls*' signal achievements is subtly building and expanding on an intricate narrative world. Its serialized architecture is almost soap operatic in its immersiveness, insularity, and interlocking relationships. At different points Hannah's roommates include her college best friend Marnie, then her former college boyfriend Elijah (Andrew Rannells), who comes out as gay, then Adam, her boyfriend, as well as his sister, unstable Caroline (Gaby Hoffmann). Similarly, Marnie begins the series in a relationship with Charlie (Christopher Abbott) and vacillates from seeing Booth Jonathan to a brief sexual encounter with Elijah, to reuniting with Charlie, to a clandestine sexual relationship with Ray (Alex Karpovsky), and then to an affair with Desi (Ebon Moss-Bachrach). The tropes of emerging adulthood; identity exploration; instability in love, jobs, and living arrangements; self-focused behavior; feeling in-between adolescence and adulthood; and an optimistic sense of possibilities flow throughout its stories largely because it is a show about the uncharted territory of growing up in the early twenty-first century.[24]

*Talking about Entitlement*

*Girls* often weaponizes dialogue as a tool for illuminating who characters are and how they perceive the world. The tension between financial precarity, socioeconomic privilege, and entitlement is a recurring dialogic theme that reflects the instability of emerging adulthood. Multiple examples from season one illustrate this theme as a staple of the series.

In the pilot episode (1.1) we learn that Hannah has an unpaid internship, and her parents have supported her financially for the two years since completing her degree at Oberlin. While her parents are compassionate and understanding, her mother pushes back on this arrangement declaring, "We're not going to bankroll your groovy lifestyle." Hannah's statement that, "I think that I may be the voice of my generation . . . or at least *a* voice . . ." speaks to how her self-focused behavior and optimistic sense of possibilities supersedes practical considerations. While her entitlement irritates her friends, she has at least one ally in self-focused and unstable behavior in Jessa (Jemima Kirke), a college friend who did not complete her degree at Oberlin. Jessa, who lives rent free with her cousin Shoshanna (Zosia Mamet), an NYU student, tells Hannah she should demand money from her parents because "she's an artist." This casual attitude about spending other people's money to fuel one's dreams is an adolescent notion that pervades the series.

*Girls* avoids character assassination by placing this enabling behavior in the context of familial wealth. While Hannah is an easy target, this entitlement also informs the lives of her peers. In "Diary" (1.4) Ray and Charlie are in Hannah and Marnie's apartment and Charlie notes Marnie's struggles adjusting to adult life, to which Ray, a curmudgeon by nature, says, "It's not an adult life if your parents pay for your Blackberry," to which Charlie responds in deadpan fashion, "She pays for half of her Blackberry." This acerbic exchange encapsulates the privileged nature of Marnie's finances, Charlie's empathy toward it, and Ray's frustration with the codependence of his friends, most of whom are younger than he. He dropped out of his PhD program in Latin studies and manages the coffee shop Café Grumpy, so he is understandably bitter about working so hard while others around him have easier access to money. Though Hannah's boyfriend, Adam, does some woodworking and has a grizzled working-class affect, he has no discernible job and casually reveals to Hannah that his grandmother gives him $800 per month.

For those lacking access to family wealth, partners also serve as a source of dependence, though this is precarious. At the end of season one Jessa quits her babysitting job and rushes to marry a successful banker, Thomas John. Though their marriage is short-lived she demands money to end the relationship. Similarly, in season two Elijah tells Hannah and Marnie his older boyfriend George pays for everything. Though he is trained as a dancer and actor his source of income is elusive (1.10, "She Did"; 2.1, "It's About Time").

*Girls* makes it clear in its first two seasons that most of its characters have ambition but struggle to envision a path beyond long-standing reliance on family resources. This tension between adult dreams and an adolescent dependence on family places them in the liminal space of emerging adulthood and partially compels us to wonder about their next steps. We know Hannah wants to be a successful writer, Marnie aspires to a place in the New York art scene, and Adam wants to act professionally, but we're less certain about how and if they will get there. Similarly, it's unclear how long Jessa or Elijah can survive on other people's money before their fortune runs out. The lives of many White affluent and upper-middle-class emerging adults are subsidized by families or lovers. The contrast between them and Ray is also telling, making him an important foil throughout the series. As the series continues careers change, but season one concludes with a powerful fusion of pointed dialogue and purposeful staging that speaks to *Girls*' development of an internal visual language.

While Hannah's reliance on her parents is somewhat understandable for a young adult at the early stage of independence, her reliance on her friend and roommate Marnie is an important thread that furthers the emerging adulthood theme. Notably, both characters are experiencing the life stage, and the innate tensions between adolescence and adulthood eventually grow too large for the friendship they have forged to continue in the same form. This conflict plays out mostly through dialogue and parallel behaviors in season one's episodes three and nine, and culminates in a scene fusing *Girls*' emphasis on the adolescent tendencies its characters are still sorting through and its visual language (1.3, "All Adventurous Women Do"; 1.9, "Leave Me Alone").

In "All Adventurous Women Do," Hannah learns from her gynecologist she has been exposed to HPV and calls Marnie, who responds very sympathetically. At the end of the call Marnie reminds her rent is due in a week and Hannah abruptly ends the call claiming her "pre-cancer" concerns are her main focus. Marnie does not mention rent again until episode six when Hannah assures her she has the money, despite quitting her job. Marnie also follows her verbal inquiry with a text in the episode (1.6, "The Return").

By episode nine the tension reaches a climax inseparable from Hannah's ambitions. Despite her desire to be "a *voice*" Hannah is disconnected from the literary communities in New York. At a book signing by a former classmate she encounters a former writing professor who invites her to read an essay at a local gathering of writers. Instead of reading a humorous essay about a hoarder she once knew, she reads a hastily written piece about a friend's death, in an effort to appear more "serious," which is poorly received. Just as she hung up on Marnie when asked her about rent, she scurries the moment her professor asks her to consider coming back. She is still learning how to respond rather than just react, or flee challenging situations.

When she returns to the apartment Marnie is compiling old clothes in her bedroom, and Hannah inundates her with the events of the night. Sensing Marnie's disinterest, she tells Marnie she could be more supportive, which leads Marnie to comment, "Hannah, I support you, literally. Do you have any idea how much money you owe me at this point?" Hannah responds that she took a trial shift at Café Grumpy to cover her expenses. In typical Hannah fashion she refuses to acknowledge Marnie's point or own her choices.

Viewers who have followed the series up to this point know Hannah has not been vigilant about covering her costs or figuring out the world of work. She tried to force her supervisor to convert an unpaid internship into a paid position, which led to her dismissal in the pilot. Instead of reporting inappropriate touching by her boss she escalated the situation by coming on to him, which forced her to quit (1.5, "Hard Being Easy"). Though Ray gave her a shift at Café Grumpy, she cut short her shift on the first day for her reading. The show's serial structure has led us to this moment of reckoning because we have access to the same information Marnie has witnessed.

They continue arguing with Marnie recalling how she covers all the bills and is tired of talking about Hannah's problems. Hannah claims the opposite, that Marnie's problems with Charlie and her efforts to secure a boyfriend in general have dominated their conversations. The argument escalates to an adolescent pattern endemic to the interpersonal nature of the series' characters:

> MARNIE: Okay, you just flipped this around in a really crazy way. I am the one that has the right to be mad here, okay? I'm taking a very brave chance to discuss my feelings.
> HANNAH: Well you should maybe bring things up while they are actually happening, and then we could avoid these overwrought conversations.
> M: Okay, then I don't want to talk about it anymore.
> H: Well, I do.
> M: Well, now I don't.
> H: Well, now I need closure okay?
> M: You are so selfish. This is why you have no friends from preschool.
> H: Uh, I have a lot of friends from preschool. I'm just not speaking to them right now.

Though the status-seeking Marnie is also a "flawed" character, Hannah's entitlement, financially and emotionally, comes through most clearly in this often absurd, juvenile dialogue. Something the episode's writers (Dunham and Bruce Eric Kaplan) do effectively is juxtapose juvenile aspects of the characters with the more serious aspects of existence, which they are often pushed to do in these climactic sequences. The next passage speaks to this quality:

> M: No, but you judge everyone and yet you ask them not to judge you.
> H: That is because no one could ever hate me as much as I hate myself, okay? So, any mean thing someone's gonna think of to say about me I've already said to me about me probably in the last half hour!

Throughout season one Hannah has managed to mask many of her insecurities and anxieties about the next phase of her life by bouncing from job to job, fixating on Adam, and trying to maintain the same social relations she had in college. For her to admit self-loathing is an important grown-up moment for the character. Hannah reaches a similar moment of personal revelation in "She Did" (1.10) during an argument with Adam. Shortly after Adam offers to move in with her she offers the spare room to her ex-boyfriend Elijah, so Adam won't "worry" about getting too serious, which offends Adam. After yelling at her for pursuing him then not trusting him when he's ready to commit, she says, "I'm scared okay? I'm really scared all the time. I'm like, very scared all the time." This revelatory moment is intricately tied to episode nine as Hannah and Marnie's argument escalates into Marnie declaring she no longer wants to live with Hannah. These moments illustrate how the serial format *Girls* employs helps it introduce, develop, and execute themes in ways that illuminate characters and advance its narrative emotionally rather than plot-wise.

*Staging Conflicts and Vacillations*

Alongside patterns with characters, internal repetitive visual cues that anchor certain types of interactions among characters are another way *Girls* rewards close viewing. Visually, Hannah and Marnie's argument ends with a wide-angle symmetrical shot of the bedroom hallway, as each character enters their bedroom and slams the door the visual is akin to two siblings having an argument except they are *twenty-four years old* (figure 2.1). The camera lingers on the closed doors for seconds before we hear music and the end credits roll. This ending feels heavier and more ominous than the typical *Girls* ending in season one and rightfully so. The episode signifies a need for these characters to recognize their habits and shift from these patterns of behavior toward something more thoughtful and generous.

*Girls* used a similar symmetrical shot in the opening of episode three to signify conflict and the emotional distance between characters. Marnie and Charlie are having a tense conversation, and the camera shifts from a series of reverse angle shots to a wide angle shot that amplifies the tension between them. Marnie views Charlie as annoyingly sensitive and anodyne, and their argument serves as a pretext to a strange, near-sexual encounter with a pretentious conceptual artist, Booth Jonathan, at a gallery opening.

Season two begins with two pairs of legs belonging to two people cuddling, which the camera reveals in a tracking shot to be Elijah, Hannah's gay ex-boyfriend cuddling with her in her bed (figures 2.2, 2.3). Though she felt blindsided by his revelation in season one, she has

Figure 2.1. *Girls* uses a wide symmetrical shot to capture the sibling-like fight between Hannah and Marnie, who are both navigating new emotional territory in emerging adulthood. The symmetrical shot recurs in the show's visual language, which uses the technique to signify narrative turning points.

displaced her anger at him conveniently so he can supplant both Marnie, who has moved out, and her guilt about alienating Adam. The opening shot of season three also finds two pair of legs enveloping each other. This time it is Hannah and Adam who reconciled at the end of season two when Adam rescued Hannah from her self-seclusion in her bedroom (figures 2.4, 2.5). Both scenes center the ongoing displacing of people within the circle of Hannah's life. The recurrence of the visual in the intimacy of the bedroom might also speak to a certain emotional and physical neediness in Hannah. Hannah continually vacillates between her "old" college self and her presumably "newer" more mature self but seems stuck. While she has made peace with Elijah's disclosure about his sexuality, and seemingly her sense of betrayal, his ongoing dishonesty, in this case his brief sexual encounter with Marnie at the beginning of season two, is what leads her to evict him. He, too, is experiencing stasis, bouncing from apartments and lovers, with no clear career. The series is quite resourceful in its ability to visualize the instability and in-betweenness characteristic of emerging adulthood.

A further example of this internal language is the way *Girls* uses the camera as a roaming eye to survey its main characters in large-scale spaces beyond the usual confines of apartments and offices. These "bottle episodes" occur a few times per season and engender anticipation from viewers accustomed to this pattern. For example, two episodes set in a Bushwick warehouse, including a party where Ray develops affection for Shoshanna and Hannah learns Adam is in Alcoholics Anonymous (1.7, "Welcome to Bushwick a.k.a. The Crackcident"), and Jessa's surprise wedding, establish this as an occasional setup on *Girls*. These allow us to learn more about who the characters are and/or how they exist socially beyond their time with each other. Routinely the addition of one person, whether it's a new partner or a stranger, changes the dynamic. The dialogue in side conversations where characters interact in small groups and feel freer

**Figure 2.2.** The opening scene of the first episode of *Girls*' season two shows two pairs of legs intertwined in bed, which suggests a romantic coupling but has an ironic twist.

**Figure 2.3.** Once the camera pans upward, we discover the characters lying together are Hannah and her gay ex-boyfriend, Elijah, which captures her breakup with Adam and inability to move beyond college.

expressing themselves are often especially revealing. This becomes something of a signature approach in season two's "It's a Shame About Ray" (2.4), when Hannah hosts an awkward dinner party where Marnie, her ex-boyfriend Charlie, and his new girlfriend Audrey clash. Similarly, in season three's "Beach House" (3.7) Hannah's spontaneous invitation for Elijah and his friends to crash a retreat Marnie planned for her, Jess, Shoshanna, and Hannah on Long Island's North Fork sparks a new set of tensions.

These directing choices contribute to an intimacy the series establishes with viewers who can draw from a variety of situations to weave

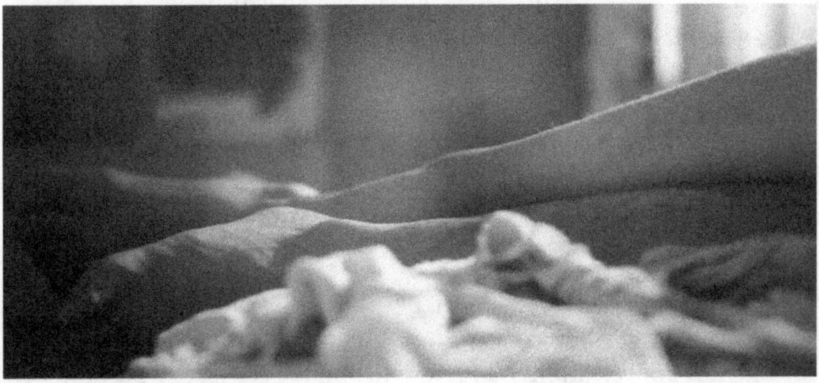

**Figure 2.4.** The opening scene of the first episode of *Girls'* season three mirrors the image of two pairs of legs from season two—a visual link that rewards close viewing.

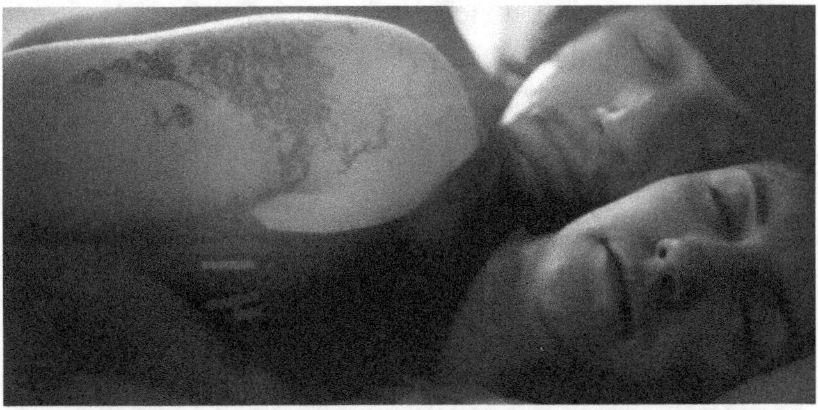

**Figure 2.5.** Similar to season two's opening shot of legs, we understand that a transition has occurred. Elijah has moved out and Hannah and Adam have reconciled and moved forward.

together its intricacies and develop curiosity and empathy for the characters. In doing so *Girls* cements itself as one of the first series to depict emerging adulthood for Millennials complexly. The series employs a range of narrative tools to build and sustain a unique dramedic universe not easily reducible to generational clichés.

## Intimate and Outward: *Shrill* Politicizes the Personal

*Shrill*'s primary contribution to the women's indie television conversation is not its visual style, which falls within the stylistic tropes *Girls* established years earlier. Rather, the way it employs indie style bridges between the genre's typical insularity with the larger political world. Tonally it oscillates between intimate and "speechifying" approaches by linking intimate personal experience into more relatable, historically grounded conversations with a broader reach. Structurally, the series locates Annie in familiar Millennial and emerging adulthood territory: she's a single, unmarried woman who lives in an urban setting with a friend and we see her struggles to find her voice personally and professionally. Along the way the series acknowledges race and racism, names fat stigma, and depicts how conversations about identity and social justice play out in a media industry increasingly driven by outrage and provocation.

*Girls*' lead character Hannah aspires to be viewed by writers, critics, and people in her life as a great creative writer of essays and fiction, and "a voice" for her generation. Her individual experiences are the crux of her writing. Annie's desire to shift from coordinating calendar listings to writing full-time as a journalist reflects her curiosity about the wider world. While her experiences and curiosities fuel her writing, the forum she writes in seeks to change society and spark meaningful conversations. Her choice to write about invisible and misunderstood people, and experiences, connects her to advocacy journalism and offers a different way to think about the aspirations of Millennial characters.

### *Visual Style: Meaningful Close-Ups*

One of the ways Ford connects *Shrill* to *Girls* is visually noting how *Shrill* "uses very similar visual language to *Girls*, including gentle (almost imperceptible) push-ins, planimetric frame composition and close framing of facial reactions."[25] The *context* for these aesthetic choices differs from *Girls*, however, because *Shrill* chooses to address topics beyond relationships even if it does so with a milder version of speechifying. Two notable examples speak to this quality.

In "Pool" (1.4) Annie attends the Fat Babe Pool Party, an inclusive party for plus-size women (figure 2.6). After showing up wearing a shirt and jeans and distancing herself from the activities, she loosens up, drinks a margarita, speaks with an attendee about plus-size clothing, and dances. When she sits down and gets her feet wet the camera focuses on her face (figure 2.7). We see her taking in the scene of plus-size women

Figure 2.6. In season one's "Pool" episode of *Shrill*, Annie and Fran enter the Fat Babe Pool Party, a space for fat women to celebrate their bodies unapologetically, which disarms Annie.

Figure 2.7. This close-up shot of Annie's face at the pool party registers her personal joy about being surrounded by fat women, and inspires her to write the online article "Hello, I'm Fat."

enjoying themselves unapologetically, which is a struggle for her. This contemplative pause serves as a prelude to her stripping down to her swimsuit and diving into the pool. No longer an observer, she is a participant who sees herself as one of them, not just a chronicler. After leaving the party she writes a pivotal piece, "Hello, I'm Fat," and uploads it to the *Weekly Thorn*'s website. Though Hannah occasionally comments on her weight and eating habits, as do other characters, the series does not overtly politicize her body or gesture toward body positivity discourse; doing so would remove viewers from its intentionally insular tone and is out of step with a "matter of fact quality" of indie film elements the series employs.[26]

Another symbolic example of a noteworthy *Shrill* close-up is when Annie leaves an interview with an infamous White racial separatist family at their compound in "Ranchers" (3.4). In typical fashion, Annie is very patient and gracious toward the family, taking a tour with its matriarch, Clara, shooting a gun for the first time at the ranch's shooting range, and eating lunch. Once she starts asking questions about the separatists' beliefs Clara turns cold, lambastes feminism, and personally attacks Annie for having publicly written about her abortion. We see Annie peel out of the driveway of the remotely located ranch, and she mutters to herself what she couldn't say directly, "Oh, you wanna talk shit about me. Bad news bitch, I'm a huge fucking bitch too, okay, and I don't give a fuck, woooo" while a punk song plays in the background.

Her abortion in the pilot (1.1), and its resonance, is not a stand-alone plot point. Rather, her choice symbolizes the uncertain status of her relationship with her boyfriend Ryan at the time as well as the importance of her best friend and roommate Fran's support. In a poignant moment in "HR" (2.8), Annie's mother, Vera, explains a random trip she took to Vancouver as respite to care for herself for a change. Inspired, Annie shares her experience getting an abortion with her mother who responds with great understanding. The series does not imply that Vera has experience with the procedure but based on her warm response she clearly understands and respects Annie's decision as a mother who appreciates what it takes to care for others. The gravity of this conversation registers on the political level for depicting the broader social acceptance of abortion *and* within the intimate space of Annie and Vera's often contentious relationship. The show's serialized structure provides the pathway for understanding the weight of this seemingly small moment as a turning point for these characters.

Both examples encapsulate how *Shrill* carved out an identity even though it debuted six years after *Girls* and toward the latter end of the series I discuss. Though less iconic than some of the other women-centric series, its bridging of the intimate and the outward warrants critical consideration. In addition to her observation about *Shrill*'s style Ford addresses how *Shrill* "explores how idealized constructions of femininity shape women's social and cultural value."[27] This is an important aspect of the show's focus, especially during the first season, but throughout three seasons it expands the boundaries of how relevance emerges in a Millennial-themed series. While it follows a familiar pattern of relationship and career struggles these coexist, and overlap, with the social context of the era. The series depictions of the contemporary salience of platonic friendships for women, including the intersectional imperative of multiracial friendships, the pervasiveness of fat stigma, and the digital mediation of social justice content challenges a tendency of women's indie series to downplay race, avoid "politics," and/or gloss over the disproportionate influence of media in how we understand ourselves. *Shrill* offers a different way to locate bits of humor from contemporary life in a more socially conscious Millennial voice.

### *Recognizing Race in Multiracial Friendships*

Annie is more removed age-wise from college than the twenty-four-year-old Hannah of *Girls*, and more similar in age to *Insecure*'s Issa. Though she shares an apartment with her former college roommate, Fran (Lolly Adefope), the series rarely references her college life and focuses more on her relatively stable position as an editorial assistant at the fictional newsmagazine the *Weekly Thorn*. She is positioned more closely to her career aspiration to work as a journalist than Hannah or Issa to their goals. Though it has some stylistic parallels to other indie television series the imprint of larger social issues and trends inflects its content more overtly.

Annie lives with Fran and interacts with her as a friend, confidante, and adviser on virtually everything. Though she dates Ryan (Luka Jones) in the first two seasons his initially condescending treatment of her, the ambiguous nature of their relationship, and his immaturity limit him as a resource. The kind of support women in their mid- to late twenties might have sought from a partner is subordinate to the input of her friends. One of the defining characteristics of Millennials is "delaying or foregoing marriage" and "forming their own households" compared to previous generations and being more likely to "live alone, with roommates, or with their parents."[28] As a woman in the eighteen to twenty-nine range who is college educated, unmarried, and childless, and living with a friend, she embodies elements associated with emerging adults and Millennials.

Collectively these factors inform the unique salience of friendship as an integral texture of the series and as a generational marker. My analysis focuses on her relationship with Fran not just because Fran is a woman but because she is a woman of Nigerian descent, born and raised in London, who is also a sexually active lesbian and hair stylist. The fact that she, as a Black woman supporting character, has a fully developed storyline distinguishes her role from the absence of Black women on most women-centric series. Within their relationship we witness comforting moments as well as conflicts and tensions informed by their respective social locations. Rather than avoiding race altogether by excluding Black characters or employing a "color-blind" approach, the series acknowledges Fran and Annie's coworker Amadi (Ian Owens), the *Weekly Thorn*'s creative director, as Black people whose experiences are informed by who they are, not just their personalities. *Shrill* has a racially diverse writing and directing staff, which seems to inform its multicultural view of who populates the professional and personal relationships it depicts.

Annie's unexpected pregnancy is the pilot's primary conflict, and Fran helps her decide to have an abortion. After Annie reveals her status to Fran we learn that Annie took a morning-after pill to make Ryan happy. Fran recommends she have an abortion, which leads to Annie crying and sharing how this might be her last chance to become a parent because her looks have made her insecure about her ability to attract a companion. Fran gently advises her to stop hating herself and tells her to end her relationship with Ryan. Annie is accompanied by Fran to the procedure, and the episode shifts from the clinic to Fran and Annie lying in bed together after the procedure.

Fran embodies the value of women's friendships as a site of meaning by recognizing how Annie has contorted herself for Ryan and his inability to serve as a true partner for Annie. Whereas the character Maude

Finley's choice to have an abortion on *Maude* engendered national controversy Annie's decision to have an abortion is presented as one of many options available to women at the time. Her ability to confer with Fran reflects an evolution in women's friendships on television that Spangler has traced from slapstick to more realistic depictions that integrate social issues relevant to women.[29] We can see similar examples of the unique salience of friendship in other "good" and "complex" series such as *Broad City*, *Crazy Ex-Girlfriend*, and *I May Destroy You*.

Annie lacks a reliable romantic partner throughout *Shrill*, and though her parents are a resource, Fran is typically her first choice. There are countless other examples of Annie turning to Fran for advice and support, but *Shrill* is also willing to depict moments when their friendship challenges Annie by requiring her, as a White, straight woman, to recognize Fran's positionality.

In "No" (3.5), Annie's story about White separatists is posted on the *Weekly Thorn*'s website with a clickbait headline ("Separate But . . . Charming") that angers viewers who email her directly, post negative comments, and attack the newspaper as racist. Annie is mortified by the personal attacks and feels betrayed because she originally submitted it under a different, less provocative headline. In a parallel to the contemporary power of social media, her colleagues joke that she has been "canceled." In the same episode Fran is put off by her White lover Em's curiosity about her Nigerian identity. In the midst of processing the feeling of being exoticized with her Chilean-born coworker, another stylist shows her a smart phone displaying an article titled "Annie Easton Is Cancelled."

When a disheveled Annie returns home and describes her day, Fran responds coolly, telling Annie she is not the victim because the headline was changed and also questions why Annie felt compelled to write the story. She notes that Annie spent the day with the ranchers, shot the gun on the shooting range, and ultimately decided to provide the group a platform. Feeling exasperated, Annie tries to justify her choice by noting she wanted to avoid being pigeonholed in her writing. Fran rejects this by asking her to consider what would have happened if she, as a Black lesbian, had gone to the ranch to write the story, and tells her, "I can't help you through this, this is your problem" (figure 2.8).

These details are important because they reflect *Shrill*'s willingness to go beyond the optics of multicultural casting to dig deeper into the

**Figure 2.8.** Fran tells Annie, "I can't help you through this," after she chooses to write about a White separatist group and has to bear the consequences in season three's "Ranchers." *Shrill*'s Black characters disrupt the typically silent White racial politics of indie television.

tension between *being* a White liberal and *thinking critically* about Whiteness. Annie's desire to be seen as more than a writer about "body stuff" precluded her willingness to consider its potential impact especially in a cultural landscape where popular misogyny and racist backlash are rampant.

Annie's tensions with Amadi in "No" and the following episode "Sorry" also reflect this dynamic but with a dash of humor. In "No" a White barista who has seen Annie's story denies Annie coffee but offers Amadi anything he wants for free. This leads him to joke with Annie about her feeling a lot of White guilt, which she affirms earnestly, for which he then asks "What's that like?" Later in the episode when Annie asks the editor and publisher to take the article off-line during a meeting Amadi also agrees that is not an option, which disappoints her. At the beginning of "Sorry," Amadi invites Annie to his thirty-ninth birthday party and addresses the tension between them by noting that as he is the only Black editor at the *Weekly Thorn*, taking down an article accused of being racist would have felt like a disingenuous attempt to hide the newspaper's mistake in running the article. She brings an "apology cake" (with the phrase "Sorry I'm A Dumb White" frosted on top) to his birthday party and the matter is ostensibly settled.

Like Fran, Amadi is a confidant and advisor, but as an older coworker in a leadership role with a family, and a Black man, he has professional responsibilities and personal obligations that sometimes come before his friendship with Annie. He is a well-written Black supporting character with a life and identity apart from his relationship to the White lead. For example, we meet his daughters at the birthday party and his diverse friend group. Similarly, *Shrill* includes Fran's family in multiple episodes, including an episode devoted to her cousin's wedding where we get a fuller look into her complicated relationship with her family (2.5, "Wedding").[30] Further, the same navigations of friendships, romantic partners, and family characteristic of many Millennial women define Fran's character arc.

While racially coded themes do not entirely define either of these friendship relationships, *Shrill* does not shy away from the racial dynamics that exist even in the liberal enclave of Portland, Oregon. By refusing to exclude Black characters, avoiding the "color-blind" approach to characterization, and declining to limit Black characters to addressing racism the series depicts multicultural friendships authentically and credibly. Both relationships also amplify the salience of friendships for Millennial women, especially since many are also housemates who play a more prominent role in each other's lives than in past generations.

### *Spectacular Fat Bodies*

Annie's ability to access her voice and articulate a unique point of view, and the awkwardness it entails for her, and her readers, is central to the series title and design. The richness of author Lindy West's experiences writing about fatness play an important role in the adaptation. Annie's epic speechifying moment comes in her and Fran's apartment living room toward the end of "Pool" (1.4). After Annie rushes from the party to attend a *Weekly Thorn* sponsored bicycle ride, her boss Gabe scolds her for being late, and quips about "lazy bodies lazy minds." At home she tells Fran and the pool party's host, who are seated together on a sofa, the following:

> Every fucking magazine and commercial and weird targeted ad telling me to freeze my fat off or to drink a tea so that I'll shit my brain out of my ass. And at this point I could be

> a fucking licensed nutritionist because I have literally been training for it since the fourth grade. Which is the first time that my mom said I should just eat a bowl of special K and not the dinner [*Annie's intonation gets teary*] she made for everyone else so that I might be a little bit smaller and so that she could . . . so that boys would like me.

The host says her mother said the same things to her, and Annie continues, "I don't even blame her because it's a fucking mind prison, you know. That every fucking woman everywhere has been programmed to believe, you know. And I've wasted so much time and energy for what? You know, I'm fat, I'm fucking fat, hello." This dialogue excerpt connects her experience to the larger issues of fat stigma but renders it in a context and language befitting of a Millennial, especially its references to "targeted ads."

Immediately after speaking she grabs her laptop and types the editorial "Hello, I'm Fat," which she uploads to the *Weekly Thorn*'s website. *Shrill* regularly employs different techniques to capture different scales of "emotional spectacle," which speaks to its efforts to be both intimate and outward looking.[31] Whereas her close-up at the pool captures her quiet internal sense of discovery and bliss, her personal rant renders her intimate experience of fatness public, which the article furthers beyond the confines of her apartment. The personal gets *politicized* through her writing and the mostly affirming responses it generates.

Embedded in her rant are subtle indicators of the systemic ways that fat stigma operates for women pervasively.[32] She verbalizes pressures from within her family but recognizes the broader problem. The series complements what she verbalizes in its design. From the obnoxious trainer who tries to push her services onto Annie at a coffee shop to a pharmacist who tells her morning-after pills are restricted to women under 175 pounds her body is a constant source of commentary and shame (1.1). Annie's internalization leads to recurring tensions with her mother, such as the contentious family dinner in "Freak" (2.4), and leads her to reject a man she feels paired with simply because they are both fat in "Will" (3.2). We are able to experience her individual struggles with fatness and see how they manifest socially.

*Shrill* operates on multiple levels that curb some of this stigma by presenting Annie and Fran, who is also fat, as physically attractive, desirable women. Though Annie's lovers vary in maturity and worthiness there's no question men appreciate her as a voluptuous woman. Similarly, Fran's sexual appeal is integral to her character. One of her challenges is finding a meaningful relationship beyond sex, leading her to take a hiatus from dating and focus on self-development in "Freak." The depiction of both as sexually active fat women breaks from US television's tendency to desexualize fat women.

*Shrill* distinguishes itself by depicting fatness and anxieties about fat stigma as a reality woman, of multiple generations, negotiate *constantly*. Though the episodes "Pool" and "Article" (1.5) center on the authoring and aftermath of Annie's article "Hello, I'm Fat," the series refuses to isolate the issue as something incidental. Instead, it insists the issue pervades women's lives. *Shrill*'s approach to fatness works on multiple levels. It employs comedy as a platform to connect individual experiences with collective issues concerning fatness and normalizes diverse bodies on television by starring fat women whose characters own their identities as fat while redefining how we understand it.

### *Outrage Media*

Given *Shrill*'s roots in Lindy West's experiences being trolled and harassed for her writing about women's issues, it is fitting that the series routinely depicts Annie's complicated experiences navigating reader response to her writing in the digitized age.[33] The series treats online harassment as not only a broad social concern but one especially salient for women. Though trolling, harassing, and doxing behaviors are well researched and well known the series approaches them as personally disarming with a blend of humor, irony, and sobriety.[34]

For example, in "Ribs" (3.1) Annie has a routine medical appointment, and her doctor, unprompted, comments on her weight and recommends surgical options for losing weight. Annie is quietly offended but says nothing. Once she is seated in her car in the parking lot and sees the doctor she screams at the doctor belligerently about her presumptions. When the doctor turns around we see she's wearing wireless in-ear headphones and hasn't heard a word. After she removes them Annie, feeling sheepish, greets her politely. Many indie series would leave this as an ironic, bittersweet moment, but not *Shrill*. In the next episode "Will," Annie has written about her experience for the *Weekly Thorn*, which generates positive feedback from readers and coworkers. The doctor even calls and tells Annie that based on negative feedback toward her, the office will now employ a "healthy sizes approach," which Annie appreciates. When asked if the article could be removed Annie says no. As discussed earlier Annie has the inverse experience in "Ranchers" when negative feedback toward *her* results in her requesting the article's removal and the editors refusing.

Because Annie's budding career at the *Weekly Thorn* is so central to her growth the series routinely depicts the increasing precarity of print media like the *Thorn* in a contemporary media landscape so rooted in commodifying outrage. In season three the weekly paper reduces the hours of many of its employees, and in "Retreat" (3.3) Amadi informs the staff everyone, including the distribution staff, is a "content creator," echoing the lingua franca of the social media age. In the same episode after Amadi expresses reservations about them covering the separatist group, editor Gabe dismisses him saying the paper used to be about controversy. Annie, desperate to branch out from fat content, takes the bait, in a sense, and has to deal with the consequences when the provocative headline Gabe publishes reduces it to clickbait.

Again, *Shrill* deftly bridges the personal and political by illustrating the tensions between Annie's sincere desires for social change *and* her career ambitions, and placing them in the outrage economy that drives contemporary media. Though "Hello, I'm Fat" is a breakthrough for Annie, the aggressive trolling from an online persona named "The Awesome" rattles her as does the negative response from readers, colleagues, and friends, to "Separate But . . . Charming?" Rather than telling us, it *shows us* how central media is for how we engage the world. The layer of insularity print media previously provided writers, such as the filtering of letters to the editor, has shifted toward online forums where writers who take on social issues must prepare themselves for immediate feedback. Instead of presenting Annie as a plucky, earnest career girl, in the classic sitcom tradition, and limiting her challenges to the personal realm, *Shrill* makes the point that these arenas are not so discrete. Its approach to her career shows us that for Annie to mature into her chosen career she must contend with the persistent social and cultural barriers affecting women in the personal and political facets of their lives.

## Specific Yet Relatable: *Insecure*'s Black Millennial Complexity

Among the series I examine, *Insecure* most overtly borders between the surreal and the unspectacular in many ways. Stylistically, *Insecure*'s pilot episode (1.1, "Insecure as Fuck") employs a high degree of spectacular and surreal elements, including voice-overs, fantasy sequences, and a split screen. Subsequent episodes, however, are leaner in their use of these elements, with Issa's fantasy rap sequences and the occasional montage or flashback as the recurring elements. Otherwise, it embodies many of the aesthetic elements Ford identifies as characterizing women-centric indie dramedies but inflects them racially. Most notably, just as many of the series she cites take an "unspectacular" approach to depicting a feminist sensibility (e.g., no speechifying) and integrate this sensibility into mundane and domestic spaces, *Insecure* depicts aspects of the "black familiar," including certain rituals and language, as a common element of Black life.[35] We rarely see these cultural practices in the largely White women-centric indie series world. It also treats racial microaggressions as a common enough occurrence in mixed racial settings to appear mundane.[36]

Though *Insecure* is not focused on "educating" audiences about Blackness, nor is it particularly polemical, its focus on the lives of diverse Black Los Angelenos defies the presumed indie norm that White-dominated shows are universal and generic, thus "un-raced."[37] Notably, it depicts situations and conversations specifically inflected by Blackness that could resonate also with people beyond the Black diaspora. This cultural specificity constitutes an important intervention that disrupts the generic unnamed Whiteness of the genre and offers a different way of experiencing the indie aesthetic. Ever since the height of media attention lavished on her web series *The Misadventures of Awkward Black Girl* Rae has intentionally questioned the terms of relatability, noting why she began her production work on web platforms at the outset.[38] For example, as Rae has noted, "But [I'm more interested in] the quirk that African Americans were not allowed to have on-screen. You were either the extreme pretty girl or the nerd; there was no in-between. I was interested in the in-between. There are so many different types that are representative of black people, from the nerd to the quirky to the cool."[39]

Rae also created a lead character who defies clichés about Black women, especially the "strong Black woman," archetype. In a bonus segment that aired immediately after the pilot, Rae and her showrunner Prentice Penny and coexecutive producer Dayna Lynne North discuss the intentional design of her character "Issa" as a "weak Black woman" who reveals the insecurities all people experience.[40] This might seem odd but it's helpful to consider the context. Black hip-hop feminist Joan Morgan broke new ground in 1999 when she "retired" from the "strong Black woman" (SBW) archetype her generation inherited from their foremothers. While recognizing the virtues of knowing how to survive the challenges of racism and sexism she was unwilling to "be the consummate professional, handle any life crisis, be the dependable rock for every soul who needed me, and . . . require less from my lovers than they did from me."[41] Smith-Shomade located examples of relief from the SBW on television in the "dizzy Black woman" archetype featured on several 1990s–'00s sitcoms (e.g., *Living Single*), which she frames as offering alternatives to "the confining space of the strong Black woman" and opening audiences to the reality that "Black women make mistakes, are multifaceted, and sometimes surprisingly soft."[42] I further unpack and explore the terms of the show's unique approach to relatability and resistance to stereotypes by examining the interplay of dialogue, plot, and tone within the "unspectacular" style of "Racist as Fuck" (1.3).

The episode begins with Issa (Issa Rae) and her boyfriend Lawrence (Jay Ellis) preparing for bed. Issa preps for bed by putting on a head scarf to maintain moisture and texture in her hair, a common practice among many Black women. The moment itself is unremarkable but uncommon in television. A similarly casual nod to Blackness occurs later in the episode when Issa and Molly attend a predominantly Black house party where we meet their friends Tiffany (Amanda Seales) and her husband Derek (Wade Allain-Marcus), and Kelli (Natasha Rothwell). Kelli tells her friends a story about dating a "White boy" and jokes about how he took her apple picking—understood in the conversation as a very "White" activity—and having sex in the orchard. Within the same group she comments on Black men with college degrees as highly arrogant, and Derek says Black women struggle to attract them because their standards are "too high," leading Kelli to joke that she's going to call noted Black feminist scholar bell hooks. The commentary on interracial dating, the challenges of intraracial dating, and the reference to hooks are so culturally specific they would not likely surface on most series in the White indie world. As such the show also interrupts conventional television practices by showcasing the inner lives of college-educated Black urbanites, which evokes the ways the indies *Love Jones*, *Hav Plenty*, and *Medicine for Melancholy* told different stories from the predominantly White indie film scene of the late 1990s–2010s.[43]

In many ways Kelli and Derek's conversation extends a thread the pilot established about the challenges for professional college-educated Black women seeking similarly situated Black male partners. This theme, which also appears in showrunner Rae's essay collection *The Misadventures of Awkward Black Girl*, is central to the pilot's opening scene when Issa gets defensive about why Black women should be "more willing to settle for less." As a complex series with a serial element this topic comes up in multiple conversations between Molly and other women of color. In the pilot Molly expresses her concern with her coworker Diane (Maya Erksine) about her surprise at not being with a Black man and how Black men seem more intent on loving women who aren't Black. Later when Diane shares her engagement she calls Issa to ask why some people are "marriage eligible" but she isn't? In "Messy as Fuck" (1.2) at a nail salon with Issa we see a humorous flashback montage of Molly's frustrating dates from dating apps. In "Racist as Fuck" (1.3) Molly dismisses Jared (Langston Kerman), a prospect she met in the pilot who is not college educated and works at a rental car company, once she's accepted into an elite dating service called The League. She justifies her choice to Issa by stating he is "not on her level," a harsh assessment that exposes her as a "flawed" character and defies the bland edict for "positive" and "uplifting" characters in Black stories rather than complex ones. This textured approach to Molly reflects Rae's intentional approach to presenting Black women's navigations of dating complexly rather than settling for tropes of victim or villain,

> Molly's single status gave her the chance to explore what her friends—and the single women in her writers' room—are experiencing on dating apps. "I wanted to put out there what it's like to date as a black woman and feel like you're not that desired. We're getting swiped left the shit out of, and that'll

> be taking its toll," she says. "There's a feeling of, *Why not me? What's wrong with me? I'm successful, I'm driven, I think I'm a catch, so why doesn't anyone want me?*" But by showing that Molly has ridiculously high standards, Rae also makes the answer more complicated than "All men suck." "A lot of men do suck!" she says. "But at the same time I wanted to ask, 'What is it about you?' I didn't want to have this thing like, 'Oh, poor black women victims.' What can you look at within yourself that might be the problem too?"[44]

A similar culturally specific challenge that emerges is the prevalence of racial microaggressions in the workplace, a theme Rae explored buoyantly in *Awkward Black Girl.* The visual representation of We Got Y'all, a youth organization Issa works for, in the pilot uses a brief visual montage to establish a theme of problematic White liberalism. The organization's logo featured on the building's front door is a white hand stretched out with the image of three black silhouettes standing in its palm in front of an orange background, signifying a rather condescending racial dynamic. As we view Issa entering the door she narrates the scene noting, "My boss founded a nonprofit to help kids from the hood but she didn't hire anybody from the 'hood." As the camera pans through the office we see various hallmarks of White liberalism, including a large Amnesty International poster on a bulletin board surrounded by smaller posters with clichés ("Make a Difference," "Think Outside the Box") and a larger poster of multicultural youth performing neighborhood cleanup. In the interior of We Got Y'all's director Joanne's (Catherine Curtin) office, camera close-ups reveal a framed image of Martin Luther King Jr. near the heads of several African sculptures (figure 2.9), a Beyoncé poster juxtaposed next to an antiwar and antiapartheid poster, and Joanne leaning back in her chair wearing a blue dashiki as Issa sit across from her (figure 2.10). As she wraps up a phone call we see a framed image of Joanne shaking President Obama's hand in front of an American flag. In less than a minute the scene establishes the cultural context for Issa's work environment.

The pilot finds Issa telling us that "being aggressively passive is what I do best," which she tells us after her White coworkers at the community group We Got Y'all ask her "What's on fleek?" a Black slang term, and she

**Figure 2.9.** These objects comprise a subtle montage of close-ups on Black-oriented material objects which relay the pseudo-liberalism of Issa's White boss and overall tone of the community-based non-profit she works for, We Got Y'all.

**Figure 2.10.** Issa's often condescending boss wears a dashiki and is surrounded by iconic Black diasporic images in her office during her conversation with Issa, symbolizing a performative racial allyship defied by exclusionary behavior at her workplace.

pretends to not understand the question. This behavior continues in episode two when Issa blanches at the notion that the mostly Black students served by the organization are interested in activities related to sports. She also scoffs at a recommendation for the students to perform community service in different neighborhoods. In a fantasy, characteristic of its blend of indie and surreal elements, she exclaims, "That's the whitest shit I ever heard," but once she returns to "real time" she recommends an activity that exposes students to the arts. In response, the all-White group expresses skepticism around the budget and various risks and proceeds to reference stereotypically "Black" themes such as the African American museum, and hip-hop Shakespeare. These moments illustrate, with overt and subtle humor, how stereotyping pervades even so-called progressive spaces.

Episode three offers us a more extended version of this microaggressive behavior in multiple scenes that build toward the series' astute understanding of how Black people regularly navigate land mines of different types of aggressions in the workplace. In the office of We Got Y'all Issa overhears her coworkers chatting about a beach trip with the students. Frustrated, she asks her coworker Frieda (Lisa Joyce), a White woman she seems to trust, what they were speaking about and voices her annoyance at back-channel conversations noting, "I wasn't cc'd." This is followed by her conversation at the apartment she shares with Lawrence about "secret White meetings" and the double standard of having to be perfect (figure 2.11). Though at this point the series has established Lawrence's struggle to find gainful employment and how Issa's frustration with him have led her to spend the last few nights at Molly's, as a Black man he recognizes and empathizes with what she is experiencing. The sense of exclusion and exceptionalism is expressed plaintively as a reality for Black people and requires no explanation. This depiction illustrates how a seemingly microlevel experience is common enough to register as a macrolevel issue specific to Black people and other minoritized people.

**Figure 2.11.** Despite tensions in their relationship, Issa and Lawrence bond while discussing the frustrating racial microaggressions she faces in her professional life while working at We Got Y'all.

As the students and staff travel by bus we hear Issa's coworkers making passive aggressive comments about the trip, which annoys Issa and leads her to stand up and chat, somewhat awkwardly, with the students to help them feel excited and comfortable about the trip, breaking the wall between staff and students. At the beach the students collect refuse and Issa overhears a coworker ask, "Why don't any of them swim?," a common stereotype of African Americans. Issa passive-aggressively responds, "Slavery," in a deadpan manner. She also responds to comments about whether the students need sunscreen, yet another stereotype, by tossing several bottles of sunscreen to the coworkers and commenting about one of them beginning to burn. Aggressively passive indeed. Rather than filtering these moments through self-conscious technique we see Issa's unfiltered frustration, which she expresses in pointed but largely indirect ways, staying true to character and the emotional spectacle approach of indie-inspired television. The beach trip turns out to be a success, ultimately, which becomes palpable when one of Issa's few coworkers of color describes how well it went and "how people always doubt us." One of the children, Dante, also hugs Issa and thanks her for the experience. The episode balances what would be generically frustrating behavior for anyone with the racial, and gender, scripts that add sting to such presumptions.

Molly's workplace also poses a racialized challenge we rarely see in women-centric dramedies. At the beginning of episode three she meets her law firm's newest intern Rasheeda (Gail Bean), who is a young Black woman. Later she hears Rasheeda talking loudly to other lawyers and is horrified by her volume and the slang she's using. Concerned about her fit at the firm Molly calls her in to check in with her. Though she gently suggests Rasheeda be mindful of the established culture, lest she appear "too ethnic," Rasheeda is offended by her suggestion that she "switch it up," sometimes referred to as "code switching." Molly's protective instinct appears motivated less by a desire to control or restrict Rasheeda than a learned self-consciousness of being one of the few, if not only, Black people in a White professional space.

In the following episode (1.4, "Thirsty as Fuck"), Molly walks past a conference room where Rasheeda is speaking boisterously, and she shakes her head. Later in the episode a partner approaches Molly about speaking to Rasheeda, which tacitly places Molly, who is not the intern's supervisor, in an awkward position. Molly declines and recommends the partner has a conversation with Rasheeda. Walking through the hallway Molly notices Rasheeda sitting and listening to several partners in a conference room with glass walls. They are presumably addressing proper behavior in a professional environment. These scenes seem less about Rasheeda being problematic than Molly, whom Issa described as "the Will Smith of corporate" in the pilot. She navigated the work environment successfully and saw herself as protecting Rasheeda and helping her fit in. The partner's presumption that Molly was responsible for "handling" the other Black woman in the office was handled deftly by Molly, who had already tried, and illustrates her empathy with other Black women and her ability to finesse her White-dominated workplace effectively. By season three Molly decides to leave the firm for a Black-owned one.

As I noted earlier *Insecure* employs the unspectacular aesthetics of women-centric indie dramedies to convey quotidian aspects of Black life, including distinctly Black rituals and experiences recognizable within the milieu of its characters. Rather than explicating on Black life for viewers it assumes viewers will catch on (or not), just as minoritized viewers have traditionally adapted to cultural references in predominantly White series. This feels less like a political gesture than an unapologetic embrace of lived Blackness. Relatedly the series flexes its cultural politics by rendering covert forms of racism as common enough to warrant a range of "low-key" strategies from aggressively passive comments to deft negotiations that never boil over into overt spectacle.

*Insecure*'s use of indie-film-oriented techniques, including its understated approach to racial and gender realities, and its tonal bordering between comedy and drama, makes it an urtext for contemporary Black women's comedy. As the first series created by and starring a Black woman on the prestigious HBO, it launches Black Millennial women in the "quality TV" realm associated with premium cable.[45] Its lack of laugh track and formulaic sitcom rhythms commonly associated with broadcast network comedies focused on Black women enables a different kind of storytelling more reliant on visual markers, character development, and dialogic subtlety than conventional elements like slapstick and linear plots.

## Women-Centric "Indie" Series Forge New Creative Blueprints

The distinctive imprint of contemporary American indie films clearly connects *Girls*, *Shrill*, and *Insecure* formally. The indie-film-inspired, serial style they employ fosters a spaciousness and clarity that allows us to focus on the emotional lives of characters and the intricacies of their relationships. Their narrative focus on women, particularly Millennial women navigating aspects of emerging adulthood, such as their professional interests and personal identity, amplifies the value of feminine culture as a worthwhile arena for television. This stylistic and thematic approach endures across the seasons for each series.

Dunham, who wrote or cowrote forty-one of sixty-two *Girls* episodes and directed nineteen of its episodes, has cited several generations of independent and "indie" directors as inspirations, including Noah Baumbach, Nicole Holofcener, and Whit Stillman.[46] Dunham, and her creative team, clearly understands the nature of the milieu of White, young, urbanities she depicts. Like Stillman, she is a meticulous chronicler of their aspirations, neuroses, and eccentricities, which has a built-in specialized appeal. The difference lies in how television scales elements of film to fit the demands of television as a medium.

Stylistically Stillman's "understated approach to film style" and lack of "tightly structured" plots are evident in *Girls*. They also share a focus on ensembles of White characters whose everyday musings and experiences constitute their essence with limited melodrama and rare depictions of extreme sex or violence.[47] As a premium cable television series, however, *Girls* locates a wider variety of situations to stage its plots to foster believable character growth and to compel audiences to remain interested over multiple seasons. The series also has a unique role as one of the first to depict the inner lives of Millennials experiencing emerging adulthood, making its stylistic departure from previous comedies a kind of generational marker signaling the emergence of new sensibilities.

*Insecure* and *Shrill* are stylistically and thematically linked to the pioneering *Girls* in numerous ways. They diverge by using the "indie" film tools to subvert the form's insularity by depicting how less visible women experience the quotidian mundanities indie films frequently seek to capture. *Shrill*'s Annie is searching in the many of the same ways as Hannah but has more distance from college and is not as insulated financially or socially by the friendship structure that sustains *Girls*. She also has a professional orientation and persona more geared toward challenging deeply ingrained perspectives on social issues such as fat stigma. Further, the multicultural nature of her relationships and workplace world requires her to interrogate her Whiteness and attune herself to the nuances of people with different realities. The characters Fran and Amadi are essential to the larger story of *Shrill* rather than stock characters. The show depicts them as complex people independently of Annie.

*Shrill*'s multicultural creative team is integral to this vision. For example, "Pool," was written by Samantha Irby, a Black woman, and directed by Shaka King, a man of Bahamian and Panamanian descent. Self-identified Korean American genderqueer Hye Yun Park cowrote episodes for seasons two and three of *Shrill*. Biracial writer Sudi Green, who is of Iranian and White American descent, wrote four of *Shrill*'s twenty-two episodes.[48] *Shrill* models how indie-oriented women-centric series can embrace racial and gender diversity even when the lead and the primary storyline are not focused on a woman of color. Writers and directors of African American, Asian American, Indigenous, and Latinx backgrounds remain underrepresented in the women's indie television arena, as are gender nonconforming creatives, so there are still many opportunities to open up access in television writing and direction.

*Insecure* is a benchmark series for subverting aesthetic and representational norms of US indie-inspired television. The choice to depict multidimensional Black characters onscreen, and its hiring of multiple generations of Black women creatives in writing and directing roles behind the scenes, has changed the face of television, literally. In addition to the diverse directing staff, the diversity of its writers is also notable. Sixteen writers have received credit for *Insecure*, including nine women and seven men. Thirty-one writing credits were assigned to women and sixteen to men. Among the nine women, seven are Black women and two are White, and among the seven men, five are Black, one is Asian American, and one is White. Though Rae has written or cowritten the greatest share of episodes (nine total), the writing duties are spread across a range of voices with Prentice Penny (a Black man) and Laura Kittrell (a White woman) writing/cowriting five episodes, Amy Aniobi (a Black woman) writing/cowriting four episodes, Dayna Lynne North (a Black woman) and Ben Dougan (a White man) writing/cowriting three episodes, and eight writers receiving credits for two episodes, and two writers receiving credits for two episodes.

*Insecure* has served as an inclusive incubator of creative talents by providing opportunities for women and men from diverse racial and national backgrounds. This is especially poignant for directors like Thembi Banks and Lacey Duke, who directed episodes in season four and had few television credits before *Insecure*.[49] The show's willingness to honor veterans like Debbie Allen and to provide opportunities to emerging creatives speaks to the ethos of Black creatives addressing historic marginality through building supportive networks and lifting up each other. One of the key aesthetic values of employing diverse personnel is the show's conscious choice to function as an "insider creation" focused primarily on telling stories inflected by Black culture and identity told from Black women's creative perspectives. This is an industrial and creative gap that has necessitated an intervention and inspired other creatives.

For example, writer, producer, and actress Lena Waithe created and served as executive producer of the Black women-centered comedy series *Twenties*, which focused on a "Gen Z" character. In December 2020 she launched The Hillman Grad Mentorship Lab focused on providing "opportunities for marginalized storytellers to connect, grow and accelerate their careers in television and film"[50] Just as *Insecure* offered diverse creators with opportunities to gain experience as writers and directors, Waithe's investment in nurturing new generations of creatives is evident in her staffing choices. Notably, she has hired numerous creatives who have been mentored by diversity-, equity-, and inclusion-themed programs focused on nurturing emerging talents from underrepresented and minoritized creatives. Waithe has also served as a mentor in AT&T's Hello Labs Filmmaker Mentorship Program.[51] By creating opportunities for storytellers from diverse backgrounds and drawing their staff from mentoring programs, future women-centric series can continue to incubate new talent, challenge the notion of people of color, center creative work as "niche" or "exclusionary," and demonstrate the potential for a range of creatives who can tell a story in the era of "good" and "complex" contemporary television. This potential pivot synthesizes the creative innovations *Girls* initiated, the more inclusive storylines and creative participation *Insecure* pioneered, which *Shrill* embraced, and works to advance the notion of "indie" television as not only a style but as a way of operating independently of television's gender and racial conventions.

# 3

# GOT TO BE (SUR)REAL

## *"Remixing" Gender through Genre*

By the early '00s comedies, especially prestige comedies, had shifted from multicamera to single-camera formats (e.g., *Parks and Recreation*, *Modern Family*) and toward serialized storylines (e.g., *Arrested Development*). Dramedies, blending comedic and dramatic elements, were also increasingly common. These genre shifts contributed to a discernible reimagining of the boundaries and possibilities of television comedy by the time the series I discuss premiered between the early 2010s and 2020. As these shifts were occurring most of the creatives this study chronicles were already producing content, in various mediums, and likely consuming a range of television programs, films, and web series. As witnesses to the sea change in television, including the way innovations from cable, open TV platforms, and streaming services were offering audiences more choices, addressing underserved audiences, and displacing the dominance of network television, they were uniquely poised to push creative boundaries.

The three series this chapter focuses on, *Crazy Ex-Girlfriend* (*CXG*), *Broad City*, and *Jane the Virgin* (*JTV*), are notable for employing a range of surreal audio and visual techniques that play with genre conventions. This "play" subverts the gendered scripts common to their respective genres through a distinctly media-savvy, Millennial women-informed lens. One particularly notable strand distinguishing these series is the primacy of friendships among women and the decentering of romantic relationships. *CXG* and *Broad City*'s focus on single women leads themselves to this, but even the title character of *Jane* expresses ambivalence about centering marriage over other interests and ambitions. The elevation of women's friendships is a significant pivot from earlier television eras that often characterized single women as unfulfilled and treated friendships with women perfunctorily.

Each series has a storied production history informing its aesthetic approach. FX originally expressed interest in producing *Broad City* but declined, and Comedy Central picked up the series. Comedy Central has traditionally targeted a young male audience, however, in the 2010s it sought to expand its market by signing shows with more diverse representation and broader themes, which included *Key & Peele* (2012–15) and *Inside Amy Schumer* (2013–16).[1] *JTV* and *CXG* were both broadcast on the CW, a broadcast network that targets the eighteen to thirty-four demographic and consciously pivoted toward female audiences within this demographic in the 2010s.[2] *JTV*, adapted from Venezuelan television for the United States, preceded *CXG* by a year. *CXG* was originally pitched to Showtime, which declined to move forward with it; this created an opportunity for the CW. Other series CW acquired with female appeal included *Supergirl* and *Riverdale*, and a reboot of *Dynasty*.

Though each series has distinct origins, its stylistic daring and synthesis has established a creative blueprint that has expanded and shaped narrative possibilities in contemporary television. Chapter 3 focuses on the diverse ways the showrunners, and creative teams, of "good" and "complex" series flex their aesthetic mastery of genre conventions in their storytelling. Episodic analyses of *CXG*, *Broad City*, and *JTV* show how they consciously recycle, remix, and subvert various genre elements as part of their creative process. The shows might differ thematically, but each focuses on women-centered stories infused with visual and aural surrealism. They also frequently subvert the gender conventions of the highly gendered genres they depict, including romantic comedies (*CXG*), stoner comedies (*Broad City*), and soap operas and telenovelas (*JTV*). Their genre subversions are not merely stylistic exercises; rather, embedded within them are important questions Millennial-focused stories frequently explore, including the following: How might our understandings of concepts like "maturity" or "completeness," or the utility of these notions, shift when women in their late twenties–early thirties embrace their single, uncoupled status and/or friendships as their primary relationships? Similarly, what are the implications of friendships becoming more salient than romantic bonds for women? Finally, what happens when women seek to honor culturally inflected values related to family in tandem with their individual need to grow into their individual identities? The three series "play" with popular culture out of both appreciation for it and a desire to reassess some of the gendered themes inherent to the forms. The ways women showrunners tell stories, in terms of tone, genre, and narrative techniques, are often adjusted by aspects of feminist thought that shape their content and themes.

## Cue the Meta: *Crazy Ex-Girlfriend* Reassesses the "Rom-Com"

### *Our Tale Begins with a Little Exposition . . .*

*CXG*'s pilot (1.1, "Josh Just Happens to Live Here!") begins with a flashback of sixteen-year-old Rebecca Bunch (Rachel Bloom) singing the showtune "A Wonderful Guy" (from *South Pacific*) onstage at a summer camp showcase. Soon we meet her camp boyfriend, Josh Chan (Vincent Rodriguez III), who breaks up with her as summer ends. Flash forward to the present where the miserable adult version of Rebecca lives in New York City. Though she is on the verge of being made partner at her law firm she's depressed and uninspired . . . until she encounters the adult Josh on the street. After telling her he's leaving the city to return home to West Covina, California, she quits her job and moves to be with him, which he does not realize and Rebecca repeatedly denies.

When Rebecca breaks into the ballad "West Covina" to celebrate this "meet cute" moment and we see her move across the country in pursuit of love we recognize the series as a romantic comedy with original music and choreography. As the pilot unfolds, however, we witness West Covina's blandness, see her lie to coworkers and neighbors about why she moved, and the episode ends with her attending a party with Greg (Santino Ferrara), Josh's best friend, under false pretenses. Greg is disappointed she is only there in hopes of seeing Josh, and the party concludes unexpectedly with her coworker Paula (Donna Lynne Champlin)—who has hacked Rebecca's work computer and uncovered her cyberstalking of Josh—confronting her at the party about her obsession. They conclude the episode singing a duet with lyrics that pays homage to modern romantic comedies and centers her pursuit of Josh as *CXG*'s focus.

From there *CXG*'s episodes continually use romantic comedy tropes to set up the audience to expect a reunion of the high school sweethearts only to defy them through plot and dialogue as well as a unique combination of music, choreography, digital media, and pastiche. The more we watch the more we experience its inverting of romantic comedy clichés toward revealing harsher truths about the limitations of culturally mediated myths and fantasies about love, sex, and romance.

Among season one's eighteen episodes, "That Text Was Not Meant for Josh!" (1.11) best encompasses how it synthesizes surreal audio and visual narrative techniques to tell a complicated story about how Millennial women navigate conflicting social pressures to assert their independence professionally and socially, *and* define themselves as "complete" and "balanced" through heterosexual romance. The pilot's use of flashback, the "meet cute" scene, theatrical musical forms, and homage, as well as its integration of texting and social media, add layers to the serialized storytelling complexity frequently lauded in contemporary dramas. The series' blurring of comedic and dramatic elements is equally central to its subversion of romantic comedy. Examining episode eleven illuminates the narrative perspective of this "good" and "complex" subversive musical dramedy.

### *A Quick Recap . . .*

In "I'm Back at Camp with Josh!" (1.10) Rebecca donates $10,000 to a children's camp where Josh volunteers, which gives her access to attend, under the pretense of delivering a "women's empowerment" seminar. Her real purpose is to rekindle her summer camp memories with Josh, which she shares in a sentimental love letter (sung as "Dear Joshua Felix Chan") he quickly dismisses as overly dramatic. Later he digs the letter out from a trash can and realizes how supportive she had always been toward him. After they encounter each other early in episode eleven Josh thanks her for the fun time they had at camp. He is on his way to martial arts practice wearing his martial arts gi and mentions he left his phone at home. At the law firm Whitefeather & Associates Rebecca and Paula sit in the conference room for an arbitration with the two clients, opposing counsel, and the arbitrator. Elated by her and Josh's hug earlier, Rebecca mouths words to Paula, who struggles to read her lips, and texts her instead. On the screen the text is displayed and reads as the following:

> Just saw Josh, he looked so 🔥 [fine] that I almost 😵 [died]. I ♥ [love] him so much and I think he ♥ [loves] me now too. God, I can't wait until we're finally together and can stop lying and tell him I love him and moved here for him. (figure 3.1)

Paula looks at her phone, then Rebecca looks at Paula and assumes she got the text before Rebecca realizes she sent it to Josh. We hear dramatic, rumbling percussion as an extreme camera close-up register's Rebecca's look of shock. She then screams "No," which is distorted and slowed down for dramatic effect. Paula asks what's wrong and Rebecca hands over her phone. Paula's jaw drops and she screams "Mother . . ." In this brief scene the accidental text, visualized onscreen, the use of nondiegetic music, audio distortion, and dramatic camera work combine forces to establish the episode's central conflict. In this instance the text is not merely a form of quotidian communication; it is integral to the plot itself.

After a quick transition Paula stares at the phone and the client asks Rebecca if things are OK. Panicked, Rebecca asks for a temporary stay to the disdain of the opposing counsel, then Paula shares the phone and explains the situation. Tonally, this shifts the scene into a fully comedic, surreal dimension. Once everyone has seen the text they unanimously

**Figure 3.1.** Rebecca uses text messaging to convey her clandestine feelings for Josh to Paula, which backfires, a common trope of *Crazy Ex-Girlfriend*'s depiction of the limits of digital technology.

abandon the arbitration, declare it as a problem, and collectively agree she needs to spin the text. Rebecca remembers Josh left his phone at his apartment and runs from the room with Paula to beat him to the apartment. Paula, who is having issues with her husband Scott (Steve Monroe), abruptly remembers she can't join her because of her obligation to have dinner with him.

The drama builds: The client, defendant, and lawyers urge Rebecca to go, and the arbitrator says he'll get her a police escort. Rebecca jumps in her car and we begin hearing the melody of the song play and a siren in the background—the arbitrator has promised her a police escort. The scene morphs into an arena rock stage with the arbitration group onstage dressed in rock costumes, playing instruments, and singing the rock flavored song "Textmergency," which narrates the action (figure 3.2).

There is a lightheartedness to the interspersion of the music and action—we see Rebecca arrive at Josh's apartment building and pretend she's texting someone until someone opens the front door and she charges in. The goofy lyrics reference multiple non sequiturs (rhyming "erection" with "yeast infection") and shift to a conflict between whether to call the situation a textmergency or a "textastrophe." Then the ghost of Steve Jobs appears and comments on the harms of modern technology—a cheeky bit of metacommentary on the root of this dilemma. The lyrics also direct Rebecca to find the key, which helps her open the door and the song concludes. She locates his phone, deciphers his passcode, deletes her

Figure 3.2. As is typical of *Crazy Ex-Girlfriend*, Rebecca's accidental text inspires the generically familiar rock song, and intentionally clichéd video, "Textmergency," which narrates her actions.

original message to Josh, and texts Paula confirming successful deletion. Suddenly, Josh arrives and is puzzled to see her in the apartment.

From the moment the arbitration team declared Rebecca's errant text as a "textmergency" ("textastophe?"), to the video to her entrance into the apartment we root for her to not be caught. Though we know she has been dishonest about why she moved, has feigned interest in Greg to access Josh, without regard for Greg's feelings, and is essentially breaking and entering Josh's apartment, the promise of a happy ending, a staple of romantic comedies, alleviates us of moral responsibility.

The difference between *CXG* and a stock rom-com movie is its unwillingness to resolve conflicts easily. Generically speaking, season one initially adheres to the blueprint of many contemporary women-centered romantic comedies (e.g., a heterosexual narrative between a man and a woman resolved by a happy ending).[3] Deleyto offers a useful definition for examining *CXG* by referring to the romantic comedy genre as the "intersection of three, closely interrelated elements: a narrative that articulates historically and culturally specific views of love, desire, sexuality and gender relationships; a space of transformation and fantasy which influences the narrative articulations of those discourses; and humour as the specific perspective from which the fictional characters, their relationships and the spectator's response to them are constructed as embodiments of those discourses."[4] Deleyto addresses the form's dynamism, which parallels the changing social climate *CXG* embodies as well. In season one, it challenges some of the more common conventions associated with the genre by offering familiar characters, settings, and narrative devices, and then defying expectations.

The opening sequence in the pilot episode of Rebecca running into Josh in New York represents a "meet-cute," which in the terms of the genre "is prophetic in that it can often suggest the nature of the couple's relationship."[5] Rebecca's ability to quit her job and move, in pursuit of Josh, reflects elements associated with the "girly film" genre. These films, made from 1990 to 2010, depict the realistic challenges for urban heroines trying to balance their professional and personal lives infused with a vision of a happy ending that includes romance. They frequently employ an ironic tone, and the central heroine is often "motivated by individual fulfillment expressed through some form of consumerism (often manifest in a shopping sequence and a make-over for the heroine) as its defining trait."[6]

Throughout season one Rebecca uses her economic resources to pursue Josh, including donating to the camp and purchasing a plane ticket and travel wear to surprise Josh in Hawaii at a surfing convention in "Josh Is Going to Hawaii!" (1.14).[7] This reflects the integral role of fashion in romantic comedies and the ubiquitous makeover montage trope of such films, as well as her professional agency and economic resources to invest in Josh, literally.[8]

Following this pattern of conventions episode eleven allows Rebecca to avert disaster, using multiple devices to illustrate and elevate the drama of the crisis, and music to resolve it. "Textmergency" thus "buys her time," which is integral to the dramatic role of music in the musical form. *CXG*'s staging of musical scenes in concert with its visualization of social media are narrative forms of "perfect eavesdropping" new to romantic comedies.[9] When we consider their functions collectively, they parallel McMillin's theory that the song-and-dance routines of most stage musicals transport audiences into "a second order of time, which interrupts book time in the form of songs and dances" that enriches characterization rather than merely advancing the plot. As he notes, "the musical gives its characters a dimension that lies beyond realism and increases the range of their presentation," which "plays against our normal sense of identity and story." Thus, the song-and-dance routines leaves us with layered characters, the character understood as the "multiple" rather than the "one."[10] Musicals are often upbeat in tone and romantically themed, so *CXG*'s blend of romantic comedy with music creates a natural expectation for audiences that music and choreography will lead us to positive narrative conclusion. Alas, *CXG* has something different in mind.

Josh's arrival returns us to "real time" realities, and Rebecca scrambles to explain herself, which involves lying, once again. Her solution is to tell Josh her apartment was burglarized and she needed a safe haven; he is inspired to join her and help clean things up. Panicked, she stalls Josh and calls Paula to ask her to stage a break-in. As per usual, the self-involved Rebecca is oblivious to Paula's needs, notably her struggle to rekindle her flailing marriage to Scott. Paula's willingness to disrupt her dinner and devote more of her energy to helping Rebecca pursue her storybook ending with Josh than to her marriage also reflects *her* investment in rendering real life in rom-com terms.

Scott accompanies Paula to Rebecca's apartment; they grab decorative rocks from inside her apartment and throw them through the patio door before fleeing. Though this miniadventure invigorates Scott and Paula it creates problems for Rebecca. Once Josh begins helping her clean up, she relays how safe she feels with him and orders fondue to make it romantic. Josh surprises her when he answers the door for a police officer. Flummoxed, Rebecca tries to explain the situation to the officer. As Josh cleans up the glass shards he notices a decorative rock that is one-third of a trio of rocks that spells "Happy Ever After," a winking nod to Rebecca's romantic aspirations. When Rebecca spots the rock the arbitration rock group sings a brief interlude called "Where Is the Rock?," which elevates the drama. Josh examines the lettering, Rebecca plays dumb, and he leaves in frustration.

The episode's tone suddenly shifts from a surreal, clandestine adventure to something more grounded and sobering: Rebecca, sitting on her living room floor littered with glass, is alone. Her attempt to kindle romance with Josh followed the blueprint of "screwball" romantic comedies, and yet she failed to find a happy ending. These efforts serve as a prologue for the staging and performance of the musical soliloquy "You Stupid Bitch," a power ballad that reflects the show's adept approach to music metagenericism.

Olson's description of iconography, archetype, and setting as tropes of metagenericism illuminate *CXG*'s audio and visual presentations of original music in season one.[11] Broadly speaking, the series' composers rely heavily on highly recognizable song pastiches, drawn from popular American song forms (e.g., power ballads, Broadway musicals) and visual tropes (e.g., music videos, mainstream films) readily familiar, or easily discoverable for audiences.

Among the plethora of songs from season one, "You Stupid Bitch" most effectively illustrates the unique role of musical interlude metamoments in the series' layers of narrative construction. *CXG*'s filming and staging of "You Stupid Bitch" correlates strongly to audio and visual iconography, archetypes, and settings associated with inspirational power ballads (figure 3.3).[12] "You Stupid Bitch" is a forty-two-bar soliloquy Rebecca sings onstage in a glittering nightgown with a slit to an imagined audience. Musically, "Bitch" adheres to the mold of "inspirational" power ballads, notably "The Greatest Love of All," popularized by

Figure 3.3. The plodding music and quasi-concert setting of "You Stupid Bitch" mimics the fashion and staging of Whitney Houston's "Greatest Love of All" and Mariah Carey's "Hero" music videos.

Whitney Houston in 1986, and "Hero" cowritten by Mariah Carey and Walter Afanasieff, and sung by Carey in 1994.

Power ballads exceed the emotional scope typical of ballads through a "continuous escalation."[13] Their build could include more prominent instrumentation, "a sudden modulation to a key a step higher," and a singer who "abandons the hushed tones of the opening and puts on ecstatic displays, including elaborate runs and catapulted high notes."[14] The song is written to be sung in E flat major, then in bar 29 the song modulates abruptly toward a conclusion in F major, adhering to the power ballad formula. E flat's relative minor is C minor and F major's relative minor is D minor, the saddest of all keys. This is significant because symbolically Rebecca never commits to C minor then suddenly tries to end the song "perfectly," mirroring the tension between her low self-esteem and the perfect persona she projects publicly.

Musically, Rebecca begins singing in an almost parlando style of speak-singing, then builds to the chorus "You ruined everything / You stupid bitch" and returns to a second verse, followed by the chorus and the litany of flaws. In bars 37–40 she lists her flaws in an angry, sprawling verse whose lyrics include the following:

*You're just a poopy little slut who doesn't think*
*And deceives the people she loves*

*Now he knows I'm not some innocent lamb*
*He sees me for what I am*
*Which is a horrible, stupid,*
*dumb and ugly, fat and stupid, simple self-hating*
*Bitch!*

In the concluding bars 40–41, notably the word "Bitch," Rebecca attempts to finish the song "perfectly" in the key of F. What should feel triumphant sounds like a forced attempt to undo the sporadic tone of the previous bars.

"Bitch" is clearly a ballad, and its lyrics are overtly self-hating. Lyrically it inverts the positive affirmations of "Greatest," whose lyrics emphasize how learning to love ourselves is the greatest love of all, and "Hero," whose lyrics urge us to look inward and access our inner strength to combat obstacles. If the Houston and Carey ballads seek to boost our confidence, "Bitch" is a savage takedown. Thematically, the tension between the pleasure of listening to a predictable song form, with a familiar build and resolution, and the dark subtext of its lyrics, reflects a pattern in several of season one's songs. After articulating her situation, notably, feeling alone after a frustrated Josh abandons her in the episode when she struggles to explain an improbable burglary at her apartment, Rebecca blames her loneliness on her dishonest and deceptive behavior. She compounds this inward turn through unearthing deep emotions, including nihilism ("And wants the world to burn"), body shaming ("And lose some weight"), loneliness ("When there's no me to complete"), selfishness ("You're just a poopy little slut who doesn't think / And deceives the people she loves"), and deep physical and emotional self-loathing ("Which is a horrible, stupid, dumb and ugly, fat and stupid, simple self-hating / Bitch"). "Bitch" amplifies subdermal emotions Rebecca has hinted at during the season but that have never fully emerged. The song makes it plain that Rebecca's pursuit is partially motivated by a fear of being by herself, a self she is hostile toward.

One of third wave feminism's tropes is women's conscious reclamation of the term "bitch" alongside other sexist and misogynist terms.[15] The term's use in this song's title and lyrics is complex in that Rebecca references social markers of female stigma regarding her appearance ("ugly," "fat") as critique and simultaneously sings the song as a personal reckoning.

As a soliloquy it is a genuinely introspective attempt to own her behavior. Despite the title the song is a vehicle for genuine female self-reflection.

One of the notable visual allusions connecting "Bitch" to "Greatest" and "Hero" is the visual presentation. Like "Greatest" and "Hero," "Bitch" adheres to the "staged performance music video" subgenre.[16] This video style features a performance explicitly staged for the production of the video and only takes place so that it can be filmed, features performers who address cameras directly, action is removed from the real world, space and time are ambiguous, and for musical artists this style of video "reinforces the mediated image of the artists(s) it promotes."[17]

In Houston's case, the "Greatest" is a staged video whose storyline juxtaposes a young Houston, filmed in sepia tones, participating in a vocal talent contest with an adult Houston returning to the same stage singing triumphantly before an audience. At no point does the adult Houston sing into a microphone, so there is no pretense of live singing. "Hero" was filmed as part of the *Here Is Mariah Carey* documentary in July 1993 and aired as Carey's *Thanksgiving NBC Special*. Both videos reinforce their singers' personae as emotionally affirming, politically neutral, girl-next-door types who sing in a technically proficient pop-soul vocal style. Houston is clearly lip syncing whereas the presence of a live audience reinforces the "Hero" video's dual purpose as footage of a filmed concert and as a serviceable music video.

Like Houston, Rebecca lip syncs (via a microphone) to an anonymous audience. The audience, filmed in distant aerial shots, is clearly a CGI style digitized audience whose purpose is purely functional. Though she sings "Sing with me!" to elicit a response the generic crowd noise and enthusiastic applause is clearly canned. Unlike Houston and Carey, Rebecca's performance is not meant to convince us of her vocal talents or her ability to connect with fans. The visual homage to "Greatest" and "Hero" uses a predictable song style form—the inspirational pop ballad—and a static video subgenre to expose the underbelly of emotions masked by self-love songs, including doubt, anxiety, ambivalence, and self-hatred. The presentation of these visceral negative emotions in this bland form is disarming in its inversion of the inspirational ballad's musical and visual formulas.

*CXG*'s ingenious use of music emerges in two other key moments, which speaks to its cohesive serialization. First, after Paula and Scott return home and discuss their marital issues Paula admits her addiction to Rebecca's love life. In classic *CXG* fashion she traces the origins of Rebecca's story by recounting, line for line, the lyrics of season one's theme song. After this the title card for the series appears in a nod to its attentive audience. The series uses the theme song as part of its humor throughout the series. Second, after the fondue has been delivered and "You Stupid Bitch" has been sung, Greg, who is visiting, Rebecca's neighbor, Heather (Vella Lovell), enters Rebecca's apartment through the patio. She asks him if he can stay because she does not want to be alone and offers him fondue. He agrees to stay and as she hugs him we hear the melody of "Settle for Me" a mid-tempo song of yearning sung from Greg to Rebecca in "I'm Going on a Date with Josh's Friend!" (1.4). Filmed in black and white and staged like the Fred Astaire and Ginger Rogers sequence from *Top Hat* the melody is reprised throughout season one to capture Rebecca's willingness to use Greg as a substitute for Josh and to illustrate his self-loathing. These seemingly small moments speak to the series' attention to the resonance of music as a kind of narrative shorthand. Music creates a second order of time and its use extends this to yet another order.

## What It Feels like for a *Broad*: (Unruly) Millennial Women's Swagger and Friendship

From the strutting theme song ("Latino & Proud" by DJ Braff) that accompanies its modular title card to Abbi and Ilana's references to hip-hop icons, hip-hop is one of the prevailing rhythms of *Broad City*. The musical blueprint of hip-hop—a synthesis of previously recorded music reconfigured into something new and distinct—deeply informs *Broad City*'s aesthetic. Like many of that genre's more notable artists, *Broad City*'s creative team, led by Ilana Glazer and Abbi Jacobson, remixes beloved elements from other genres, including film and television, into a personal story.

Though Glazer and Jacobson have noted their characters mirror aspects of their younger selves, the "personal" element I refer to here is less about literal autobiography than a panoramic view of postbaccalaureate, Millennial womanhood in New York.[18] Hannah Horvath's declaration that she might be "*a* voice of *a* generation" is delivered earnestly in the pilot of *Girls*, as she tries to convince her parents to extend their subsidizing of her. *Broad City*'s characters are too iconoclastic for that kind of dialogue. Abbi and Ilana's voices often are loud, confrontational, impolite, and unapologetic. This is certainly not true all of the time during its six seasons, as that would make their characters one dimensional and grating. Yet even when they bluff their way through bombast, essentially drafting themselves in real time and stretching their own personae, there's a certain playfulness that lets us into the experiment. We feel what they feel and imagine ourselves walking alongside them on the streets of the city with its dazzling array of sights, sounds, odors, and characters. Their mastery of different genres and strategic use of surreal elements is the most resonant aspect of their stylistic "remix."

A recurring example from season one illustrates this emotional access succinctly: When Abbi (Abbi Jacobson) encounters her attractive neighbor Jeremy (Stephen Schneider) in a hallway in the pilot we embody her panic: nondiegetic music overwhelms the audio feed as Abbi says "J-E-R-E-M-Y" in slow motion, continues speaking with distortion, and the camera tilts to the right throwing us off balance (1.1, "What a Wonderful World"). In the second episode when she spots a reminder note on her door and realizes she has missed a package she promised to intercept from a delivery service for him: a high-pitched audio sound surges, Abbi panics, a man in the hallway asks her if she's OK, and she collapses, and we do too (1.2, "Pu$$y Weed"). Rather than confining her "crush" to neurotic dialogue, as is common in television comedy, the series translates desire into a corporeal embodiment that catches us unaware and overwhelms our senses sonically, visually, and physically. In these moments we see what she sees, feel what she feels, and develop empathy. Abbi is financially strapped, feels cramped in her apartment, and is painfully single. Knowing she is an aspiring artist miserable working as a custodian at the Soulstice Gym and frustrated by the presence of her (invisible) roommate's omnipresent and obnoxious boyfriend Bevers (John Gemberling), we *want* her to experience some respite with Jeremy. She's experiencing the post-2008 financial and social precarity blues and trying to maintain some levity.[19] Abandoning herself to her senses and collapsing occasionally feels more like survival than surrender.

I explore the world of the creative duo of Abbi and Ilana by exploring *Broad City*'s narrative focus on the experimental lives of twenty-something Millennial White women navigating the precarity of the 2010s. This section addresses what *Broad City* is generically and who these "broads" are archetypally, and delves into its boundary-breaking "remixes" of genre and characterization by exploring Abbi's highly stylized narrative progression in season one. *Broad City* employs multiple expressive devices to convey the complexity of the Millennial women archetypes that emerged in television of the 2010s.

"Man! I Feel Like a Woman!" (Shania Twain), "What It Feels Like for a Girl" (Madonna), and "Make Me Feel" (Janelle Monae) are songs popularized by women vocalists and understood as reflections of women's intimate feelings and experiences. Though the songs vary in origin, when we hear them we imagine a link between the song and singer. Arguably popular music listeners are comfortable hearing women sing about their feelings, especially those pertaining to romance and sexuality. Television, however, has struggled to represent a broad spectrum of women's feelings. The housewives and career-women roles that long dominated comedic television gave way in the 2010s to single-women characters with less well-defined futures. One of the innovations of the women-centric "good" and "complex" series is their willingness to depict the broad affective range of Millennial women. One sign of how effective many of these programs were relates to a 2023 article chronicling the resurgence of Millennial women rewatching *Girls*. The women interviewed, now in their thirties, note the "trial-and-error" of being a woman in your twenties "who do not have it all figured out" and view the series as a poignant touchstone for "reintrospecting" shorthand for the ways they have grown.[20] Though the article was about *Girls* (*Fleabag* and *Insecure* are also referenced) this renewed interest seems to reflect how these shows captured something very specific generationally that felt new in the 2010s.

Collectively, many of the series that aired between the 2010s and early 2020s focus on "the feels"—what it feels like to end college and have limited job prospects; to struggle to find an intimate partner, short or long term; to attain financial independence; to navigate patriarchal biases; and to have fun, at least, occasionally. *Broad City*'s creators approached this task armed with a wide knowledge of audio, visual, and textural tactics for capturing the wide-ranging emotional essence of its lead characters. It is telling that in a 2014 interview regarding the series Glazer defined "broad" as "A full person."[21] This perspective informs my sense that the show is aware its stories are being channeled through two women and equally committed to demonstrating how this presents an opportunity rather than a limitation. Unbridled in its narrative ambition the series employs homage, audio distortion, flashbacks, and montage to various combinations to capture what it *feels* like for a "broad" and invite us into their world. The show's creative team members are aesthetically sophisticated storytellers who filter women-centered values and concerns through formal approaches that reflect their understandings how popular culture shapes their creative sensibilities. Their subversions riff on different forms and remix how we understand women on television by challenging the norms of women's buddy comedies and traditional stoner comedies, and depicting Millennial-style "unruly" women whose physical comedy and pop-culture-fueled personae distinguishes the series.

*Broad City* blends familiarity and novelty, which has fostered unique stylistic and thematic interventions into established genre conventions that have expanded the representational scope of Millennial women and the look and feel of television. The series is also immediately recognizable as a female buddy comedy in the tradition of *Laverne & Shirley* (1976–83, ABC), *Kate & Allie* (1984–89, CBS), and *Hope & Gloria* (1995–96, NBC), among others. Unlike these shows its characters are single women in their twenties who are Jewish, sexually fluid, and living separately, as well as Millennials living in the post-2008 economy. *Broad City* also originated as a web series created by its lead actresses and adapted by them for television rather than the mainstream "legacy TV" network production cycle. The series eventual broadcast on Comedy Central stemmed from the network's conscious effort to expand its appeal to female audiences.[22] Its women-led creative team cultivated their voices before reaching the mainstream.

*Broad City* is also a "stoner comedy" in the tradition of Cheech & Chong films, and derivatives like *Friday*, *Half-Baked*, *Harold & Kumar*, and *Pineapple Express*, among others.[23] Both "broads" get stoned throughout the series: Ilana is a chronic marijuana smoker whereas Abbi partakes more selectively. Abbi and Ilana are among the few women represented in the genre. Rather than being romantic partners or incidental characters, which is more common in the male dominated genre, they share the lead roles and have developed subplots and whole episodes around being stoned, such as the animation and live-action hybrid episode "Mushrooms."[24] Further, *Broad City* is a basic cable show that has adapted select aspects of stonerdom within the standards and practices regulating basic cable channels.

*Broad City*, which premiered in 2014, is also notable as one of several post-*Girls* depictions of Millennial women navigating a primarily urban environment that includes *Fleabag* (London), *Insecure* (Los Angeles), *Shrill* (Portland), and *I May Destroy You* (London). Like many of its "sister" series the city is more than a backdrop; its character and rhythms are represented in exterior shots and filming in specific city neighborhoods, and integral to understanding how the characters move through space and time.

Abbi and Ilana's corporeal choices and positioning offer a key way to distinguish Millennial "broads" from television's ladies. In the pilot Abbi and/or Ilana do the following: engage in sexual acts in front of trusted friends on video, lie to an employer to evade responsibilities, steal office supplies, engage in hygienic acts while doing daily activities, swoon over a crush, use drugs, shortchange friends, engage in quick money-making schemes, abandon said schemes when they become difficult, break things when they get angry, drink alcohol publicly, impersonate "alpha" type behavior to scare someone, vomit, and possess a sex toy.

Contextually, the duo frequently embodies and expands on aspects associated with Rowe's schema of unruly women, which includes behaviors perceived as physically and emotionally "excessive" for women, such as loud laughter, overt sexuality, and associations dirt, among others "rending her above all a figure of ambivalence."[25] They constantly defy traditional television femininity through overt or implied behaviors pertaining to sex, deceit, drug consumption, property destruction, and/or bodily functions. Slovenly, dishonest, impatient, impulsive, reactionary, vulgar, unrefined, and often engaged in illegal behavior, they are also thoroughly likable and highly entertaining. We can observe these elements in individual episodes throughout the first season from the duo laughing on the subway after failing to exchange stolen office supplies for cash (1.1) to Abbi and Ilana donning tuxedos to enter a gentleman's club (1.8, "Destination Wedding") to Ilana overeating shellfish despite her allergy (1.10, "The Last Supper") they exemplify a new generation of comediennes willing to push boundaries. Freed from the wives, mothers, and desperate single career women tropes, their existence juxtaposes social privilege (White, college-educated, middle-class backgrounds) with the realities of striving for financial independence. Abbi and Ilana are frequently the main source of joy, emotional support, and motivation for each other. They cheer each other on even when the other's pursuit seems impractical or uncertain. Their adventures—whether romantic or entrepreneurial in nature—typically lead them back to *each other*.

Watching them behave in an "unruly" fashion feels less like imitations of rebellious bad boy behavior and more like women resisting the boundaries for women's bodies in the comedic format. As Paumgarten has observed, the duo mirror raucous behaviors associated with men "but with an ease that absolves them of the lingering accusation, levelled elsewhere, that women comedians who work unclean are merely using shock to get attention—just trying to out-dude the dudes."[26] Their actions parallel the remarkably unremarkable presentation of "unconventional" female bodies, especially Hannah Horvath's in *Girls* and the often-grotesque depictions of Rebecca Bunch's in *CXG*.[27] As Branfman observes, the duo's "gross-out routines thus doubly mark them as unruly: for violating bodily boundaries, and for blurring masculinity with femininity."[28] A notable aspect of women-centric, "good," and "complex" television is the way it has expanded how we understand women's physicality in comedy toward a spectrum that includes awkwardness, slapstick, cringe aesthetics, and combinations of these elements.[29] The new generation of showrunners is authoring a new kind of articulation of comedic corporeality.

In my analysis Abbi and Ilana's bodies are a component of their surreal approach. They are physical comedians, and understanding what they are *willing* to do with their bodies as creators and actors simultaneously helps us engage with the intentionality of how their bodies allow us to access their affect. It is a consensual act between the performers and audience, and surreal techniques most consistently foster this curated access in a manner that feels intimate and welcoming, rather than exploitative or objectifying.

As the first episode indicates, Ilana has the least amount of caution among the duo—she mounts her lover Lincoln (Hannibal Burress) on a video chat with Abbi, tries to redeem stolen office supplies, and responds to a Craig's List ad on the phone while seated on the toilet—but Abbi actively participates even in a slightly more subdued way. She pretends to be a trainer rather than a custodian at her gym and participates in schemes such as attempting to cash in the supplies, pretending to be a bucket-playing percussionist in the park for money, and stripping down to her underwear to clean a creepy man's apartment for money. One of the episode's most telling moments is when we see her vibrator with a sticky note that says "Wednesday or Thursday." Abbi's defiant unruliness is slightly more contained than Ilana's, but barely. The pilot, and subsequent episodes of season one, build on these themes and offer multiple variations of grotesque, illicit, and erotic behavior.

Contrasting personalities are central to Abbi and Ilana's dynamic. Though both characters are unruly Ilana is bolder, more outspoken, and unfiltered compared to the more cautious and politer Abbi. In "Knockoffs" (2.4) Ilana jokingly refers to Abbi as a "WASP-y Jew" from the Main Line of Philadelphia to her mother to distinguish their personalities. As a series with serialized elements, a recurring thread season one introduces is Abbi growing into her personality, which often involves awkward attempts to adapt popular culture elements to attain confidence. The series combines aspects of absurdist humor, chick flicks, hip-hop videos, parodic techniques, and audiovisual special effects to take us on Abbi's journey toward self-realization. Abbi's effort to access a mediated notion of "swagger" is not a solo affair; Ilana is with her throughout her journey and is her biggest champion. The show's absurdist humor and sense of awareness enables the duo to be there for each other without lapsing into sentimentality.

In "Fattest Asses" (1.5) Ilana invites Abbi to attend a rooftop party in SoHo.[30] Determined to come out of her shell Abbi declares the following to Ilana as they stroll down the sidewalk:

ABBI: No more Mr. Nice Abbi. No more—no more cleaning up other people's pubes [a reference to her custodial job]. And you know, getting screwed by people that end up not having cancer. No. From here on out, I am stepping it up. If anyone's going to pretend like they have cancer it's gonna be me. You know what? I look too nice.

ILANA: You look really nice, yeah.

A: No, I look vanilla.

I: Oh, let's go shopping.

Suddenly we see a black high heel shoe as a "wipe," or transition between scenes, and upbeat pop music plays as we watch Abbi and Ilana enter a boutique (figure 3.4). In this abridged homage to the shopping montage scenes in movies like *Pretty Woman* (1990) and shows like *Sex and the City* (1998–2004) Abbi tries on *one* outfit, a blue dress Ilana lauds for highlighting Abbi's posterior, and decides to buy it. After learning its $438 she rationalizes the expense and asks about the return policy. As she attempts to exit, excited about her "new" persona, the cashier stops her and reminds her to sign the receipt, then the upbeat music resumes. The wipe, the music, and the truncated nonmontage shopping scene are knowing moments that affectionately send up multiple media tropes of women's films and TV shows.

Before entering the party's decorative archway their movements are filmed in slow motion briefly and the camera offers a close-up of Abbi and Ilana's butts as hip-hop music plays. Entering in her blue dress Abbi responds to Ilana's comment about how attractive they look stating, "Yeah, I mean, look at all these fashion chic basic bitches" (8:42–8:45).

**Figure 3.4.** *Broad City* humorously frames Abbi and Ilana's shopping scene montage with a high-heeled shoe "wipe," a winking visual nod to romantic comedy film and television conventions.

After Ilana discusses her own party persona as the "real" her, Abbi says "Let's get drunk" and asserts herself physically and verbally, forcing her way through the crowd. Her dialogue is a comical mix of a forced brashness and her natural politeness:

> Move, honk, honk. Pardon me [Looks at a woman]. Out of the way clavicle [Looks at another woman]. Okay five-nine, I can't even, like, deal with you right now.

Then she sees a group of people huddled holding drinks near the bar and responds sarcastically:

> Oh, do you guys all have drinks already? Maybe you should, then, get the hell away from the bar, great.

No one responds to her directly; she asserts herself obliviously. At the bar she shouts: "Is anyone even working at this bar?" To her embarrassment a very polite bartender comes over and says "Yes, hi." Then she orders a cocktail sheepishly, disarmed by the bartender's politeness.

One of the metajokes of the episode is New York hipsterism. The duo learns that the party's theme is "Change," as uttered detachedly by a partygoer, an homage to the Obama campaign. At the bar Abbi drinks a "Tsunami" whose proceeds allegedly go for tsunami relief. When asked which one, he responds, "whichever one" is happening.

In the clothing store, her party entrance, and the bar Abbi experiments with new ways of being, largely appropriated from popular culture affects, and we empathize with Abbi and also see the humor in how hard she is working given the juxtaposition of her "boldness" with her fundamental politeness. Her body might do unruly things, often in private settings, or with Ilana, but her comfort asserting herself remains at odds with other aspects of her personality.

After Ilana and Abbi nosh on appetizers, accompanied by earnest recitations of hunger statistics by the waiter, Abbi heads to the restroom. Eyeing the long line for the women's restroom, she heads to the men's room. Entering the restroom, she kicks open a stall door action-star style and finds a nervous young man about to snort cocaine. He shares some with her and is surprised when she says she's never done it before.

Upholding the "new" Abbi persona she snorts and starts speaking with bravura . . . then apologetically notes she seems to have snorted a lot and offers to pay. These scenes poke fun at the party's earnest hipster themes and amplify Abbi's ridiculous performance.

High on cocaine and feeling emboldened we see a minimontage of a man doing a shot off her butt, and high fiving another man, as she lies on a table. She kisses her biceps triumphantly as a hip-hop song plays in the background (figure 3.5). She leaps up and dances frenetically, by herself, in front of the bar. Ilana walks over, with the party's two DJs, and Abbi—who no one is paying attention to, says "I'll see you later" to no one, and she and Ilana agree to leave. The "new" Abbi has the gestures but lacks the conviction to fully transform. Rather than questioning why she *needs* to change she tries to embody a cartoonish version of an "empowered" woman that feels like an assemblage of mannerisms derived from popular culture. The staging of these scenes through pop culture tropes like the door kick and the body shot capture Abbi's angst and mock pop cultural formulas deftly.

Four episodes later in "Apartment Hunters" (1.9) we experience what "success" feels like for Abbi, and to some extent, Ilana, and it is imagined through a popular culture lens. The scene begins with customers doing banking transactions with tellers stationed behind glass partitions in a marble-lined lobby. Suddenly we hear the opening of

Figure 3.5. Abbi celebrates her generically over-the-top cocaine-fueled behavior, though it does not change her actual persona.

Drake's "Started from the Bottom" and see a blue strobe of light surges horizontally as Ilana saunters in—in slow motion—dressed in a blond wig, a pink lace brace, gray leather skirt, and fur coat, like Nicki Minaj. Ilana is dressed in a black, puffy, rubber suit wearing a hat and yellow shades, like Missy "Misdemeanor" Elliot in "The Rain" video of 1997 (figure 3.6). The sequence is shot like a late 1990s Hype Williams video with close-up shots and a convex lens, and Abbi and Ilana dancing in front of each other, similar to figures in the "Mo Money, Mo Problems" video of 1997.[31] In one shot Ilana pushes a customer aside and smashes a large check, which reads "EIGHT THOUSAND F*KING DOLLARS," in the window of the teller who reacts with her mouth agape and gleefully hands over cash to Abbi and Ilana. The duo throw the bills in the air and people in the lobby dance in celebration. Suddenly, we see the teller's mouth say "Ma'am" multiple times and the music and dancing ends abruptly—we are back in real life.

Like the musical sequences in a Broadway musical and *CXG*, the fantasy sequence places us in a different order of time.[32] We learn, from Ilana's exuberant boast to the teller, that Abbi received $8,000 for a graphic she designed. Unimpressed the teller deposits the check, and as Ilana holds up a cell phone to show off the graphic, we see a "low funds alert" on her screen, which the teller notes to Ilana's mild embarrassment.

**Figure 3.6.** Abbi and Illana celebrate Abbi's profitable sale of her artwork at a bank through an imagined visual homage to hip-hop icons Nicki Minaj and Missy "Misdemeanor" Elliott.

Abbi's triumph is grounded in the socioeconomic realities of living with a service job in New York circa 2014. It's worth noting that both characters come from middle-class families, and it is implied they could borrow money from their families if they needed to, much like many characters on *Girls*. In "Knockoffs" (2.4) Ilana's mother Bobbi (Susie Essman) treats her and Abbi to a spa treatment, and it's clear Ilana is not in serious danger of losing her apartment or starving.

The expert video homage juxtaposed with Drake's triumphant lyric fuses late 1990s hip-hop video imagery and 2010s-era hip-hop music to let us in to Abbi's budding sense of achievement and Ilana's mutual enthusiasm. Whereas the party scenes in "Fattest Asses" primarily allow us to witness Abbi's actions externally, this scene—whose fantasy belongs to the duo rather than either of them individually—approximate what it *feels* like. Their affection for hip-hop—alluded to by Ilana's request to the DJ's in "Fattest Asses" to replace hipster music with 1990s hip-hop—offers a specific conduit for their joy in Abbi's success. Minaj and Elliot are two iconic hip-hop personae who offer temporary respite from everyday banality; the duo imagine themselves moving through the city with the swagger of hip-hop superstars if only for one minute and twenty-three seconds.

After the opening fantasy sequence, the title card, and commercial break Abbi builds from its energy, somewhat, when she confronts her slovenly tacit roommate Beavers. After entering and observing him preparing to masturbate in their living room she says:

> I'm done. I'm moving out. I am moving the (bleep) out! You know why? 'Cause I have money now. I got money now. 'Cause I'm a boss. 'Cause I'm a bad ass boss! Yeah see how it goes. You see how it goes. [*She exits and slams the door*]

As she confronts him she hesitates slightly and repeats herself; her volume increases, nervously, she takes on an abrasive urban accent (pronouncing money with a hard "u" as in m*u*ney) and her body lurches ever so slightly. In her mind an $8,000 payment makes her a "boss" poised to change her life.

In season one's finale Abbi and Ilana dine at an upscale restaurant, which serves as a backdrop for understanding their individual personalities and what unites them as friends. Though we learn early on in the episode that Ilana has a shellfish allergy her bravura approach to life guides her more than common sense. About midway through the episode they get high with restaurant staff in the back alley. As they return to the restaurant's interior the second half of the episode becomes more surreal and "cinematic" in scope: the camera tilts, we hear nondiegetic rock guitar music, and the camera acts as a surrogate for our stoned leads panning in slow motion showing the horrified the faces of patrons as they return to the dining room. Once seated, Abbi notices Ilana's face breaking out, her eyes swelling, and her speech slurring. Ilana attempts to downplay her condition and asserts Abbi doesn't know everything about her, to which Abbi responds:

> You text me every time you take a dump, I know about the pimple on your nipple and I'm like, the holder of your social security card.

This reasserts the corporeal boundaries the pilot establishes; Abbi leaves the table and Ilana continues consuming more shellfish as her condition worsens. When Abbi returns she locates Ilana's EpiPen. Ilana resists her efforts and they squabble briefly before Abbi stabs herself accidentally. The adrenaline hits Abbi and she jumps on the top of the table, like an action hero leaping into action. As she ascends Ilana loses consciousness and falls to the floor via an aerial shot, which amplifies the dramatic "cinematic" effect. Feeling empowered Abbi picks up Ilana's limp, weakened body and carries her through the dining room in a scene reminiscent of Richard Gere carrying Debra Winger out of a factory at the end of *An Officer and a Gentleman* of 1982. Instead of the melody of that film's ballad, "Up Where We Belong," "Ave Maria" underscores the action as Abbi carries her valiantly. The camera uses a long shot to capture the patrons looking on in shock with Abbi roaring voraciously like the comic superhero the Incredible Hulk as she tries to maintain her grip on Ilana whose head flails around and hits tables. With a little help from weed, an EpiPen, and a little inspiration from romantic dramas and action movies, Abbi becomes a hero rescuing her friend from shock. Whereas Abbi clumsily adapts pop culture versions of swagger in earlier episodes to limited ends this episode allows her to channel tenderness and strength toward something nobler and more daring, her deep friendship with Ilana, while showcasing the show's signature humor. Next, we see Ilana recovering in a hospital bed with Abbi by her side and they discuss their progress completing their bucket list.

They made it to the end of season one, which opens up a door for future adventures of these urban, Millennial stoners. Tellingly, just as *CXG* upends the rom-com genre by ending the series with Rebecca rejecting three suitors (Greg, Josh, and Nathan) and focusing on her personal development, *Broad City* challenges the typical arc for women in their late twenties in its series finale. Though we witness Abbi and Ilana's various sexual partners over the course of its five seasons their friendship remains the most salient relationship over romantic partnership and children. In the series finale, "Broad City," Abbi leaves New York for Boulder, Colorado, to pursue her dream of being an artist, and Ilana remains in New York (5.10, "Broad City"). The episode simply ends with them remaining in touch and maintaining their open-ended intimate connection reflecting the observation that these characters are "goofy, gross, and devoted to women friends above all else."[33]

## Telenovela? Soap Opera? Dramedy? Yes . . . and No: *Jane the Virgin*'s Balancing Act

*Jane the Virgin* was one of the most promiscuous shows on television—stylistically. Creatively speaking, the series team is led by producer and writer Jennie Snyder Urman. Though less well known than creator-performers like Lena Dunham and Issa Rae her coauthorship is crucial to the series as a producer and writer. She wrote thirteen of its 100 episodes, including crafting the first and last episode of each season.[34] The show's creative approach draws its visual and aural language from multiple sources, including television comedy, social media, and the serialized forms of soap operas and telenovelas.

The original premise of Venezuela's *Juana la Virgen* centers on a seventeen-year-old virgin who is impregnated accidentally. The US adaptation is set in Miami, Florida, and Jane Villanueva (Gina Rodriguez) is a twenty-three-year-old college-educated woman living with her mother Xiomara (Andrea Navedo) and grandmother, Alba (Ivonne Coll). Jane is a virgin who has never been sexually active with her fiancé,

Michael (Brett Dier). In a freak accident her gynecologist Dr. Luisa Alver (Yara Martinez) accidentally inseminates Jane with her former crush Rafael's (Justin Baldoni) sperm. He is married to Petra (Yael Grobglas), and the couple owns the Marbella Hotel where Jane works.

Jane is a twenty-three-year-old college student rather than a seventeen-year-old, which connects her to this book's focus on Millennial women characters. Like other characters I study she is college educated, works a low-paying service job, and is trying to figure out her postbaccalaureate life. *Unlike* most of them Jane lives at home with her family, rather than independently, is not sexually active (at least in the first few seasons), and is a student throughout much of the series. Her pregnancy also adds a different kind of complexity and responsibility to her life compared to other characters, few of whom become mothers.

This section addresses what *Jane* has to say about its Millennial protagonist by exploring the formal vocabularies it employs to articulate its point of view. I focus on the stylistic and thematic approach of the first season because it established the series' core blueprint and critical reputation. While its range of tools is in keeping with the elevated tone of the original series we must consider how the show's intricate choreographing of different techniques enhances our understanding of Jane's complex navigation of her identities in the US context of her character.

Jane is a college-educated, third-generation Venezuelan American woman raised by a single mother, Xiomara. They live in the house of the staunchly Catholic Alba who immigrated illegally to Miami from Venezuela with her husband (1.10, "Chapter 10"). Though Jane is engaged to be married to her fiancé Michael, she is a virgin, a "virtue" ingrained in her and continually reinforced by her Alba. The first two seasons make Jane's sexuality a continual source of comedic and dramatic tension. As she vacillates from Michael to Rafael, the biological father of her baby, back to Michael, numerous opportunities emerge for her to explore her sexuality; she is repeatedly grounded by her hesitance and guilt tied to her upbringing. Alba worries her pregnancy and engagement would serve as excuses for her to lose her virginity. Xiomara simply wants Jane to be intimate with someone who values her.

Thus, in season one we continually watch Jane balance her individual needs with the cultural expectations to adhere to four values associated with Latino culture: *marianismo*, *familismo*, *respeto*, and *simpatía*.

Understanding these cultural values helps audiences engage with the gender, ethnic, and class elements its stylistic mélange frames so meticulously. *Marianismo* is "the cult of feminine spiritual superiority, which teaches that women are semi-divine, morally superior to and spiritually stronger than men."[35] The term captures both the idealization of Latina identity as "virtuous, humble, and spiritually superior to men," and the subordinate positioning in Latin American culture for Latinas to be "submissive to the demands of men, withstand extreme sacrifices and suffering for the sake of the family" and "be like the Virgin Mary who is viewed as virginally pure and non-sexual."[36] Even when Stevens coined the term in 1973 she acknowledged it as a powerful but not all-encompassing value.[37] As Cauce and Domenech-Rodríguez note, "while *machismo* and *marianismo*, like *familismo* and *personalismo*, are values that inform behavior, they are not behavior patterns themselves. There is a difference between legacies and realities." In their study of gendered values in Latino families they acknowledge the complexities of balancing tradition and modernization, noting, "Latinas are attaining increasingly egalitarian relationships within the families, but this change in role is not accompanied by a change in ideology. Latinas show some reluctance to let go of the notion that males should have the prominent roles as breadwinners and as family representatives to the outside world."[38]

Jane's access to higher education and relative financial independence give her greater flexibility and choice than her mother or grandmother in many respects. Alba's pressure on Jane to maintain her virginity and thus her "purity" reflects elements of these traditional values. *Marianismo* complements *familismo*, "an individual's strong identification with and attachment to nuclear and extended families," which necessitates women "provide physical and emotional support to the family, bear and raise children, and take care of house work." We see this value in the Villanueva family's excitement around Jane's pregnancy and her frustrations feeling micromanaged by her family. *Respeto* represents the "obedience, duty, and deference of an individual's position within a hierarchical structure," notably the family. This is a gendered notion, and for Latinas "the adherence to *respeto* has molded a Latina's gender role to be content in the home, subordinate to the husband, and obedient." As a single woman, until the end of season two, Jane behaves as a dutiful daughter, but tensions often arise when she defies their expectations and asserts her independence. Finally, *simpatía* focuses on avoiding controversy, being courteous, and projecting positivity.[39] Jane strives to be diplomatic and reasonable but occasionally flexes her independence.

### Jane the Virgin*'s Stylistic Synthesis*

*Jane the Virgin*'s intentional stylistic "impurity" helped the series develop an audience. By borrowing conventions associated with Latin American telenovelas, US soap operas, and complex US dramedies, but never falling squarely into any one category, it stands apart from other series. Updates from the original Venezuelan series to North American tastes include its metaconscious tone, more overt nods to feminism, the prominent incorporation of social media (e.g., via onscreen hashtags), its casting of prominent Latin American performers, and its acknowledgment of social issues such as immigration. *Jane* reflects the transnational nature of contemporary media forms, which was pioneered by the exportation of telenovela scripts, and the convergent nature of contemporary media. Though it was broadcast on the CW originally, it was licensed for streaming on Netflix in 2016, which broadened its audience.[40]

Here, I clarify how it borrows from and diverges from the stylistic properties of soap operas and telenovelas. Part of its divergence is its ability to incorporate genre elements without fully surrendering to either form, which allows it to relay the tonal complexity of the dramedy form. Straight adaptations of telenovelas have not fared well in the United States traditionally. ABC's *Ugly Betty* (2006–10) is the closest precedent to *JTV*'s style, though Jane's confrontation with *marianismo* figures more prominently, and it has a more surreal tone closely tied to its metaconscious approach.

Soap operas originated on US radio networks in 1930 to attract female consumers, and the format quickly grew in the 1940s to become the dominant daytime radio program format. Television networks began airing versions of radio programs as well as new series by the 1950s.[41] Levine's analysis of soap operas traces their different historical phases. These include the early 1960s to mid-1980s when daytime soaps were "a powerful force in the TV industry and in American culture," and the mid- to late 1980s decline in the ratings and profitability of soap operas.[42]

Formally, soaps are "open serials" focused on a large community of interrelated characters. The open format is "predicated upon the impossibility of ultimate closure," and its ensemble format means "there is no central, indispensable character . . . to whose fate viewer interest is indissolubly linked." Additionally, they focus more on dialogue than action and tend to repeat certain plot points or revelations as "each retelling affects relations among the community of characters." The emphasis on talk also means no single event "will push the open serial narrative any closer to ultimate closure." Common narrative tropes include the resurrection of previously dead characters, "revealing of parentage" plotlines, the prominence of occupations requiring abundant talking (e.g., doctors), and locations where characters "regularly have occasion to meet," such as hospitals.[43] In *JTV*, Jane is devastated when she learns Xiomara has been withholding that her father is telenovela star Rogelio de la Vega for over twenty years. Similarly, much of the narrative action in *Jane* occurs in Jane's workplace, the Marbella Hotel. Where Jane works, Rafael is boss, and he and his wife Petra live here.

Levine acknowledges soaps as a dynamic genre that changes shape as broadcast network television changes, including their visual and aural approach. For example, soaps of the "Network Era" of the 1970s to 1980s distinguished themselves via new aesthetic approaches, including the use of extreme close-ups, music cued to certain characters and moods, the increased use of workplace settings, more quickly paced episodes with shorter episode recaps and flashbacks, and brisker, more stylized editing techniques between scenes.[44] In *JTV* unique recurring "love themes" underscore conversations between Jane and Michael, and Jane and Rafael. In terms of pacing many scenes transition pointedly to the next to amplify dramatic or comedic elements in scenes.

Soap operas are also a form "associated with women" whose construction of femininity "gets regularly complicated and even fractured." An especially relevant observation for *JTV*'s use of soap operatic elements is the "changing construction of their audience," including their "reimagining [of] narrative fixtures such as the supercouple and the family," some of which "progressively confronted constructs of race and sexuality as well as gender admitting to a new degree nonwhite and nonstraight characters."[45] *Jane* is arguably more about Jane figuring out what she wants in her personal life, including her choice to have her baby and seek intimate relationships, without sacrificing her aspiration to become a professional writer. Her marriage to Rafael in the series finale (a lot happens in between) is far more of a willful choice on her terms than a concession to social norms.

The first telenovelas, including Cuba's *Sua vida me perence*, Brazil's *Senderos de amor*, and Mexico's *Ángeles de la calle*, debuted in 1951.[46] These three series aired once or twice a week until Mexico's *Senda prohibida* became the first to air daily in 1958.[47] Unlike soap operas, telenovelas are "closed serials" with "clear-cut stories with definite endings that permit narrative closure."[48] Telenovelas are a pan-Latino form with national variations. For example, Mexican telenovelas tend to be romantic and melodramatic, whereas Colombian telenovelas often incorporate humor. This transnational quality is amplified by the global exporting of telenovela scripts to multiple countries generating billions in revenue especially for telenovela producers.[49] Given these national variations, my descriptions of the form are necessarily broad.

Structurally, telenovelas are influenced by a range of melodramatic forms, and their stories unfold in multiple phases, including initial episodes that introduce multiple characters and plotlines, twenty to thirty episodes where themes, characters, and plotlines deepen, and the final third focused on resolving the major plotlines. The series end is usually promoted very heavily to generate discourse and build anticipation.[50] Telenovela plots usually focus on events affecting families, such as "lost children and family members, confused paternity, lost inheritances," or unusual twists on common situations family members experience such as "marriage, sibling relationships, [and] engagements."[51] Like telenovelas *JTV* is very family centered with its recurring storylines focused on the awkwardness of Jane and Rafael coparenting their son Mateo when she and Michael are married; Rafael and Petra's eventual coparenting of twins who are step siblings to Mateo; and the volatile relationship between Xiomara and Rogelio. *JTV* aired 100 episodes over five seasons, and while US viewers would not expect a primetime television series to air as long as a soap opera they would not necessarily anticipate its eventual closure the way a telenovela viewer might anticipate it.

Acting styles on telenovelas are calibrated to melodramatic excesses integral to the form. Examples include "overdramatization, emphasis on emotion rather than logic, use of music to mark key relationships, characters as symbols of ethical values."[52] In *JTV*, Rogelio's comic vanity and lack of self-awareness, and Xiomara's need for attention frequently lead to flare-ups between them in which they each accuse the other of behaving dramatically. Like soap operas, telenovelas are a dynamic form shaped by a range of factors.

Soaps became so culturally ingrained several shows used the form for humor and social commentary. In the 1970s the syndicated series *Mary Hartman, Mary Hartman* (1976–77) and ABC's *Soap* (1977–81) employed the soap opera form for humor. *MH2* was a satire of American cultural norms that employed elements of US soap opera production design, including the lushly scored theme song, melodramatic organ music, and domestic and workplace interior settings, to cosset its absurd plot elements, deadpan humor, and lack of a laugh track. The series aired daily like a soap opera but during the evening and generated controversy for its unconventional approach and mature themes, including mass murder and domestic violence.[53] *Soap* was a more conventional sitcom with a laugh track. More parodic than satirical it had a serialized structure and began each episode with recaps of previous episodes chronicling the dysfunctional behavior of the Tate and Campbell families. *Soap*'s often sexually suggestive and provocative content generated controversy before it even aired, but it ultimately lasted for four seasons.[54] Both series are benchmarks for the fusion of comedy with the serial narrative form.

The adaptation of telenovelas for US audiences occurred more slowly and with mixed results. In the early '00s Fox's MyNetwork TV's two English-language telenovelas, including *Desire* and *Fashion House* (2006) made a minimal impact.[55] In the early '00s US daytime soap operas, such as NBC's *Passions*, began experimenting with the form by incorporating elements of musicals, supernatural genres, and telenovelas. ABC's *Port Charles* also adapted aspects of the "closed serial" form of the telenovela. Though laudably experimental, low ratings ultimately led to its cancellation.[56]

Within primetime US television ABC's adaptation of Colombia's *Yo soy Betty, la fea*, *Ugly Betty*, was the first successful fusion of comedy, soap opera, and telenovela elements.[57] The series is primarily a coming-of-age dramedy focused on the professional and personal growth of Betty Suarez (America Ferrera), a Mexican American woman who lives with her family in Queens. *Ugly Betty* was critically acclaimed and popular. As such, *Jane* is not the first series to blend comedy with US and Latin American melodramatic forms, but it incorporates aspects of the telenovela more prominently than any US series to date, including *Ugly Betty*, and fits with the stylistic homage and aesthetic mastery of the other good and complex series.

*Between Marianismo and Millennial: A Close Reading of "Chapter Seven"*
I focus my episodic close reading on "Chapter Seven" (1.7) because it is a pivotal episode in the first season, and stylistically it employs a broad range of narrative, visual, and aural elements that represent the show's fundamental stylistic hybridity.[58] Many of the features I highlight define the entire series. My reading emphasizes how it combines melodramatic tropes associated with soap operas and telenovelas with metaconscious elements, including visual captions and voice-over narration, anthropomorphized objects, and other stylistic nuances associated with complex TV. The reconfiguring of these genre tropes with more contemporary televisual elements parallels Jane's own positioning between the traditional and the contemporary. Her family supports her education as well as her engagement to Michael, but Alba expects her to remain a virgin. When her engagement ends Xiomara expects her to follow her advice about men. Jane, however, is faced with the dilemma of wanting to honor her family, develop her own voice, and have her own experiences. Drama!

In soap operatic fashion the episode begins with a recap conveyed via voice-over. The brief yet dense recap brings the audience up to speed and links it with the telenovela tradition immediately. First, it reiterates Jane's virginal status, linking her to *marianismo* values, by flashing back to a scene where a doctor tells her she's pregnant and she declares, "But I've never had sex." This scene is repeated frequently in the first season's recaps; this repetitious quality is an oft-mocked element of soap operas *Jane* employs for humor.

Next, it reiterates the soap opera and telenovela tropes of ensemble structures and the dominant themes of family and romance. Jane is in a hospital bed surrounded by the people for whom her pregnant virgin status is "a problem," according to the narrator, including her family, Rafael, Michael, and Petra. Finally, the narration briskly unpacks the most germane aspects of conflict. For example, we learn Jane has reunited with the father she never knew, Rogelio; Xiomara is growing closer to him but fears moving forward to protect Jane; two girls, who attend the school

(Our Lady of Sorrows: A Catholic School for Girls) where Jane is student-teaching are Rogelio's stepdaughters, know Jane is pregnant and plan to reveal pictures; and the nuns who run the school have created a "Jane the Pregnant Virgin" website to cash in on her miracle pregnancy, unbeknownst to Jane. The narrator (actor Anthony Mendez) does this with greater flair than I could, but hopefully I've captured the essence. Because the episode has so many threads I focus on Jane's dilemma because it most inspires the fusion between traditional forms and more surreal elements.

The episode transitions to a flashback of Jane and Rafael kissing five years earlier, her enchantment with him, Xiomara's skepticism toward the kiss, and Jane's disappointment when he does not contact her after the kiss. Though flashback scenes are common on soap operas *Jane* differs by beginning each episode with a flashback and depicting whole scenes rather than just a few lines of dialogue from a past episode. When Rafael fails to call, Jane is picking the petals off a white rose. As the petals descend to the floor then there is a seamless dissolve—drawn from soap opera editing techniques—that brings us into "real time" as petals continue to fall from a tree where Rafael and Jane kiss in the moonlight at a bay near the Marbella Hotel. Xiomara, who is skeptical of Rafael, interrupts them abruptly and reminds Jane that she and Alba are waiting in the car for Jan to drive them home.

As Jane drives them home the voice-over tells us her head was spinning, and when she stops she sees something unusual for soap operas and telenovelas. The stop sign's signage morphs from "STOP" to "STOP NO RAFAEL" (figure 3.7). This visual anthropomorphism adds a layer of humor and magical realism distinct to the series mix of soap opera and telenovela tropes. Once home the narrator tells us Jane has a feeling, and she tells Xiomara she feels like she is meant to be with Rafael. Xiomara warns her to consider her current situation and Rafael's past and present, signified by an onscreen caption with five emoji type graphics, including a crying baby, a voluptuous woman's silhouette, a champagne bottle, a wedding ring, and Petra's head. This is the first of several appearances for the caption, which punctuates the emotional stakes and reorganizes information the audience is aware of into another form, extending the theme of repetition. Like the anthropomorphized objects this is another distinguishing visual element of the series from the soberer tone of soap operas and telenovelas.

Figure 3.7. A communicative stop sign is one of several anthropomorphic objects "Chapter Seven" of *Jane the Virgin* uses to convey Jane's contentious attraction to Rafael.

The next morning Xiomara, Alba, and Jane are discussing her situation briefly when we hear a knock on the door from Rafael. When Jane opens the door and sees it is him the title card "CHAPTER SEVEN" appears onscreen with a percussive beat. Like telenovelas *Jane* is organized into chapters rather than episodes, which implies the closed serial structure, as all "books" must come to an end. Since the audience could not know how many seasons the series would last, however, its seriality is somewhat ambiguous, like the open structure of soap operas, so arguably it exists in a more liminal space between the forms.

On the porch Rafael offers to take Jane on a date and as she is about to kiss him the baby-silhouette-champagne-ring-Petra caption reappears and she asks him to give her some time, especially given her recent break from Michael. When she re-enters the house, she gets a text from Michael who asks her to bring him the watch he left during their previous encounter. This minor interaction creates an opportunity for them to interact in person later in the episode.

At the school, a married couple speaks with Jane about their family planning and hug her. As she leaves them the nuns who run the school discuss the divine blessing Jane represents, and we see a coin featuring a picture of a pregnant Jane dressed in a white gown with a protruding belly and a crown of thorns around her head over a powder blue background. The text bordering the image reads "OUR LADY OF SORROWS" at the top of the circle and "JANE THE VIRGIN" below the picture. A similar encounter with a couple happens again, except they show her the coin, and she confronts the nuns about exploiting her image. The series title, Jane's declaration of her virginity in the recap, her student-teaching at a Catholic girl's school, the nuns, and the coin's detail reflects the show's awareness of and engagement with the prominence of Catholicism throughout the pan-Latin American world.

A few scenes later at the hotel Jane gives Michael the watch and asks about a computer case she left. Similar to Jane's encounter with Rogelio we hear music, but the score is a noticeably melancholic guitar strum. Michael admits he lied to her and was nervous about being engaged and ambivalent about the baby. Frustrated Jane exits the scene and we hear a reprise of the score.

Meanwhile in the lobby Jane processes her feelings about Rafael with three coworkers. They change the subject to a desire to celebrate Frankie's birthday at an exclusive new club, Viento, and ask Jane to see if Rafael, a club investor, can get them access. As she listens to their request and types information into a digital cash register its text shifts from "Is $44.50 the correct total?" to "Will you tell your friends you kissed him" (with a heart above the "i" in him) and her eyes expand in shock (figure 3.8). She sees Rafael in the lobby and he agrees to help her friends and notes he will be present since it's the club's opening. Based on previous patterns in the episode we know this is a setup for them to interact.

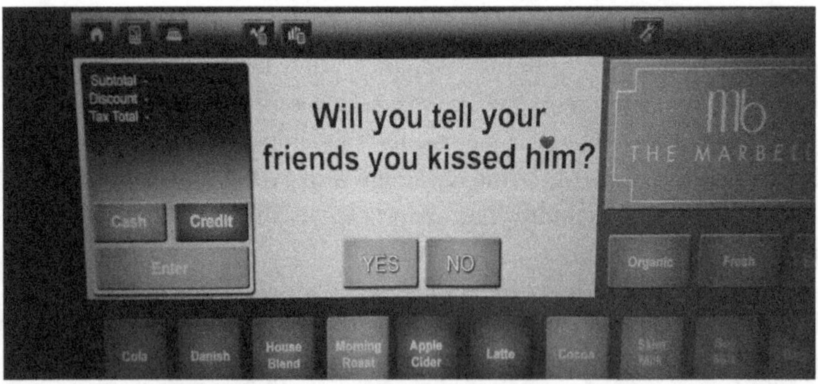


**Figure 3.8.** A cash register continues the anthropomorphic theme of "Chapter Seven," humorously testing Jane's willingness to be honest about her internal romantic struggle.

The narrative intricacy of *Jane* as well as its stylistic density assume its audience is sophisticated enough to pick up on its various cues. These characteristics allow it to transcend the "low" culture stigma of primetime US melodramas (e.g., *Dallas*, *Dynasty*, *Melrose Place*) and aligns it with "quality" television of the "peak TV" era of prestige television. Being cast in a telenovela is a prestigious milestone for actors in Latin America, and the form has gained a modicum of critical respect in scholarly communities. In the United States, however, soap operas remain a "low culture" genre rather than an aspirational form. *Jane*'s fusion of melodramatic elements and its alignment with qualities of "complex" series and a tacit "sophisticated" viewer steeped in multiple media forms allow it to appeal to viewers who like a "great story" and those who revel in their understanding of the narrative's componentry. To return to the melodrama . . .

Like the highly opinionated stop sign and digital cash register, objects continue speaking to Jane. On the bus home with Xiomara she tells her mother she is going to Viento, to Xiomara's dismay. Jane then sees the bus sign text morph from "NEXT STOP BISCAYNE BLVD" to "RAFAEL-DANGER, JANE." As such the series defies any semblance of realism by acknowledging its status as a highly constructed piece of fiction and engages the audience in a kind of knowing dialogue that enhances the viewing experience.

As the episode continues various storylines begin winding down toward their "cliffhangers" in a few additional scenes. Most importantly, Michael brings the computer case to the staff locker room area and stares angrily at a bouquet. When Jane enters he hands her the case, says the flowers are for her but not from him and declares, "You're not the person I thought you were," as he exits the room, in a parallel to Jane's exit from their prior encounter in the space. Through an onscreen caption we see the note Rafael has written to Jane. She confronts him in his office to recall the intensity of the situation, including recounting her recent broken engagement with Michael, which we know but in the tradition of soap operas repeats an obvious detail. Operating in the *marianismo* mode she sacrifices her feelings for others noting they have to consider other people's feelings beyond their own.

The birthday celebration at Viento, and its aftermath, illuminates what Jane is seeking to protect from the influence of others.

When she enters the club with her coworkers she immediately notices Rafael surrounded by several women in the VIP section and feels "not fine," as the narrator tells us. As time passes in the club Rafael catches up with a disengaged Jane and explains the women are just friends and assures her if they date they could be discreet. Once again, the silhouette-champagne-Petra-wedding ring-baby caption appears though in a slightly different order (figure 3.9). As he makes his case for how he will prioritize the baby, feels estranged from the moneyed world he occupies, and wants to get to know her, the emojis disappear one by one and we hear an earnest strummed melody. He asks her to meet him outside, and as Jane approaches the exit sign the narrator notes how if she went after him it would defy all the advice she has been given, and the sign's language changes from "EXIT" to "DO NOT EXIT." Jane meets Rafael at his car and the voice-over informs us, "For the first time Jane throws caution to the wind."

In many romantic comedies these moments would culminate in a romantic and sexual climax, but the series has to delay this element to maintain its seriality. As a result, we see lighthearted scenes of Jane and Rafael bonding in very rom-com-like fashion. At one point they lie down next to each other gazing up at the stars, and we see them cuddling, with their clothes partially covered by a blanket with a small fire burning. Then a row of hearts appears as a caption.

Figure 3.9. A recurring visual motif in "Chapter Seven," more broadly representative of *Jane the Virgin*'s visual density, is a screen caption with various symbols corresponding to dialogue.

The next morning, Xiomara calls Michael and says Jane has not returned home and she is trying to track her down. When it registers to them that she is with Rafael, Michael looks devastated and Xiomara looks surprised. Michael is jealous of Jane for spending time with Rafael, implying that she *spent the night* with him while denying him during their relationship. Xiomara is shocked that Jane defied her advice. In his final scene in the episode Michael sees images of Jane and Rafael on his phone and is short with his fellow detective Nadine. After Michael and Nadine argue for a bit they gaze into each other's eyes and begin kissing as he rips his shirt off and they begin kissing and caressing on a table. Drama!

In a parallel to Xiomara waking up abruptly and not seeing Jane, Jane wakes up and urges Rafael to drive her to school because she is late. When she pulls up in his red convertible and gets out wearing the dress from the previous night the head nun criticizes her. Jane, feeling empowered after trusting her instincts with Rafael, confronts the nun about the website and the coin. Later in the episode Rogelio confronts Rafael about keeping Jane out all night and notes *his* former background as a playboy. Rafael alerts Jane who confronts both Rogelio and Xiomara at the house about their treatment of Rafael. She recounts how she has always made sensible choices. Xiomara agrees and says she should continue to do so, but Jane notes she feels her cautiousness has hindered her; pursuing a relationship with Rafael is her last chance before she has the baby. This is one of the key moments in the first season where Jane challenges the *marianismo* trope by defying the advice of her family to pursue her own happiness.

In the evening after, Jane is standing at the bayside that opened the episode, wearing a dress and heels ready for her second official date with Rafael. As he ends his text to her and is exiting his office his father enters and fires him. The episode ends with Rafael calling Jane from a limousine and noting he is traveling to Mexico City. The episode ends with the usual text projected onscreen "TO BE CONTINUED . . ."

## The Art of "Remixing"

Though *CXG*, *Broad City*, and *JTV* differ in plot, setting, and structure, their commonalities inform my choice to discuss them in a collective context. Each series "remixes" familiar genre and subgenre elements from a vast range of styles and synthesizes these into something distinct and recognizable. The richness of these series and the narrative "worlds" they have generated reflects how "U.S. television has devoted increased attention in the past two decades to crafting and maintaining ever more complex narrative universes, a form of 'world building' that has allowed for wholly new modes of narration and that suggests new forms of audience engagement." The worlds these series create "depend on the long-term viewer's knowledge and appreciation of the modes of narration and emplotment characteristic of the series as a whole."[59] Relatedly, Mittell eloquently describes how complex television targets and rewards more discerning viewers, encouraging them to rewatch and "to notice the depth of references, to marvel at the displays of craft and continuities, and to appreciate details that require the liberal use of pause and rewind." In these highly stylized programs we witness a generation of series unafraid to create their own narrative worlds and vocabularies. Such familiarity, with *CXG*'s musical interludes, *Broad City*'s stoner sequences, and *JTV*'s visual anthropomorphism, has a unique effect among their fans of "rewarding regular viewers who have mastered each program's internal conventions of complex narration," reflecting "trust in the payoff" among viewers.[60]

Equally important is their central narrative focus on the interests and concerns of Millennial women. The tension between Rebecca's relentless pursuit of rom-com-inspired ideas about romance and the importance of attending to her mental health, the ways Abbi and Ilana adapt different forms of swagger and fantasy to explore their ambitions and stretch their personae, and Jane's efforts to honor her family while pursuing her professional aspirations and forming her own family are distinctly women-centric. Their dilemmas are not interchangeable with man-identified characters, giving them a unique pathway. The series' stylistic "play" exposes the gender-specific scripts of romantic comedies, stoner comedies and buddy films, and melodramas, and inverts them, asserting the value of feminized culture in the contemporary discourse of complex television.

Series like *Buffy* and *Ally* are important precedents for the more surrealistic elements of 2010–20s era women-centric series in their narrative focus on women and innovative approaches to genre. *Ally*, for example, pioneered the hybrid dramedy category and integrated the single career women narrative trope with animation, fantasy, choreography, and music in unprecedented fashion.[61] The way *CXG*, an hour-long network dramedy that also focuses on a woman-identified lawyer, expands from *Ally*'s approach informs the genealogical connection between the series *and* the generational and contextual difference. In the fifth and final season, Ally purchases a home, adopts a ten-year-old daughter, and becomes a partner in her law firm, all hallmarks of success.[62] Comparatively, Rebecca, who rejects a partnership at a prestigious law firm in the pilot of *CXG*, is a renter, is child-free, and quits the law firm to run a pretzel shop. Most importantly her journey in seasons three and four entails confronting the popular culture fantasies that have distorted her sensibility and also entails striving toward personal clarity, which is more salient for her than pursuing a romantic relationship. Similarly, we can trace influence between the post-*Ally*, *Buffy*, and *Sex and the City*, and pre-*Girls* series *Ugly Betty* and *Jane the Virgin*, which is more surreal and explicit in its genre play.

Another key way to connect the series is to note their impact on other series. In the context of post-*Girls* women-centric series, *CXG* influenced the choreographed musical fantasies of *Zoey's Extraordinary Playlist* (2019–20, NBC), which centers on a Millennial woman and spotlights an ensemble of coworkers. The slapstick element of *Broad City* is also evident in several series focused on women's friendships, including the adolescent friendship on Maya Erksine and Anna Konkle's *PEN15* (2019–21, Hulu), and the sexual and professional antics featured on the 2022-era series *Harlem*, and *Everything's Trash*. Just as *Girls* established the indie stylistic blueprint for many women-centric television series, *Broad City* pioneered the Millennial women's buddy comedy. The US adaptation of Venezuela's *Juana la Virgen* inspired the South Korean adaption *Woori the Virgin* (2022), suggesting the core story's ongoing resonance across continents.[63] The series "Got to Be (Sur)real" discusses have effectively made the familiar *unfamiliar* through deft genre synthesis. Their efforts have inspired audiences to pay closer attention to how Millennial women challenge familiar tropes, romantic fulfillment, friendship, and family, to suit their needs and modeled how emerging storytellers can continue to take creative risks and stretch the boundaries of televisual storytelling.

# 4

# ALL IN THE TIMING

## *Temporal Play and Women's Hidden Subjectivities*

*Fleabag*, *I May Destroy You* (*IMDY*), and *Orange Is the New Black* (*OITNB*) tell very different stories but are linked by the way they employ different orders of time to offer narrative insight about characters and context that go beyond exposition or mere plot advancement. In the context of musicals McMillin refers to this quality as "a dimension that lies beyond realism and increases the range of their presentation."[1] The art of the flashback, flash out, and flash-sideways, combined with other effects like breaking the fourth wall and the use of fantasy, are dominant stylistic innovations essential to each series. Whereas flashbacks to the past and flash-forwards to the future might be obvious, Levy defines "flash-sideways" as presenting "an alternative present, perceived as a form of temporal play that moves sideways across the present without shifting forward or backward in time but offering a parallel present that visualizes what would happen in the present if circumstances were different."[2] The way the three series use different temporalities is central to the narrative structure rather than an affectation or gimmick. While this quality is self-evident in the musical context informing McMillin's theory, in a nonmusical it can be equally effective and distinguishing.

It's worth noting some of the post-2020 women-centric series that liberally employ flashbacks: *Feel Good* (2020–21, Channel Four and Netflix), *Single Drunk Female* (2022–23, Freeform), and the miniseries *Tiny Beautiful Things* (2023, Hulu). *Fleabag*'s temporal structure pushes boundaries on the default trope of "likability" for women in comedy through a daring sleight of hand in its first season. *IMDY* uses intimate experiences with sexual trauma to depict its social pervasiveness; it is equally insightful about the limits of social media as a tool for wellness. *OITNB* mimics its theme song's refrain of "you've got time" by using space and time creatively to constantly expand and deepen our understanding of its panoply of characters and contexts over seven seasons. The notion that there is more to the story is integral to its design. For example, in an astute analysis of the series opening credits, which show extreme close-ups of the faces of multiple diverse women, McHugh notes, "the sequence's structure, series, title, and women's faces connote a tone that is ironic and double-edged, suggesting there is more to see or know than is immediately evident or discernible in the text and images."[3]

This chapter unpacks what can be understood more clearly and fully about women characters, and aspects of women's lived experiences, when stories go beyond the confines of linear storylines associated with earlier eras of television. Levy chronicles the proliferation of "temporal play" among twenty-first-century television series and argues, "Televisual resistance to narrative order can thus be read as resistance to social order—temporal complexity not only as a metaphoric or aesthetic structure affected by industry, economy, and technology but also as a political instrument."[4] Levy's observation should pique our curiosity regarding the following: What is hidden, illuminated, and/or distorted by different orders of time? How might addressing these concerns through storytelling reveal something meaningful about women's subjectivities less visible to audiences traditionally? The following series analyses explore these questions in the context of a "posh" (or "posh" adjacent) White London woman processing her friend and business partner's death alongside romantic and familial drama; a working-class woman of African descent processing sexual trauma while making a living as a writer and coexisting in her close friendships in London; and a diverse cast of women trying to maintain some semblance of humanity in the confines of a women's prison.

## Flawed in a Flash: *Fleabag* Puts Likability in Crisis

Likability is such a common trope of what audiences expect in comedic female leads that critics frequently label series as bold for writing women who are "unlikable." Hagelin and Silverman observe this about television's contemporary female antiheroes, noting, "Selfish, vengeful, often deeply unlikeable, they fly in the face of our expectations for women. . . . The women are the outlaws and outcasts of contemporary TV—the new female antiheroes."[5] Bogutskaya similarly refers to the recent resurgence of antiheroines as "a third golden age," following similar character trends in Hollywood films of the 1910s–1930s, and film and television of 1990s, in her study of unlikable female characters. Regarding recent characters, she notes, "They can be flawed, malicious, self-serving, ruthless, hapless characters—but ultimately unlikeable female characters are liberating, because they are not meant to be seen as morality lessons within their stories."[6]

What exactly constitutes likability, and its inverse, is debatable but implied in the implicit notion that we root for likable women. We want them to get what they want, and the goal-oriented narrative structure of popular media genres, from mainstream films to soap opera, usually posits various forms of companionship and kinship as women's primary desires. In the (so-called) postfeminist era of post-1960s television, women are presumed to have relatively equal access to education and careers, compared to men. As such, even the most ambitious and successful career women of television (e.g., Ally McBeal, Carrie Bradshaw) feel unsatisfied and incomplete.

These issues of likability, audience perspective, and desire get particularly knotty when we consider the protagonist of *Fleabag*. The comic conceit hinted at in titles like *Jane the Virgin* and *Crazy Ex-Girlfriend* is ambiguous enough to be intriguing, and a series title like *Insecure* broadcasts its focus on awkward, vulnerable, and misunderstood people. *Fleabag*, however, connotes something dirty and repellent. The colloquial term does not signify likability or heroism, yet the lead character, whose name is never revealed to the audience in its two seasons, but for whom the series is named, challenges the boundaries, and utility, of "likability" in refreshing ways.

Iconic antiheroic men such as Tony Soprano, Don Draper, and Walter White have been lionized as symbols of television's daring.[7] Though they are undeniably complex, they adhere to certain ideals of masculine behavior and are taken seriously by virtue of appearing on acclaimed dramatic series. The closest analogue in comedy is *Curb Your Enthusiasm*'s misanthropic Larry David. The character is selfish, vindictive, inconsiderate, inappropriate, and very difficult to like. Yet, these qualities are understood as a guilty pleasure and relief from the stale, inoffensive men typical of mainstream comedies. Women characters have rarely had parallel opportunities to emulate this behavior without severe critical backlash. Rowe's analysis of the public outcry toward comedienne Roseanne Barr's "unruly" femininity in the early 1990s is nearly indistinguishable from the body shaming and relentless scrutiny Lena Dunham received for her depiction of Hannah on *Girls*.[8] This limited permission to be unlikable is even clearer when we consider racial and gender barriers. Issa Rae has commented, for example, on wanting room for flawed Black women characters in the vein of Larry David.[9]

On a macrolevel the "flaw" is stepping outside of the gendered script television expects of women, which is where *Fleabag* excels. During its first season, composed of six episodes, Fleabag—a narrator who breaks the fourth wall, often in service of setting up a flashback—informs us that her best friend and business partner, Boo, has died, which engenders empathy (figure 4.1). Their relationship is central to the arc of the first season and remains a thread in season two. As she breaks the fourth wall, and flashes back, we simultaneously witness a range of morally questionable and antisocial behaviors.

Yet, we want her to triumph against the characters we meet, from her uptight sister Claire (Sian Clifford), to her noncommittal lover ("Arsehole

Figure 4.1. The finale of season one of *Fleabag* initially relies on its unnamed protagonist's usual direct address through visual and verbal fourth wall breaks.

Guy" played by Ben Aldridge), to her obnoxious stepmother (Olivia Coleman). The series origins in Phoebe Waller-Bridge's one-woman show bake a certain level of audience empathy into the work.[10] Once we view her betrayal of Boo in an extended flashback sequence, we question the narrator's reliability and integrity. She emerges as flawed and antiheroic, yet compellingly disruptive. She is "likable," in her judgment, but the pivotal flashback tests our tolerance. It asks us to confront the question of what women are allowed to do on television before we as an audience draw the line—if we ever do.

The show uses temporality as an instrument to develop narrative subtext much like a musician employs different time signatures to draw out the essence of a song lyric. In season one of *Fleabag* the "song" became a surprise "hit" when it returned for its second and final season. Whereas the first season tiptoed quietly into the Amazon Prime Video accounts of US viewers in 2016, the second season, which premiered in 2019 and continued the style and tone of the first, was decidedly buzzy. In addition to garnering critical acclaim, it won three Emmy Awards for its lead showrunner and actor Waller-Bridge, making it the first series made outside of the United States to win best comedy.[11] Multiple factors shaped the second season's reception, including its narrative daring to push "unlikability" from banal flaws to one that proved fatal for another person. How did Waller-Bridge manage to accomplish this feat and generate praise rather than backlash? Arguably, it's all in the timing.

Like *Broad City*'s lead characters Abbi and Ilana, Fleabag is a contemporized version of the unruly woman archetype Rowe described through television. Unruly women are assertive, excessive, self-deprecating, sex positive, and cross boundaries of proper feminine embodiment.[12] Fleabag's actions and personal commentary in the first five episodes of season one's six-episode run illustrate her taboo breaking vividly for viewers: She lacks self-awareness and bodily boundaries (strips down to her bra at the bank); makes poop and hygiene jokes to her sister, Claire; self-describes as a bad feminist; steals money from her date's wallet; steals an allegedly "valuable" piece of sculpture from her stepmom; calculates the timing of her breakups with her boyfriend, Harry, so her apartment gets cleaned; is obsessed with sex; likes sexually explicit pornography; and admits she would fuck anything.

I intersperse moments when she refers to herself as "bad" with moments when she behaves in ways that lead others to comment on her behavior for crossing boundaries of taste, propriety, and expectations, invoking Rowe. I do not need to declare her jokes "inappropriate" because the society she inhabits in the series *does this* for us. The expectations she admits to flouting and many others are highly gendered. In the pilot she labels herself a "bad feminist" when a lecturer asks if they would trade five years of life for the perfect body, and she and Claire are the only ones to raise their hands. Of course, feminists—good, bad, and otherwise—are aware of the social pressures for women to reject themselves and conform to certain manufactured notions of "perfection." By "admitting" what she would prefer she's tacitly reflecting and indicting a social expectation of women.

Fleabag's sexuality is also paramount to her sense of herself and the way others respond to her. Her rather uptight boyfriend Harry (Hugh Skinner) is almost pathologically sensitive, which offers a contrast to her brash and stereotypically masculine sexual behavior. These moments range from his jealousy at Fleabag masturbating to a video of President Barack Obama while he's asleep (1.1) to her scaring him in the shower (1.2) to the point of him having heart palpitations and descending into sobs. He is presented as more stereotypically feminine in his emotionality compared to her. The Obama moment stands out both for her disturbing him in his sleep and for reflecting his possessiveness of her sexuality. We also learn in episode two how the sour underscores the sweet within Harry, such as when he "compliments" her intelligence, noting, "You aren't like other girls. You can keep up." Waller-Bridge, as a writer, understands how to bring out the dark underbelly of characters, which emerges later and more pointedly in the season.

Fleabag's refusal to belong to her partners sexually in the first season is also notable. She opens the pilot episode admitting her calculating routine for having sex, including "performing" spontaneity. In an episode two flashback, after Harry breaks up with her she realizes he is not returning, by virtue of a toy dinosaur he usually leaves behind so he can retrieve it. Sitting on the toilet she delivers the following monologue: "Gonna think about all the people I can have sex with now. I'm not obsessed with sex. I just can't stop thinking about it. The performance of it. The awkwardness of it. The drama of it. The moment you realize someone wants your body. Not so much the feeling of it. Probably got about 48 hours before Harry comes back. I should get on it." Then she rises from the toilet and wipes her frontal area. Fleabag's plaintive description of her sexual appetite delivered from a toilet—repeated in episode three when we see her taking photos of her vagina for a former boyfriend—literalizes Rowe's description of unruly women pushing boundaries and taboos. The bathroom scenes do not appear to have been shot in the spirit of "cringe" humor; there's a straightforwardness about them, as her commentary is more central than the acts or locations themselves. For all of her stated guilt about being a "bad" feminist she is far less cautious about her sexuality.

Fleabag also flirts with taboos in various throwaway moments, such as when she turns to the audience and says, "The next man who walks in [to the café] is getting ridden to death," and it's her father (Bill Paterson) in episode two. Later in the same episode she has reunited with Harry, who only wants to "make love" rather than "just fuck me," which leads her to flashback to an older man who "breathed with every thrust" and keeps screaming "you're so young." She tells us, "I masturbate about that all the time." Toward the end of the episode she enters the apartment where Harry is seated at a table looking at a laptop, shopping for clothing, and her browser history pops up. This exacerbates him as he lists the elaborate types of pornography, including "anal, gang bang, mature, big cock, small tits, hentai," and more. As he recites the list, Fleabag turns and smiles at the camera. Her lust for older men, acknowledgment that she masturbates, and eclectic taste in pornographic fantasies further her unruly persona.

Further, for viewers there is an unusual glee in her mostly unabashed candor about her sexuality. The character coexists on a continuum with a distinguished group of sexually frank female characters, including the iconic Blanche Devereaux (*Golden Girls*), Sandra Clark (*227*), Samantha Jones (*Sex and the City*), and her Millennial contemporary, Ilana Wexler (*Broad City*). Though these characters vary in generation, race, and sexual orientation, they push the boundaries of the "proper" woman archetype. The main way Fleabag differs, especially in season one, is that she is the lead character rather than a colead or a member of an ensemble dependent on contrast. She is the primary narrative focal point so her sexuality is not just comic relief; it is central to the series and a source of the series' innovative approach to time.

By the time viewers reach the finale of season one (1.6) her persona is solidified and little about her behavior surprises us, until we see how her unruliness places Boo in a compromised position that leads to her accidental death. In the episode, Fleabag comes undone in multiple ways. Notably, at her stepmom's garish "Sexhibition" the "Arsehole Guy" dumps her, her stepmother forces her to hold champagne trays and serve guests, and Claire behaves distantly toward her.

After getting sloppily drunk and being scolded by her father, Fleabag flees to a back room serving as a makeshift coatroom and catering station. Claire follows her and asks why she is behaving so erratically. Fleabag declares, "You're not going to Finland" (referencing a professional opportunity), to Claire when her husband, Martin (Brett Gelman), enters. Despite Fleabag's admonition to Claire about his behavior, Claire defends Martin and says she does not believe he attempted to kiss Fleabag, instead asserting it was the opposite. Shocked, Fleabag asks how Claire could consider her a liar, especially as her sister, to which Claire says, "After what you did to Boo?" (figure 4.2).

Suddenly a melancholic musical tone emerges, Fleabag winces, looks into the camera for reassurance, and we see flashbacks of hands

Figure 4.2. Claire confronts "Fleabag" about her betrayal of Boo, which catalyzes the episode's abrupt reveal of the fuller truth obscured in the season's fragmented flashbacks.

unbuttoning a pair of jeans and of Boo crying. Trapped—literally and metaphorically—Fleabag turns around in one direction and the camera blocks her so she is forced to turn around and look at the audience directly (figure 4.3). In a flashback Boo tearfully explains how her lover told her he "fucked somebody else." Fleabag, in real time, looks bereft, and her eyes dash between the audience and Claire, who says, "I'm sorry but you have to see it from my point of view." This line of dialogue slyly disrupts what has been a one-sided perspective of events in Fleabag's life.[13]

We see a montage interspersing flashbacks with "real time" events, beginning with the flashback of Fleabag and Boo's ex-lover Jack spotting each other in a shoe store, followed by Fleabag welling up in real time, and Claire staring and leaving with Martin. Fleabag, now alone with the audience, turns to the camera as it zooms in on her and corners her; she nearly falls into the coat rack, underscored by a dissonant harmony. Another montage sequence begins—Fleabag watches Boo and Jack flirt in a bar, in real time she tries to move to the side of the camera and elude being seen, to no avail. More follows with a flashback of Jack caressing Boo's hair, Fleabag turning a corner in the coatroom away from the camera, and a flashback of Boo saying, "I think I love him" juxtaposed with Fleabag dashing down a dark hallway away from us; we can only see her back in silhouette, making her appear monstrous (figure 4.4).

The next series of juxtapositions finds Jack flirting with Fleabag as she drinks wine in a flashback, Fleabag standing in front of a cage-style

Figure 4.3. After Claire confronts Fleabag about her past, the camera corners her, disrupting the trust her fourth wall breaks established with the audience.

**Figure 4.4.** The camera shows Fleabag from behind, attempting to flee from her transgression against Boo.

door turning halfway toward the camera, Jack gazing in her eyes in the following flashback, a reprise of her unbuttoning his pants then rising to kiss him, and a flashback of Boo revealing her plan. She believes getting hit by a cyclist and hurting her finger will force Jack to visit her in sympathy. Fleabag stands before the caged wall crying, followed by the flashback of her and Jack kissing with Boo's voice-over describing her plan. The sequence concludes with Boo stepping off the sidewalk into the street and getting struck.

In this sequence Claire's naming of Fleabag's most serious transgression disallows Fleabag from controlling the narrative. The series uses the tools Fleabag has employed to tell the story more "objectively" by boxing in Fleabag claustrophobically to limit her ability to turn away and avoid confronting her behavior, which is her usual pattern. No amount of wit and asides can endear her to us in this depiction of betrayal. She is forced to confront the reality that she is a "fuck up" whose behavior indirectly led to her friend's death. This element of her persona connects her with other Millennial characters in its focus on fallibility and the work-in-progress, trial-and-error ethos, especially when compared to the more common depiction of women characters as finite.[14]

In domestically focused comedies wives are often wise, pragmatic, and grounded (e.g., mother figures on *The Cosby Show*). Single women comedies focus on women searching to complete themselves with a partner and/or a more domestic life (e.g., *Ally McBeal*). Comparatively, Fleabag, like *Girls*' Hannah, *Broad City*'s Abbi and Ilana, and *Insecure*'s

Issa, is a flawed character whose surface level confidence belies insecurity and uncertainty. Like them she constantly places herself, or is placed, in narrative situations that push her to challenge her self-understanding. A comparison between Fleabag and Boo illuminates the shift she represents even further.

The flashbacks reveal Fleabag and Jack's mutual attraction and betrayal. She is dishonest in not revealing her relationship to Boo, but Boo is reducible to a mere "innocent." If Fleabag is a deeply flawed antiheroic Millennial archetype, Boo is painfully idealistic. Her notion that pity would lead Jack to salvage what is clearly a weak relationship represents an old archetype. Her death feels like the death of a certain naivete about the nature of people. Fleabag is not *directly* responsible for Boo's death or the inanity of her "plan," which seems more like something a character would contrive in a romantic comedy than a mature approach to a failed relationship. Unlike a typical television series, the sour endures over the sweet. The series is not glib about Boo's death, yet it refuses to fully sentimentalize her.

After the revelatory montage we see streetlights filmed out of focus clear up and Fleabag appears. Walking down the street she runs into her father, who is leaning on his car crying. They discuss her mother, and he notes some of their similarities. She asks if he thinks of her mother, and he asks if she thinks of Boo. She apologizes for her behavior, and when the stepmother appears in the background he says he thinks she should go. As she departs the camera goes out of focus again and then clears up. We see her walking on an empty street accelerated slightly by a series of jump cuts, where we hear Boo's outgoing voice message nondiegetically. As the night sky becomes morning, Fleabag's mascara pours down her face. Because this "became the show's primary marketing image," Nygaard and Lagerwey analyze the character's image—her apparent upper-class clothing, urban setting, and emotional expression—as one that "encapsulates the cycle's overwhelming bleakness and centralization of white precarity."[15]

While the dominance of White characters among 2010s–2020 era prestige programming is undeniable and worth examining, as Nygaard and Lagerwey do throughout their study *Horrible White People*, their reading distorts the show's focus and overlooks some of the formal work happening throughout the series. Fleabag is not a sentimental series asking us to pity (or reject) Fleabag. While its wryness and sexuality clearly mask more complex emotions, the mascara scene is quite brief and hardly represents the series' essence. The image captures Fleabag having a moment, and it passes.

This moment feels like closure in many respects. Fleabag returns to the café to feed Boo's guinea pig. Fleabag goes outside to step into the street in the same spot as Boo when a car pulls up, and halts what could be interpreted as an attempt to endanger herself in parallel to Boo. The driver is the loan officer (Hugh Dennis) who denied her a small business loan in the pilot. They enter the café and go from small talk to her confession that her relentless "fucking," including "fucking the café into liquidation," and transgressions with her family and her friend makes her question her self-worth. She acknowledges conflating desirability from others, manifested through sex, with a strong sense of self, and wonders aloud whether other people feel the same way. As much as I appreciate the myriad arguments about post-2008 financial and social precarity as structures of feeling in many contemporary programs, the gendered component—that women's value is tied to sexual appeal—is not confined to the late '00s. Fleabag is articulating a sense of confusion about broader social notions; finding herself askew of the scripts for financial success, familial propriety, and social mores, the one area where she has felt confident was her ability to perform desirability. She understands that script and has experienced some modicum of success yet feels unfulfilled. When the loan officer, several years older, notes that "people make mistakes," he is recognizing that she is unsettled and in progress. The episode's developments necessarily disrupted some of her presumptions—about her family, her friendships, her sex life—and give her permission to own her behavior and space to make different choices.

Fleabag's fourth wall breaks and use of flashbacks are narrative manipulations that draw attention to our expectations of characters and narrative closure. The fourth wall breaks endear us to Fleabag by virtue of an implied intimacy. We assume she is letting us in and revealing something we might overlook in just viewing behavior and dialogue; her breaks promise to unfold psychological, less-obvious, or even undetectable aspects of people and/or situations. Woods describes the fourth wall address on *Fleabag* (and Michaela Coel's *Chewing Gum*) as one that "establishes a privileged relationship between protagonist and viewer," which "evokes whispered feminine confidences, a shared intimacy, although both women speak with a comic bluntness."[16] This act of intimacy presumes she is credible, reliable, and well intentioned. Even when she does something morally questionable and admits it, the intention seems to be a sly forgiveness, as in "I'm doing something bad but by being honest about it, you'll forgive me."

Fleabag's face and gestures are also integral to her persona. Knowing stares, furled brows, and other types of facial responses the audience sees but the people in her life cannot see amplify the sense of intimacy. In these situations, we are in on the joke so it feels like an intimate secret between friends. No matter how unconventional or problematic her behavior, the combination of verbal dialogue and gesticulation during the breaks come so frequently they allow little time to process things, so we proceed to the next moment or scene.

Flashbacks are an even more effective structure for the series. Every episode entails multiple moments of looking back, including her relationship habits, sexual behavior, and, most poignantly, her relationship to Boo and both the café they managed together and the guinea pig, Hilary, that was largely cared for by Boo. The mix of Fleabag's more amorous moments, many of which border on slapstick, with the quieter, more tender moments with Boo ostensibly neutralize Fleabag's randiness and misjudgments. The Boo flashbacks take us out of time literally but also tonally. There is a sweet, nearly saccharine quality to Boo's relationship with Fleabag. She is nearly always gentle, smiling, kind, and generous toward Fleabag. She is delighted they are in business together, feels strong affection for Hilary, and is effusive about her budding relationship with Jack. In most of these scenes Fleabag is the benevolent receiver, grateful for Boo's trust and affection.

The starkest of the flashbacks are when Boo, dressed in a blue sweatshirt, attempts to step from a curb into the street. At first, we discern she was hit but have no clear understanding of what she is doing and why. The first time we question what we are seeing is when Fleabag does a double take when she sees a shoe salesman who turns out to be Jack. As the details emerge we realize Fleabag's previously amusing lustfulness shifts from being occasionally reckless to destructive. After seeing Fleabag flirt with Jack, we feel betrayed. Fleabag's flashbacks have covered her tracks thus far and insulated her from our judgment. Once we know the fuller picture they are as much about illuminating the past as they are about building a buffer to accommodate her presumed fall.

What we get is an idealized view of Boo and Fleabag, which earns our empathy by virtue of her loss. Seeing that her behavior is the root of the loss, in terms of the impact of her betrayal, shatters our faith in Fleabag's presumed authenticity. For once, she is not being straight with us, and we do not care for the feeling.

Fleabag's behavior up to episode six counters the characteristics we associate with likable female characters, and yet we like her. She bends certain rules and flouts conventions unapologetically. However, when Claire confronts her about her attempts to break up with Martin we witness a moment lacking Fleabag's usual curation. In *Fleabag*, the direct address of the fourth wall we are accustomed to "traps us solely in the perspective of its emotionally detached protagonist" and "is used to display her performance of femininity and attempts to control social situations." Further the fourth wall breaks help Fleabag "conceal her own moments of flailing, frustration, and fury," which are eventually revealed as "'conspiratorial' rather than benignly 'confessional.'"[17]

The "time-release" truth we see is morally repulsive but narratively daring. Fleabag asks us to love, or at least tolerate, her anyway, just as we enjoy the irascible nature of characters like Larry David. This tension suggests the series is manipulating us, suddenly, but then we *were* all along but welcomed it because of our glee for Fleabag's resistance to comedy norms for women. Fleabag sacrifices conventional morality and likability—each inextricable from the earnest emotional affect of comedies—for something more daring narratively. The series uses the sentimental trope of women's friendship to interrogate sentimentality. What we get with Fleabag is a character whose arc allows a certain bitterness to curb decades of sweetness.

Fleabag's manipulations of time and innovative approach to character led me to consider where to place Fleabag among the continuum of women-centric series. Hagelin and Silverman focus their book on US-based series but count *Fleabag*, and *IMDY*, as part of what they view as a new brand of "wonderful antihero series."[18] Though they view this archetype as a feminist disruption to patriarchal norms, confining women to "neoliberal expectations of productivity and the guilt and isolation that often follow our failure to meet them," Nygaard and Lagerwey view

*Fleabag* differently. They classify it as one of several "Horrible White People" shows. Structurally, the authors view *Fleabag*, which was produced by the BBC, with additional funding by Amazon, as an exemplar of the "transnational cultural economy of British and American broadcasting" focused on cultivating an affluent audience by catering to middle-class and upper-class, White, and progressive taste cultures.[19] Aesthetically, the authors cite *Fleabag*'s frequent skewering of artistic pretensions as a sign of its elitism, noting, "Because the show's comic sensibility makes fun of an elitist aesthetic posturing, audiences are expected to understand the art discourse in order to then understand or appreciate the joke's critical lens." As such "a specific type of bleak television comedy is being mobilized as a way for cable networks and streaming portals to target an emergent 'imagined community' or 'coalition audience'" of affluent consumers.[20]

While I do not dispute their account of media industries' targeting of affluent audiences, their reading is flawed. Though Fleabag struggles to make a profit from the café and knows she has access to resources through her family, Nygaard and Lagerwey's reading is too broad. Notably, it presumes that viewers outside of the middle-class and affluent demographics television networks routinely target would find the art discourse too elusive. This is unconvincing since the core issue with the stepmom's artistic bent is that it is pretentious, narcissistic, and reflective of her lack of self-awareness. The juxtaposition of the stolen-then-returned torso sculpture with the ridiculous penis molds featured in the exhibit border on the absurd. It's unclear these require a certain income or social status to recognize the emotional targets of the humor. Reducing the series to a ploy to court viewers—who already subscribed to Amazon Prime when the series debuted—overlooks the series' routine efforts to mock and deflate pretentiousness. Though the "posh" English culture Fleabag was raised in is often the target, the notion of challenging elite cultural norms is a staple of humor in multiple cultures beyond England.

*Fleabag*'s first season uses different orders of time to establish rapport and then adds tension to this formula with its final revelation. This narrative move contrasts it with more conventional comedic approaches by drawing attention to the way sentimentality can lull and distract us from other affective currents. Fleabag is unruly for a female comedic character *and* likable because she breaks this barrier and charms us as viewers. The final episode inverts female sentimentality by pushing the boundaries of likability.

## Are You Okay? *I May Destroy You*'s Characters Navigate Sexual Trauma in Different Orders of Time

> thank you for defending WOMEN
>
> Please share my go fund me page
>
> I hate men
>
> you okay?
>
> U so stupid lmao
>
> are you okay
>
> You mean so much to me
>
> show breasts
>
> you need to talk to someone

After Arabella (Michaela Coel) goes "live" on her phone and faces these comments, an unintelligible visual-and-aural-scramble freezes the screen. In less than two minutes the comments on her social media feed shift from adoration to spam-like self-promotion to affirmations of her video message about misogyny to trolling to questions about her well-being to recommendations for therapy to more trolling before the rapid-fire combination of text and imagery collapses visually and we see her in the office of her therapist. Witnessing this implosion is shocking and disarming but also feels inevitable and even necessary. How could this be for our titular protagonist?

*IMDY*'s lead character Arabella is portrayed by showrunner and writer Michaela Coel. Coel's most notable prior writing experience was as the creator, primary writer, and lead actress of *Chewing Gum* (2015–17,

E4). While writing the second season of *Chewing Gum*, Coel was sexually assaulted by two men. During her 2018 MacTaggart lecture she noted her decision to translate her experience into her art.[21] She also channeled her experience business-wise, declining a one million dollar offer from Netflix, which had streamed *Chewing Gum*, to work with the BBC and HBO to retain creative control.[22] Whereas the Netflix model usually makes an entire series available, Coel designed the episodes for single-episode consumption when it aired originally with BBC One airing two episodes per week, and HBO airing one episode per week.[23]

*IMDY* throws conventional expectations into disarray. From the pilot (1.1, "Eyes, Eyes, Eyes, Eyes") we know Arabella as a promising young Black-identified author, with one successful book, *Chronicles of a Fed-Up Millennial*, under her belt, who lives a bohemian life in London. Integral to her urban adventures are her childhood best friend Terry (Weruche Opia) and her close friend Kwame (Paapa Essiedu). We also discover, through flashbacks, that after enjoying a few drinks at a club called Ego Death with Terry and her friend Simon (Aml Ameen), she is sexually assaulted by an unfamiliar acquaintance of Simon's named David (Lewis Reeves). The memory of her assault—specifically that of David wearing a pink oxford shirt standing over her gyrating, anchors most episodes of series (figure 4.5). We see her replay the image in her head multiple times, including in the opening scene of "Social Media Is a Great Way to Connect" (1.9). By episodes "Would You like to Know the Sex?" (1.11) and "Ego Death" (1.12), Arabella has fully reconstructed

Figure 4.5. The haunting image of David's assault is a recurring image for Arabella in *I May Destroy You*.

the evening of her assault, and we place David and the shirt in fuller context.

Time is a constantly shifting aspect of *IMDY*. The series regularly takes us out of the present to expand our understanding of characters and their lives and simultaneously capitalizes on the status of Millennials as "digital natives" who "are used to receiving information really fast" and "thrive on instant gratification and frequent rewards."[24] These observations are prescient for understanding episode nine because Millennials "have grown up in an era that has witnessed the global proliferation of technology, thereby making the world a much more connected and smaller place."[25]

In the series social media is both mundane in frequency of use and extraordinary in how it distorts and exposes. The interplay of "real time," flashbacks, and the unique qualities of social media are different "orders of time" central to the formal structure of *IMDY*. We rarely have access to the "full story" of complex situations. Certain genres, such as police procedurals, routinely offer detailed step-by-step re-creations of crime scenes and tidy resolutions. *IMDY*'s fragmentary, ever-shifting time disallows this certainty, mirroring life itself. The reality of the actual assaults is never in question; rather, the way the characters seek to process their experiences and reclaim a sense of self is necessarily incomplete and unresolved. Though I focus my analysis on episode nine, my reading references multiple episodes, which are of a piece in the way they demand we participate in the processing and reconstructing just as its characters do throughout.

### *Depicting Collective Trauma*

The pilot seemingly establishes Arabella, and her traumatic experience, as the series' focal point. Episode four contributes to this notion when her writing mentor Zain removes his condom during intercourse without her permission. In episode five she makes his transgression public during her remarks at a book festival, and they go viral. *IMDY* defies expectations, however, by exposing the audience to Terry and Kwame's experiences of sexual assault. In "Don't Forget the Sea" (1.3), which is a flashback of Terry's visit to Arabella in Italy, she and Arabella go dancing. Terry meets two Italian men in a nightclub; they both express interest in her and claim to be strangers. After agreeing to spend the night with them, Terry invites them to Arabella's villa. As they leave, we realize the men have conspired to pretend the encounter was spontaneous rather than premeditated. Terry gradually pieces this together and processes it silently.

In "That Was Fun" (1.4), Kwame, a sex positive gay man, goes to the apartment of Malik (Samson Ajewole), whom he has met on the dating app Grindr. After Kwame fellates Malik, Malik says he wants to have sex with Kwame bareback, but puts on a condom and begins having sex with Kwame. At this point Damon leaves awkwardly and the hook-up resumes. As Kwame gets dressed to leave, Malik insists he stay, then presses his body against Kwame's, against his will, and ejaculates. Kwame leaves and walks away in a panic, with tears falling down his face. He refrains from telling anyone he was assaulted. By the episode "It Just Came Up" (1.5) Kwame goes to a police station to report his assault; a male officer, who is ignorant of Grindr and queer male sexual protocols, interacts with Kwame very insensitively. Deeply frustrated, and humiliated, Kwame leaves without reporting the incident.

The weight of his assault lingers and leads Kwame to declare to Arabella and Terry that he is taking a break from sex. Kwame seeks downtime during Arabella's birthday party and sits quietly in her bedroom (1.7, "Happy Animals"). He hears a piercing ringing sound and flashes back to his assault briefly, in a similar manner to Arabella's surreal flashbacks. Another gay man at the party, Jamal, enters the bedroom accidentally. Arabella, trying to force a connection between them, locks the door from the outside. Toward the party's end, Terry asks Arabella about Kwame and reminds her that he is taking a break from sex and dating. She unlocks the door, Jamal leaves, and near the episode's end, Kwame and Terry sit in a tub together when he reveals the incident. She insists he share it with Arabella. He dismisses her suggestion, noting he'll need to "tweet or insta to get her attention." This dialogue matters because by this point in the season, Arabella has joined a sexual assault support group, run by a former childhood enemy, Theo, and has garnered a new group of followers due to the viral exposure of Zain's assault and for some video promos she has done for a vegan food service.

Rape and sexual assault are usually topics for dramas, soap operas, and TV movies. A dramedy like *IMDY*, which seamlessly blends comedy, drama, and surrealistic elements, is an unusual genre for depicting a traumatic subject. As Benson-Allott notes, its innovations include "its structural critiques of rape television as a genre and its thoughtful orchestration of narrative and broadcast time, especially as these intersect with its fundamental queerness, which includes but is not limited to its exploration of sexual assault among Black gay men. Taken together, these devices confirm that *IMDY* elevates its genre, and television more broadly, by contesting their prior shortcomings."[26] Similarly, Jung notes its unique focus from most consent dramas, "because she is less concerned with political correctness or the failures of the criminal-justice system than with the psychology of the self: How do you become whole again after trauma breaks you open?"[27] To build from these observations, Terry and Kwame's assaults are significant because they pivot the narrative from one where assault, in various forms, is an exceptional behavior to placing it the broader context of contemporary society. For example, 2022 data reported by Rape Crisis England and Wales reports that one in four women (6.54 million women in total) and one in eighteen men (1.34 million men in total) have been raped or sexually assaulted as adults.[28] For comparison, the US-based organization Rape Abuse and Incest National Network (RAINN) reports one out of every six women has been the victim of an attempted or completed rape in her lifetime, and one out of every ten rape victims are male.[29] Sexual assault is clearly a systemic issue affecting people of many backgrounds. *IMDY* focuses on its impact on three Black British Millennial characters.

Whereas some series might focus on one character's experience and make rape a topical yet isolated issue, *IMDY* allows us to see how different people process their experiences. The series eschews didacticism by integrating their traumatic experiences with the more mundane aspects of British Millennial urbanite life, such as Terry's pursuit of acting jobs, Arabella's struggle to fulfill her second book contract, and their navigations of Blackness amid the rise of "authoritarian populism" in post-Brexit London.[30] From the character's use of slang to its eclectic musical choices, *IMDY* is informed by the nuances of Black British Millennial culture.[31] In this way it parallels HBO's *Insecure*, which depicts Blackness boldly as a complex culture and avoids a didactic, explanatory tone. Along with processing sexual trauma, Arabella's relationship with her family, especially her absent father, Kwame's uncertainty about the utility of relationships versus the fun of recreational sex, and the comic vagueness of the concept of "self-care" are also undercurrents.

Finally, the series' depiction of Arabella's social media status offers a unique order of time essential to the story. *IMDY*'s characters employ internal, external, and conversational forms to communicate. Whereas the flashbacks allow characters to process what happened individually and, in Arabella's case especially, re-create and re-imagine their experiences, "social media time" has a time frame based in immediacy that is virtually unfiltered, unregulated, and unpredictable yet capable of inspiring deep feelings of affirmation and dejection often simultaneously given its algorithmic nature. For Arabella its allure provides an immediate audience. Episode seven when she shoots videos for the vegan food service Happy Animals is where social media's power as a tool arrests Arabella's attention. At the end of the video shoot Arabella declares her hair—a wig—isn't real, removes it, and eats a piece of chicken on the livestream. We see her daring move generate instant "likes."

Arabella's growing sense of status leads her to weaponize herself (1.8, "Line Spectrum Border").[32] After the police share that their report was inconclusive she informs Terry she wants to fly to Italy to see Biagio, a former lover who dismissed her sexual trauma and was angry the police asked him to submit a DNA sample for her case. When Terry reminds Arabella how hypocritical, controlling, and dismissive he was previously, Arabella tells Terry *she* is not being affirming. By "Social Media Is a Great Way to Connect" (1.9) Arabella *appears* confident in her more prominent public status, but something seems amiss. She has traded levity and openness for a pretentiousness and combativeness that makes her nearly insufferable among her friends. To return to the question one of her followers asks during her live social media spiral: We know she has not been "okay" since the pilot. The question is: how could she be? What would "okay" look like? Silence nearly paralyzes Kwame and Terry. Arabella's public spiral forces her to get outside of her head and break abruptly from a medium with no boundaries.

### *Arabella Is NOT Okay—Stoking the Algorithm*

Arabella's bold choice in episode five to expose Zain's behavior at a high-profile venue drew attention to the pervasive and silent nature of sexual abuse and garnered her public attention. The viral videos affirmed her emotionally and leavened some of the melancholy she was carrying. Emboldened, she decided to seize on her newfound notoriety and redefine herself as a new public face against sexual assault and misogyny. She fuses two hallmarks of Millennials: an engagement with social justice issues largely mediated through digital media. Lacking in her hashtag activism was a systematic critique. Hashtag activism describes "the strategic ways counterpublic groups and their allies on Twitter employ this shortcut to make political contentions about identity politics that advocate for social change, identity redefinition, and political inclusion."[33] In their study of the #BeenRapedNeverReported movement of 2014, Mendes, Ringrose, and Keller note how "this solidarity often transforms into a feminist consciousness among hashtag participants, which allows them to understand sexual violence as a structural rather than a personal problem."[34] Jackson, Bailey, and Foucault Welles locate similar effects from #YesAllWomen and #MeToo.[35] The tension between Arabella's personal crusade for retribution and notoriety, and the potential to address root causes of sexual violence and help survivors through digital activism pulsates throughout episode nine. As much as we admire Arabella's confidence she still seems unsettled, and her actions gradually lead her to come undone and reach a new point of grace far beyond the reaches of social media.

Episode nine, which takes place on Halloween, is pivotal for gradually unmasking Arabella. The episode shows us how Arabella's intensely personal experience processing her trauma, beginning with a flashback of her assault while in bed, manifests externally in aggressive social justice posturing on social media and alienating her closest friends Terry and Kwame. Frustrated, she abandons them at a Halloween event to peruse the streets of London and is emotionally assaulted on social media, which leads her to visit her therapist, shut down her social media accounts, and apologize to her friends. Ultimately, stripped of the protective filter of social media, she returns to the scene of her assault, Ego Death, poised to address her trauma directly. My reading highlights essential moments when the show uses different orders of time, including flashbacks and social media time, to critique social media's power to distort our sense of reality and disarm us when weaponized. The bigger issue is its distraction from Arabella's need to resolve her trauma.

Flashbacks are a recurring trope of nearly every episode of the series. Despite the glee she experienced when the exposure videos went viral, her assault by David continues to haunt her when episode nine begins and she lies in bed. Whereas the fuzzy image of David, adorned in a pink oxford shirt, towering over her in a bathroom stall with malice in his eyes is the most frequent memory Arabella has had previously, in this version of the flashback the faces vary from David's to those of four other White men of differing ages and builds. These images, which occur in rapid succession, both recognize David as her perpetuator *and* suggest the existence of many "Davids" who have victimized other people. As such the flashback illuminates sexual assault as a broad social vulnerability committed by a range of actors. It suggests Arabella is aware the issue is bigger than she, yet in her actions she cannot quite access this understanding.

When her flashback ends she picks up her phone and types #IHSWG, shorthand for "I hate straight white guys." She then reviews online videos mocking White history month, straight pride day, and men's day—each an example of a reactionary backlash to racial, sexual, and gender justice movements. Her hashtag instantly garners responses from her followers, including "agrees," a person sharing their rapist's address, and "IT'S TIME WE STARTED DOXXING MEN" from @thisgirl70. Arabella searches for the term on her web browser, apparently unfamiliar with "doxing": exposing one's enemies on the internet by publicizing personal information such as their phone number and home address.[36]

Eckert and Metzger-Riftkin define doxing as a "gendered process" that "highlights the importance of identity, as the type of doxing a person experiences is tied to dimensions of their identity, such as gender and sexuality, adding to the vulnerabilities that already discriminated groups, including women, experience."[37] This resonates with evidence that cyberviolence disproportionately targets people of color and women with threats related to violence, slavery, lynching, and sexual violence.[38]

The fast-paced virtual interactions Arabella participates in are less about conversation or communication than visceral, unconditional, and instantaneous affirmations. She has yet to experience the underbelly of these affirmations—trolling. Trolls harass people through digital sources and is so disproportionately directed toward women that Mantilla coined the term "gendertrolling" to describe "image-based sexual abuse or 'revenge porn,'" rape threats, death threats, and body shaming.[39]

Tellingly, exposing, shaming, and silencing do not require digital technology, as we witness in episode nine. The episode continually reminds audiences of the prevalent nature of sexual abuse for different people based on how social media users affirm Arabella and her dismissive attitude toward Kwame and Terry. As the episode unfolds it gradually exposes how social media's power to expose sexual violence can also trivialize it.

Though much of my attention to different orders of time has included attention to musicals (in chapter 3), flashbacks, and the breaking of the fourth wall, the way social media alters our sense of time is also relevant. Almost all of the series in *Broads, Sisters, Exes* regularly feature characters texting on their phones and show us key statements characters are typing. The ways characters draft and redraft messages, the time they spend awaiting responses, their responses to messages sent mistakenly, and the issues that arise when characters have not garnered a response (e.g., the anxiety of persistent ellipses) illuminate the emotional states of contemporary characters. Their expectations around social media and other digital protocols are a relevant texture of life in the digital era. Arabella is thrilled by the instant affirmations but seems less accustomed to and ready to address trolls. Her hunger for affirmations increasingly distorts her ability to engage with counter-perspectives beyond the extremes of online trolling. This lack of preparation in the virtual space emerges as an issue for Arabella in the "real world."

At the climactic wine-and-paint event the trio has prepared for in the episode, they are dressed in their Halloween finery: Arabella wears a sheer black body suit with black angel's wings topped by black spiky horns; Kwame wears an unbuttoned shirt in a black-and-white print, white angel's wings, and a black wig; and Terry wears a white vest with white angel's wings and a fuzzy white halo. These costume choices soon inform their respective roles during the event, with Arabella serving as prosecutor, Terry as defender, and Kwame as caught between being an apparent perpetrator and victim.

As they paint, Arabella takes a photo and vapes, which leads an attendant to remind her "no vaping." Undeterred, she returns to her phone and records the moment as the "POC paint and wine movement," which she tries to justify beforehand as "helping people." Both Terry and Kwame bristle at her behavior and question how a onetime event constitutes a "movement."

Arabella continues filming, Terry joins her in the video briefly at the end, and the group begins chatting casually. Terry asks Kwame to elaborate on his failed date with Nilufer (Pearl Chanda), which opens up Kwame to Arabella's scrutiny. In episode eight Kwame tries dating a woman, and when they transition from dinner to her apartment he flashes back to his assault. She causally cites the cultural climate for making her cautious about language then notes her reluctance to use the term "fag," the British slang term for cigarettes. Continuing on, she rants about her disdain for men appropriating femininity—an echo of the Trans-Exclusionary Radical Feminists, or TERFs, perspective—leading Kwame to reveal he is gay.[40] She rejects his sexual "exploring" and demands he leave her apartment. When Kwame discloses that Nilufer said "homophobic stuff" she hugs him then challenges him for not being honest about his sexuality before the date. Empathizing more with Nilufer than Kwame she questions his intentions, responding to his comment about "feeling shit about it" with the line "I'm sure she feels absolutely superb." Kwame might state that his motivation was a need for intimacy and safety he perceived more attainable with a woman. For Arabella his behavior was dishonest and exploitative. Terry tries to temper the situation by suggesting there was confusion from both parties, which Arabella quells by declaring that as someone who hasn't experienced rape, "You should be listening and not concluding conversations."

Despite her earlier flashback and its implicit acknowledgment of rape's pervasiveness, her newfound social media status has given her license to *presume* she knows the full scope of Terry's experience and can discount her voice. In a sense she is doxing, trolling, and "canceling" Kwame and Terry in real time. Arabella's obliviousness extends to her vaping again, which the attendant reiterates as disallowed. Unwilling to comply she exits the event followed by Terry and Kwame. The conversation descends into a dizzying back and forth with Kwame defending himself, Arabella rejecting Terry's framing of the incident as a mistake, and Terry asking Arabella how she could justify locking Kwame in a room with Jamal without his consent. Incensed, Arabella asks Terry where she is going then tells her to "shut up and fuck off" since Kwame can speak for himself. She instantly tries to allay Kwame, reassuring him that she feels *she* has been a good friend to him and questioning whether he is deceiving himself about who he truly is compared to who he thinks he is, then leaves. Her words come back to haunt her surreally later in the episode.

Once again Arabella weaponizes her personal experience of trauma. She also inverts the systemic critique inherent to social justice by mistaking social justice for a *personal* crusade of "calling out" the problematic behaviors of others. The intensity of this sequence feels like an intentional staging of how so-called cancel culture or call out culture can stifle communication rather than foster authentic dialogue.[41]

Arabella's exit launches a daring dramatization of algorithmic culture. Algorithms "produce outputs that reflect the training data over time. If the inputs are biased (in the *mathematical* sense of the word), the outputs will be, too. Often, this will reflect what I will call 'sociological biases' around things like race, gender, and class."[42] One of the products of algorithms on social media sites generates and circulates content likely to generate strong responses, for example, platforms like Facebook and Twitter "encourage extreme content, and algorithms reward polarization."[43] This is compounded by the anonymity social media affords; many users engage in "technology-facilitated sexual violence and harassment," which occur via "the aid of new technologies."[44]

Walking the street adorned in her costume and surrounded by fellow-minded Halloween revelers, Arabella is distracted by her phone. Scanning it she sees the picture of her and an admirer, and that 254 new followers have joined her feeds. She asks someone to take a photo and struggles to position herself properly for a noble pose. After a man compliments her costume she dismisses him abruptly before walking away from him and delving into a "live" media spiral, which dramatizes the "data dump" of random facts about male biases and replicates the "doom scroll" element of social media.

Walking away she begins recording a video on the male biases of crash test dummy tests, which generates immediate responses. The camera transitions from her walking normally to a dolly shot that moves a backlit Arabella toward us. Still filming herself, she glides forward and comments on how smart phones were built for male hands. She feeds the algorithm by supplying a barrage of information devoid of context. Her descriptions of male biases feel like a form of "gotcha" politics lacking analysis or action with every comment hovering at the ephemeral level. This cycle generates comments about social groups ("I hate men") and reduces it to interpersonal localized conflicts. Then the barrage of affirmations, spams, and trolling begins. Its overwhelming visual and aural relentlessness becomes too chaotic for comprehension—for Arabella, for viewers, for her "feed," and it must end (figure 4.6). She turns off her phone abruptly.

We find her in a quiet well-lit space with her therapist, "disarmed" by not having the barrier of her phone. After explaining her frustrations with Kwame, she shows the therapist (Sarah Niles) her digital messages and says—without self-awareness—that she hates her responsibility to tell the truth and not to be complicit. The therapist asks her, "Do you need social media?," and unpacks how social media's business model incentivizes "speaking over listening." In addition to recommending Arabella take a break from social media, she asks about the status of the case, which Arabella reveals as closed, and engages Arabella in an exercise that allows her to affirm her sense of reality and things that contradict or challenge her perspective. The scene centers Arabella and tacitly critiques the limits of certain reactionary forms of social media activism.

In doing so it reflects on the most superficial aspects of faux hashtag activism evident in other series. For example, on *CXG* when Rebecca attempts suicide and is hospitalized, her friend Valencia transforms

**Figure 4.6.** In the episode "Social Media Is a Great Way to Connect" Arabella's feed is gradually flooded with trolls who overwhelm her and force her to stop her live broadcast. She ultimately silences her social media to focus on internal healing.

video updates about her health into corporate sponsorships, resulting in the anthemic song "This Is My Movement" (3.6, "Josh Is Irrelevant"). The humor of this over-the-top ode to vanity and self-righteousness, and its pretentious video, derives from its familiarity to digital natives—the conflation of promotion and publicity with activism and social change.

When Arabella leaves her therapist, the episode inverts the external focus of her interactions by shifting from social media toward a blend of the internal and conversational. Sitting on her bed—where the episode began—she deletes her social media accounts. She then reaches under her bed to begin the process of reviewing the contents of the investigation bag from her police intake. One of the items we see is an ultrasound image of a fetus she forgot she aborted. The bags are as much about deflection and forgetting as they are about the investigation. Her roommate Ben enters and they discuss its contents before they are interrupted and he goes to the door.

Then we experience a surreal moment when Arabella sees herself seated and she recites dialogue similar to what she directed toward Kwame earlier: "If you felt good, I would be even more horrified. When you paint things to make it look as if you're just the victim, and I find out that isn't the case, [it] really makes me question who you are. Just look, look in the mirror. You know what I mean? It's really uncomfortable and unnerving for everyone." This soliloquy is yet another disruption of the normal "order of time" that begins an internal reckoning for Arabella.

Now freed from the immediacy of social media affirmations and trolling she has to sit with herself and forge ahead. In "real time" Terry and Kwame enter and Arabella apologizes. She also acknowledges how callous it was to lock him in the room with Jamal. Kwame accepts, and after he leaves Arabella, Ben and Terry unpack the bags. Terry asks if she wants to do this, and the camera pans over the items. Terry asks what she needs, and Arabella asks her to join her on a walk. As they walk the streets, still adorned in their Halloween costumes, they approach the door of Ego Death. We see their reflection and see inside the club. They sit at a table outside and Arabella vapes. Arabella has returned to the site of trauma and seems poised to confront the assault outside of her head with the support of her friend.

Her oscillations between internal processing, external affirmation, and interactive conversational opportunities are mediated through a range of time signatures. The series depiction of her internal processing, her abrupt breaks from the conversational into the virtual, her fusion of the extreme behavior of social media in real time confrontations, and the accelerated and chaotic staging of her "live" messaging lead her to a calmer and more balanced state. She emerges readier to focus on genuine healing and interact with people who care about her, some of whom have experienced traumas. This turn does not promise justice or resolution, like a procedural, but offers the potential for movement beyond the incessant internal reconstructions of the incident and the aggressive avoidance of introspection.

### *An Ending without a Resolution*

Viewers have been exposed most fully to Arabella's navigations of trauma. For Arabella, who has mediated her experiences with assault through flashbacks, various attempts at "self-care," social media influencing, and a more therapeutically informed, nuanced form of engagement, unpacking the events of her assault at Ego Death haunts her more than anything. As a limited term series, we wonder, naturally, how things will "end."

Arabella has the fullest flashback of what transpired the night of the assault in episode eleven. In a montage we see the harrowing events of the night, from David staring directly at her during a group toast, to Arabella losing her balance, to Arabella opening her eyes in a bathroom stall and seeing David force himself into her mouth and gyrate over her. Episode twelve, the series finale, begins with Arabella sitting outside of Ego Death and staring inside at David and a friend, and we see a reprise of the full flashback at twice the speed of episode eleven.

The episode restages the night through a three-part flash-sideways sequence in a series of revenge scenarios, all of which involve the bathroom stall. As Booth notes, "contemporary television storytelling often plays with the stylistics of the storytelling to ask the audience 'what if' questions—questions that directly pose alternative viewpoints to specific characters."[45] In the first scenario Arabella, Terry, and their high school classmate Theo plot to catch David (who introduces himself under the alias "Patrick") in the act. After Patrick spikes her drink, Arabella goes to the restroom with him, and as Patrick begins undressing her, she recites a line about criminals always returning to the scene, right before

Theo, stationed in the adjacent stall, injects him with a needle filled with drugs. They chase "Patrick" on the street until he collapses, and Arabella punches him while Theo holds him down. Then she drags his body onto the bus and places his bloodied body under her bed. She marks the event by placing a blood-stained notecard on her wall alongside other plot point cards.

In scenario two Arabella snorts multiple lines of cocaine, supplied by Terry. Arabella dons a pink wig and behaves erratically, dancing frenetically with David, and reciting the lyrics of Prodigy's "Firestarter" after he hands her the spiked drink. As she stumbles and David takes her into the stall she perks up and shouts "Hello David!" He insults her and then begins lamenting himself in the third person. The police, whom Terry has called, enter the men's restroom, which is implied to be empty. The next scene finds Bella listening to David describe going to prison, recounting rapes he's committed, and describing how nicely he gets treated. We hear police sirens and a knock on the door. David gets worried and cries; Arabella hugs him, then the police enter and remove David. Arabella writes another notecard and places it on the wall.

In scenario three Terry tells Arabella she believes the two men she had a threesome with during their trip to Italy pretended to be strangers and had actually tricked her. This is followed by a surreal scene of Arabella entering different bathroom stalls and seeing different people, including a stall featuring a woman she encountered at the police station in episode two and a stall featuring the teenaged versions of her, Terry, and Theo.

The fourth scenario finds Arabella and Terry inverting the male and female gender roles with David calling himself "Patrick" and Arabella acting as an aggressor, including taking him into the stall and kissing him as well as changing locations and fucking him from behind in her bedroom. Next, we see them wake up in her bed basking in the morning light. He says, "I won't go until you tell me to go," and she says "Go." We see the bloodied Patrick stored beneath her bed leave with the investigation bag (figure 4.7). Arabella looks up at the two notecards and pulls them down.

Each scenario is creatively staged, visually stunning, and narratively daring. Collectively they speak to the unresolved nature of sexual trauma. Arabella has to manage the literal fact that the police department has closed the investigation and navigate trauma's ongoing demands on her

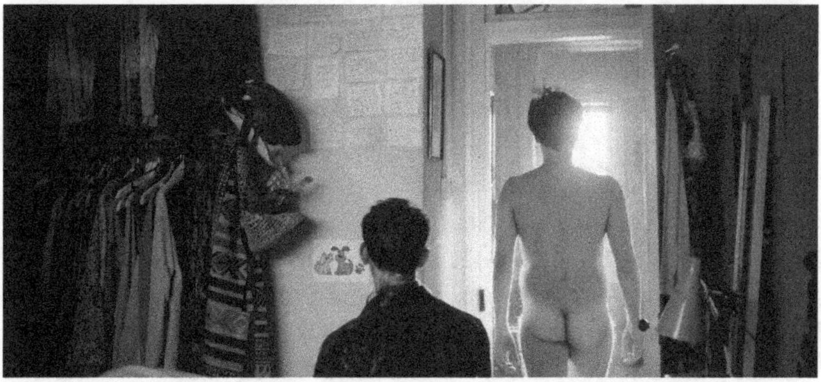

**Figure 4.7.** Arabella's "flash sideways" sequence envisions three different scenarios between her and David and concludes with the different versions of him departing, indicating both her uncertainty about specific details of her sexual assault and the evolution of her healing process.

psyche. Avenging her assault by confronting David violently—verbally and physically—offers respite temporarily, for her, and her collaborators Terry and Theo, but is insufficient. Conjecturing who David could be and what might motivate his behavior complicates and humanizes him. This does not justify or rationalize his behavior, it merely places him in context; having to relive her experience with him in her head informs a natural curiosity. She might know intellectually that the case is "closed" and she has to "move on," but these scenarios allow her to feel her way through this and work toward this awareness. Confronting and exploring a range of possibilities helps her envision her life somewhat less fixated on the what, why, and how, so she can truly move forward.

## Every Woman Gets Her Due: Temporal Displacement and Character Development on *Orange Is the New Black*

*OITNB*'s focus on women from diverse backgrounds incarcerated within the prison system makes it the most overtly "political" and critically divisive series in this study. Many scholars and cultural critics acknowledge its diverse cast and ambitious thematic scope.[46] Others dismiss the series as depicting aspects of the prison industrial complex inaccurately and question the series initial framing through the voice of the White upper-class protagonist Piper Chapman.[47] Absent from many of these analyses, which focus on the first season primarily, is attention to *OITNB*'s innovative use of flashbacks and its intentional decentering of Chapman. Reviewing some of the earliest scholarship on the series, usually published between 2014 and 2016, exposes tension between a desire for "representational correctness" and sensitivity to the nature of television as a medium. This final subsection analyzes the narrative trajectory of Tasha "Taystee" Jefferson, whose ascent from a supporting to lead character parallels the series expansive approach to telling women's stories beyond and alongside Piper. As my reading reveals, telling her individual story inevitably entails the stories of other characters. The series' intricate juxtapositions are integral to the serialized story and mediated largely through flashbacks.

*OITNB*'s topicality leads some scholars to assess it purely on its social realism and fault it for "imperfect" representations. Henderson notes emotional realism and the personal involvement this engenders from audiences as a central narrative approach of television. Ignoring this, and other formal elements, limits our understanding of the nature of dramatic series. Several scholars of serialized dramas have noted how the "open" structure of serial dramas fosters engagement with social issues differently than news and documentary forms with an informational focus.[48] As Henderson notes, "The requirements of narrative pace, cliff-hangers, and engaging the audiences are elements which are not confined to television fiction but are important factors for other television programme makers."[49] As one of the first series to foster the option of binge, or "marathon," viewing, these qualities are particularly salient to *OITNB*'s design.[50]

Despite objections to the narration by Chapman, loosely based on author Piper Kiernan's one-year experience of incarceration, several scholars have noted the subversive nature of Piper's "Trojan Horse" role, emphasizing how the classic function of such a figure is "a surprise attack."[51] Narratively, the presumably "relatable" character's fish-out-of-water role positions her as a "comic fool" whose naivete and frequent missteps illuminate the insularity of her privileged background and the futility of many aspects of her affluent status in the prison context.[52] Most notably, the circumstances force her to develop a more nuanced and empathic awareness of the complex lives of the diverse women of Litchfield.

The rush to castigate *OITNB* as an ideological reinforcer of hegemonic perspectives seems increasingly less persuasive and premature once we examine the series beyond the inaugural season. Many arguments succumb to the impossible demand for representational correctness. Schiappa's argument regarding representational correctness asserts that "a good portion of popular media analysis is guided by the idea that *if* we can attain the goal of Representational Correctness *then* oppressed groups will be empowered or at least encouraged, and mainstream consumers and users of popular media will be motivated toward a more open, tolerant and just society." Integral to this kind of analysis are critics' emphasis on accuracy, purity, and innocence that frequently mistakes the fictional landscape of narrative television for sociology, thus avoiding "ambivalence or ideological contradiction" and other nuances inevitable with complex characters.[53]

The narrative structure of a series operates in concert with ideological elements, which is key to *OITNB*'s architecture. I agree with Henderson's observation that the repetition and opportunities to empathize with characters inherent to serialized programs "is impossible to replicate in other fictional forms" and "allow[s] viewers to bring a distinctive historical context to the airing of a social problem, which would simply not be possible in news and documentary programming."[54] These formal qualities of drama combined with *OITNB*'s use of memory temporality helps us understand the scope of the diverse women's experiences. Memory temporality describes "shows that use analepses (any change in temporal structure) as a form of memory or recall for characters within a show's narrative. Shows with memory temporality typically include some type of regular visual, auditory, or textual 'clue' or trope to indicate the shift in narrative temporality, what Fiske and Hartley define as an aesthetic code." Among the various forms of temporal displacement, memory temporality is the most commonly used form of flashback *OITNB* employs, as it lends itself best to understanding characters over time.[55]

The show's execution of its ambitions is worth noting from a formal perspective because it stretches the narrative boundaries of the medium. Postman's *Amusing Ourselves to Death* argues that television is most successful as light entertainment and ephemera that requires no prior knowledge or context, noting, "Television, as I have implied earlier, serves us most usefully when presenting junk-entertainment; it serves us most ill when it co-opts serious modes of discourse—news, politics, science, education, commerce, religion—and turns them into entertainment packages."[56]

The industry and the medium he describes has changed significantly enough since 1985 that a narrative series like *OITNB* can devote multiple seasons to challenging television's superficial tendencies by attempting to present such complex characters that the sociopolitical context of their lives—and ours—is virtually unavoidable. *OITNB* reflects and embodies television's maturation toward what Sconce refers to as "sophisticated and complex elaboration of character and story world," where "viewers gradually feel they inhabit along with the characters." His original argument associates this quality with eleven acclaimed series of the 1990s and early '00s; only *Xena: Warrior Princess* and *Buffy*, both supernatural, fantasy-oriented series, are women centered. Dramedic series telling women's stories remain a rich source for exploring the character-driven nature of the more distinctive contemporary television series, and the fandom they have inspired.[57]

In this regard Henderson's argument that serial television structure "facilitates 'coming to terms' with an issue over time and can include important emotional dimensions of ambivalence, confusion, anger, and denial" is relevant. Serialized dramas have addressed social issues but avoided strong ideological commitments or "taking sides" for fear of alienating audiences and/or didacticism. However, the aesthetic choices a series creative team makes "can help establish a 'preferred meaning.'"[58]

Structurally, *OITNB*'s multiseason run combined with its perpetual availability as a streaming series means viewers can access it and review it continually. Even casual viewers who find the series entertaining could discern the numerous ways it employs the backstories of characters and their experiences to critique systemic issues such as sexual abuse, domestic violence, and the factors informing recidivism. It shows rather than tells through the contexts it provides for characters and the ways they embody these contexts. Though many dramatic forms avoid controversy, showrunner Jenji Kohan has overtly identified the show as an expression of her activist sensibilities. She also explained her reasoning for pitching the series through Piper's narration as a strategy for navigating the television industry's racial and cultural biases. *OITNB* is distributed through Netflix but produced through the film company Lionsgate, which suggests her role was to persuade the production company the series was viable.[59]

*OITNB* is a character-driven series with many unexpected moments of levity, yet its ability to push the boundaries of comedies and dramatic norms is new for television. For example, in 2014 the series was nominated in multiple comedic categories at the Primetime Emmy Awards then placed in dramatic categories for subsequent seasons.[60] Despite critical dissatisfaction with the series, especially during its first season, its attempt to tell such an array of stories is new for television *especially* in the context of women typically unseen and unheard. Regarding season one, McHugh observes, "Midseason, subplots become more significant—Dayanara and Bennett's romance, Taystee and Poussey's friendship, Red's increasing conflicts with Mendez—and temper Piper's narrative centrality."[61] Though Piper has garnered the bulk of scholarly attention, numerous scholars have analyzed characters beyond Chapman. In this vein I focus my analysis on the character "Taystee."[62] Her more prominent role in season two reflects a larger narrative tactic the series took with its supporting characters pivoting from Piper as the focus.

The majority of the younger inmates at Litchfield are Millennials, and the series tells their stories diversely. The actress Danielle Brooks, who portrays "Taystee," was born in 1989, and we can presume she is meant to portray a character approximate to her actual age. Whereas the character Brook Soso (Kimiko Glen), who debuts in season two, is presented as a somewhat stereotypical Millennial hipster with often precious politics, Taystee's life represents a very different dimension of experience among their generation. Taystee, who is introduced in the first season (appearing in eighty-nine episodes over seven seasons), was a foster child who experienced the vagaries of the juvenile detention system throughout her adolescence before Vee (Lorraine Toussaint), a woman who lives in her neighborhood, adopts her under the guise of care but largely for the purpose of selling drugs.

### *From Tasha to "Taystee"*

My reading takes a deeper look at "Taystee," who becomes one of the series' most developed and important characters. The use of multiple flashbacks over several seasons, especially season two, and a key "flash out" in season one, illuminates her background and provides context for the trajectory of her life. Her dialogue, actions, and relationships communicate the cultural and socioeconomic challenges she has mounted in an organic, emotionally resonant way that mitigates the default perception that incarceration is merely the result of poor individual moral choices. While the series cannot determine viewer responses, this is arguably the "preferred" reading, as the overall combination of scenes does more than offer narrative color or advance the plot. Taystee illustrates there is an abundance of notable stories at Litchfield besides the perceived narrative dominance of Chapman. *OITNB* introduces "Taystee" as a largely comedic character in season one who bonds closely with Poussey Washington (Samira Wiley) and finds community among other Black inmates, especially "Black" Cindy (Adrienne C. Moore), Janae Watson (Vicky Jeudy), Sophia Burset (Laverne Cox), and Suzanne "Crazy Eyes" Warren (Uzo Uduba).

Taystee provides multiple scenes of comic relief, perhaps most iconically in "WAC Pack" (1.6) when she and Poussey mock Sophia's desire for better health care at Litchfield by imitating White bourgeois attitudes in high-pitched voices with dialogue littered with references to sushi, veganism, yoga, wine tasting, and hedge funds. In "Fucksgiving" (1.9), however, we learn there's more to Taystee than her sense of humor. Various inmates throw Taystee a going away party in a lightly decorated recreation room. Toward the end of the episode Taystee shares more context about her release with Poussey, revealing she was a ward of the state until the age of sixteen, then placed in the juvenile detention system. She also voices her fears about her going into the external world with no skills. Ms. Claudette (Michelle Hurst), an older inmate, assures her that based on her time working in the prison library, she has skills and is quite smart. Right before she is released Taystee shares her optimistic postrelease plans with Sophia. We see the grimmer reality of her life, however, when she arrives at a home and the owner nearly rejects her. After pleading that her cousin told her she could sleep there and her address must be accurate for her supervision, the owner begrudgingly permits her to sleep on the floor in the corner of her crowded living room, but tells her she must leave in the morning (figure 4.8).

In "Fool Me Once" (1.12), Taystee returns to Litchfield unceremoniously. As she quietly sifts through books in the prison's library, Poussey approaches her and they discuss her unexpected return. After she laments the high level of surveillance she experienced, including maintaining a curfew and doing regular drug testing, Poussey confronts her about the hubris of complaining about being free. In response, Taystee bares her soul, soberly noting:

> Minimum wage is some kinda joke. I got part-time workin' at Pizza Hut and I still owe the prison $900 in fees I gotta pay back. I ain't got no place to stay. I was sleepin' on the floor in my second cousin apartment like a dog and she still got six people in two rooms. One of the bitches stole my check. I got lice. Everyone I know is poor, in jail, or gone. Don't nobody ask how my day went. Man, I got fucked up in the head, you know? [Taystee chokes up.] I know how to play it here. Where to be and what rules to follow. I got a bed. And I got you. (figure 4.9)

**Figure 4.8.** After Taystee is released from Litchfield during the first season of *Orange Is the New Black*, she struggles to find stable housing or community, which provides a fuller context for her life before imprisonment.

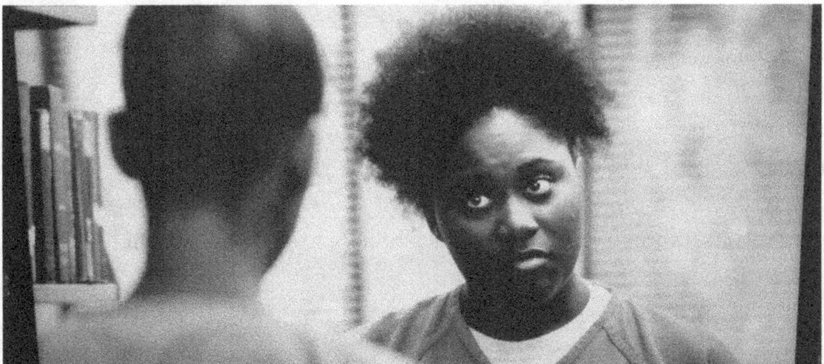

**Figure 4.9.** After Taystee returns to prison at the end of season one, she explains to her friend and fellow inmate Poussey the struggles of being out of prison without support resources.

The combination of both episodes exemplifies how "emotional realism" can illuminate structural issues. The lack of structural supports for Taystee is obvious, making her return unfortunate yet understandable given the context.

Season two offers further context for Taystee's internal and external struggles. Though I focus primarily on season two we learn about her background in "Flaming Hot Cheetos Literally" (5.6), when her foster mother presents an eighteen-year-old Taystee a letter that her birthmother asked her to withhold until she was of age. When Taystee's birthmother meets with her in person she shares why she gave her up. She also offers Taystee the opportunity to live with her family, but when this falls through Taystee is further disappointed and seeks refuge. This informs her eagerness to be taken in by Vee in "Looks Blue, Tastes Red" (2.2).

*OITNB*'s chief "aesthetic code" with memory temporality is to juxtapose a character's present-day behavior with key events from their past to offer context. The flashback scenes are too artful in design, generally, to feel like literal rationales or explanations for actions. Rather, in any given episode the cumulative effect of multiple flashback scenes paints a rich picture of the character, offering insight into the settings, relationships, and conditions of their lives prior to incarceration.

Season two builds on the expository information Taystee shared with Poussey about being in the "the system" by illustrating how and why Vee became such a dominant force in her life. Cunning, manipulative, and predatory, Vee is skilled at understanding the vulnerabilities and needs of people, which enables her to build relationships that appear beneficial for both parties, and to destroy relationships that threaten her power. Understanding her pre-prison life clarifies how Taystee morphs from a mostly jovial character, whose humor masks her challenging experiences of neglect and poverty, to a loyal foot soldier for Vee willing to sacrifice relationships and compromise the well-being of other inmates in a show of loyalty. The flashbacks continually depict how Vee garnered her trust and exploited it.

"Looks Blue, Tastes Red" shifts the narrative focus from Chapman, who is relocated to a Chicago detention center, and delves more deeply into the cast. The episode kicks off a series of flashbacks about Taystee's background in the foster system that illuminate her struggles after she is released from prison. In a flashback Vee helps a young Tasha rebound emotionally from rejection at an adoption fair. She nicknames Tasha, who is enjoying candy, "Taystee," because "everyone wants a taste of something tasty," an attempt to flatter her. As Tasha ages into her teen years, Vee tries to lure her into what we discover is a drug ring that employs teens and young adults. The next flashback shows a teenaged Tasha waiting for a bus in front of a group home on her way to work. Vee approaches her with an entourage of young protégés. Tasha dismisses her abruptly, and Vee gently reminds her of her status in the community. The third flashback finds Tasha expressing her need to leave the group home and pleading with Vee for a spot. When a derelict client/drug dealer begs Vee for a break she reminds him of what he owes, and Tasha calculates what he owes with interest if Vee grants him the "supply." Impressed by her acumen she accepts Tasha into the fold.

Flashback four from Taystee's youth prior to imprisonment finds Taystee entering Vee's kitchen and raving about the supplies she's purchased at a hobby shop to aid with packaging Vee's product. Though Vee and her protégé RJ are skeptical of her enthusiasm, they admit her idea is memorable. When she says one day she will have a career on Wall Street, Vee reminds her girls from the 'hood "have jobs not careers" jocularly. Though this moment is self-serving, for Vee it indicates Taystee's creativity and ambitions as a young person, and the lack of someone to nurture her gifts fully. The scene ends with Vee asking for Taystee to try a spoonful of her butternut squash and ginger soup, and Taystee reveling at the maternal warmth and idyllic domesticity of the meal preparation (figure 4.10). The camera captures her staring at her new life with contentment before Vee asks her to sit at the table.

The final flashback reiterates the cruelty of Taystee's predicament. We see her seated wearing black and holding a framed photo of RJ that will be displayed at his funeral. Vee comes over to comfort her and they discuss his demise due to police fire; Vee vows to protect Taystee. The flashback of "It Was the Change" (2.12), depicting Vee's audacious engineering of RJ's death, reaches a pinnacle of manipulation nearly soap operatic in its chilling effect.[63] Collectively these scenes posit Taystee as a victim of circumstance from a young age. During their first encounter Vee correctly tells the young Tasha how her race and age impact her adoptability. Further, though the episode does not take us into the group home it is implied that it is a space of survival rather than nurturance.

Figure 4.10. A flashback reveals a hopeful, adolescent Taystee basking in her adoptive mother Vee's matronly facade before Vee preys on her vulnerability and betrays her trust.

Taystee's fortitude about not joining Vee's group indicates her goal to play it straight and pursue her interests legally. Lacking a stable family structure, financial resources, or mentoring she feels compelled to work with what's available to her, Vee. Embedded in these scenes is a structural critique, but it plays out in dramatic rather than didactic fashion. An attentive viewer can observe how Tasha's youthful vulnerability, and Vee's manipulative and persuasive style, contribute to her seduction, but the lack of a safety net or support structure pervades these scenes. They also evoke her discussion with Poussey about the lack of support she found on the "outside." The adult Taystee had been lubricated socially and economically to settle for less. These scenes set us up for how and why Vee's return to Litchfield rattles Taystee and forces her to come into her own.

*Taystee Is Tested*

In present narrative time Taystee wins a "Mock Job Fair," triumphing over Flaca with impressive poise. As she pivots to exit she sees Vee standing in the doorway posed with her arms crossed in an orange jumpsuit and says "Oh, shit" before the closing credits appear. With Vee's arrival season two sets the groundwork for Taystee to rise from a supporting character to more of a lead by testing her will against the machinations of Vee. The season repeatedly depicts Taystee falling under Vee's alluring spell of manipulation, and eventually gaining agency. When Vee arrives in "Hugs Can Be Deceiving" (2.3), she instantly tries to ingratiate herself to Taystee, who feels embittered about Vee's failure to contact her when she was released. Vee tells Taystee she had to go into hiding, but she remains skeptical.

Beyond Taystee, Vee knows she must charm other inmates to build a coalition she can lead and help her smuggle in contraband. She begins by giving a hidden pack of cigarettes to lead cook Gloria (Selena Lyvas), who is the figurative head of the Latina inmates, and then she gradually attempts to build individual relationships with the Black cisgender inmates, focusing on Cindy, who dismisses her, and Suzanne, whose mental state makes her more malleable. "Hugs" ends with Flaca bringing Vee a decorated cake, courtesy of the kitchen, in the recreation room where several of the Black inmates are playing a game. Vee offers Taystee a slice as a peace offering. Reluctantly, she accepts it and then invites the others over to partake. Vee invites herself to join the game; Red observes from afar, and we see Gloria and Aleida standing in the rain smoking stale cigarettes in the alley. Gloria realizes Vee has tricked her. Vee's ability to manipulate makes an immediate impact, such that she regains Taystee's trust.

Vee's success winning over Taystee also opens up Cindy, Suzanne, and Watson, but Poussey resists her charms, leading Vee to orchestrate a strategy to separate Taystee from Poussey and isolate her socially. After witnessing an affectionate homoerotic interaction between them in "A Whole Other Hole" (2.4), Vee questions Taystee about her sexuality, and she gets defensive instantly. After Vee questions whether Poussey can be trusted and asserts how rumors about Taystee being queer could ruin her reputation back home, Taystee begins acting coldly toward Poussey. Vee escalates this further in "You Also Have a Pizza" (2.6). By this time Vee has become the self-appointed "mama" among the Black inmates and arranged to switch roles with the Latinas who now work in the cafeteria so the Black women can work in custodial. The group is not particularly excited about the reassignment until she shows the group how she smuggles in tobacco via containers of a cleaning supply.

The reassignment provides a perfect setup for Vee and Poussey to face off in "Pizza." Taystee gives up her position working alongside Poussey in the library. Poussey's protectiveness leads her to confront Vee, who she calls "a fucking vampire" who exploits younger people and abandons them. Undeterred, Vee reminds her that Taystee will never love her the way she wants.

Vee's confrontation with Poussey, and her willingness to fight, informs the episode's primary flashback, which focuses on Poussey's father being forced to relocate from a military base in Germany back to the United States because his commander catches Poussey and his daughter being intimate. We get a glimpse into her past and her willingness to resist bullying and coercion. The episode winds down with a Valentine's Day celebration in the recreation room. While Taystee, Suzanne, and Vee listen to music and dance, Poussey flirts with an inmate. Taystee invites her to join them but she declines then looks off into a distant focal point before we see her final flashback sequence.

While Cindy joins the coalition, she remains suspicious and Vee enlists Taystee as a weapon against her before going in for the kill. In exchange for the tobacco Vee wants her troops to collect postal "Forever" stamps in "Comic Sans" (2.7). We see a montage of different exchanges, including Watson passing a tampon, with ingredients for makeshift cigarettes, to an inmate in the stairwell, different inmates smoking clandestinely, and Taystee even offering a cigarette to Rosa (Barbara Rosenblat), who has cancer. In a key scene Vee asks Cindy about her profits and she reveals she has no stamps. Once again Taystee intervenes; sitting next to Vee on a bed she warns Cindy about "coming up short." When Vee reassigns Cindy to maintenance she tells her she's not afraid of her. Late in the evening while everyone sleeps soundly, Vee walks over to Cindy and tells her that her lack of ambition and tendency to address all matters through humor suggests she has given up on herself, which makes her a "loser." The backdrop of these exchanges is a series of flashbacks where we see how Cindy's recklessness in the past led her mother to gain sole custody of her birth daughter. The next morning Cindy tells Vee she will "take her medicine" and concedes to reassignment. These incidents reveal how Taystee is not the only inmate vulnerable to Vee's strategies.

Taystee continually flexes her newfound confidence as a member of Vee's coalition among the prisoners. For instance, in "Approximately Sized Pots" (2.8) she vocalizes in the cafeteria's food line how unfair it is that Piper was granted a furlough. This stirs up similar sentiments among Cindy and Poussey. Taystee also intentionally bumps into Piper as she sits down at the adjacent table, which enrages Piper who rants about her Whiteness and missing her dying grandmother. This scene helps exacerbate Vee's desire for the Black inmates to intensify the tribalistic conflict with the other "races" and confirms Taystee is still somewhat of a leader among her peers and best positioned to reinforce Vee's wishes. In scene after scene Taystee willfully defends Vee and tries to enlist her friends to follow her, despite her allusions to Vee's disappointing behavior in the past.

As season two winds down Vee's efforts to secure power and dominate Litchfield leads to an influx of drugs beyond tobacco and sparks violence, which further tests Taystee's moral will. After Leanne (Emma Myles), a White inmate who rarely speaks with the Black inmates, asks Poussey for something to soothe her pain after being hit, Poussey rejects her and realizes Vee is smuggling in hard drugs. When she approaches Taystee with her suspicion she tells Poussey to stop talking about it and "mind her business." She declares that Vee has been good to her, is her family, and warns her: "No more talking about Vee to me, or to anyone. And P, that woman don't play around. Don't get in her way (grabs Poussey). Or mine. You hear?" Poussey is shocked by Taystee's increasing fealty. Later in the episode we see Red's flashback to the rivalry that began when Vee was imprisoned at Litchfield and commanded a group of her followers to beat Red viciously. Perhaps the final straw for Poussey is when she witnesses Taystee offer Nicky, a recovering heroin addict, a "free" bag of heroin.

Taystee's journey from comic relief to cold-blooded drug dealer leads Poussey to confront her again in episode ten. At the beginning of the episode Vee, and her followers—Cindy, Suzanna, Taystee, and Watson—receive preferential treatment in the cafeteria and move through the space with a newfound swagger. Taystee reiterates that Vee will take care of them. In a separate scene Poussey expresses her anger to Taystee for lying to her about the drugs and says Vee has brainwashed the whole group. Taystee notes she does not understand her background and dismisses Poussey as a "bougie bitch." Later in the episode Vee and the girls enter the library to request Poussey allow the library to become a new spot of commerce. As she rejects Vee we see Taystee in the background with her hoodie on, nodding for Poussey to comply. Stressed-out Poussey grabs her secret bottle of hooch and enters the bathroom to vomit. Drunk, she pushes Vee against a wall and Suzanne attacks Poussey, beating her continuously until Vee calms her down. Cindy observes in horror and eyes Vee, aware of how things have escalated.

Drunk again in "It Was the Change" (2.12), Poussey enters the warehouse and destroys the cans of tobacco stored there, drenching them in bleach. When Taystee enters the warehouse and sees Vee cleaning up the mess, she lashes out, pinning the wasted stock on Taystee's relationship to Poussey and telling her she's letting her go. Taystee reasserts her loyalty and Vee's pledge to protect her. After a storm floods the prison the staff ushers everyone to higher ground on the second floor. Cindy and Watson avoid Taystee and shun her when they play a game with Vee and Suzanne to pass the time. When she asks if they're no longer speaking to her, Cindy shares that Vee is moving her back to sales.

After Poussey is allowed to go to the library to move the books to higher shelves, Taystee enters. She congratulates Poussey ironically on getting her ostracized by the group, especially by Vee who she says is the only person who has ever looked out for her. Poussey questions the notion entirely; Taystee accuses her of not being content to be friends, and for failing to understand she wants one thing for herself. They ultimately reconcile, and the episode reveals in flashbacks how Vee arranged for RJ to be killed by a corrupt cop once she learned he was attempting to be her new rival. The episode ends with Vee ambushing and attacking Red for attempting to strangle her that night and not allowing her to use the greenhouse for smuggling in items.

Once the prison begins investigating Red's severe injuries in the second season's finale, "We Have Manners. We're Polite" (2.13), Vee tells Suzanne to "confess" that she attacked Red, starkly aware of her loyalty and mental challenges. Cindy and Watson are unwilling to question Vee and reluctantly comply when investigators ask them who attacked Red. Taystee tries to convince Suzanne to not confess because of the severe consequences she could face, but Suzanne dismisses her, stating Vee had already warned her she would say bad things about her. In this moment Taystee begins changing from a stooge to the moral conscience of the group. Meanwhile, Vee, alienated from the coalition she built, spins out of control; unable to find her heroin, which Nicky has stolen, she physically confronts Cindy.

As Poussey and Taystee continue reconciling in the library, including a reprise of their comic White bourgeois voices routine, Cindy and

Watson enter the library, stating they came in peace. Poussey notes that Vee has no one left except for Suzanne. Taystee believes she has a solution to Vee's terrorizing behavior. Vee later approaches Taystee, urging her to return to "mama." Poussey, Cindy, and Watson then surround her and Vee questions the move, telling Taystee, "You know what happens when people overstep," to which Taystee replies, "Like RJ?" By this point Taystee has discerned the nature of Vee's character; whether we know when she figured out RJ's murder is less salient than her awareness of what Vee is capable of achieving through manipulation. Taystee verbalizes a different perspective on the role of a "mama" and questions what mamas are without people. Vee dismisses them all and says she will find another family. She tries to make a final appeal to Taystee, claiming she is breaking her heart, which Taystee dismisses. Vee attempts to escape the prison through the greenhouse tunnel and is struck by a van driven by Rosa, who mutters that she has always found Vee "rude."

Though all the inmates know Vee is dead, in season three Suzanne struggles to accept this as reality. Taystee intervenes when Suzanne is having an intense episode and asserting she had a vision of Vee in "Finger in the Dyke" (3.4). Taystee tries to calm her, and after declaring Vee is dead she breaks down and cries, with Suzanne switching roles and hugging and consoling her. Vee was so integral to her life she mourns her despite knowing how deceptive she was to her and others. Throughout season three Taystee takes on a tacit leadership role among the Black inmates, often serving as a voice of reason and representing their interests in various squabbles. She is shocked and humbled when Frieda (Dale Soules), an older White inmate, refers to her "Don't Make Me Come Back There" (3.12), as "the mom." Though Taystee's prominent role in the prison riot that dominates season five and her subsequent preparation and murder trial in season six are beyond the focus of this chapter, they further cement my observation about how Taystee was elevated to a central character.

Sustained temporal displacement in the form of memory temporality, largely characterized by narrative juxtapositions of the past and present, defines the narrative architecture of *OITNB*. The series maximizes the serial forms and makes room for multiple stories through its use of temporality. Though I focus on Taystee, the lives of Cindy, Poussey, and Suzanne are clearly inseparable from the larger design to imbue women-centric stories with complexity and nuance.

In 2011 Booth noted, "television is the most visible, most watched, most familiar media technology in our lives today, and the impact of these temporally displaced complex narratives is far-reaching."[64] Series like *OITNB*, *IMDY*, and *Fleabag* are part of the expansion and normalization of television's temporal play, and its emergence in other mediums. The subject continues inspiring reflections on the dynamics of television, such as Melissa Ames's anthology *Time in Television Narrative* and Yael Levy's more recent women-centric exploration in *Chick TV*.[65] Building on this tradition my discussion emphasizes how *OITNB*, *IMDY*, and *Fleabag* exemplify the ways different forms of temporal play enable viewers to reevaluate gendered character tropes and genre boundaries, and simultaneously illuminate a spectrum of sociocultural issues salient to women, including relationships, sexual assault, and the lack of social safety nets for women of color among others. This synthesis of form and content they model elevates feminized culture and the storytelling possibilities of television.

# CODA

## *Pivots, Impacts, Challenges, and Possibilities*

Though *CXG* focuses on the experiences of Rebecca, a White, Jewish, cisgender female lawyer, her two best friends, Heather and Valencia, a biracial and Latinx woman, respectively, steer one of *CXG*'s most remarkable scenes. At the end of season three Rebecca accidentally kills her stalker, Trent. At her trial, rather than plead insanity, which would reduce her sentence or absolve her, she flashes back to all of the lies and deceptions she has committed over three seasons and pleads guilty. For the first time in the series Rebecca—who is notoriously, and comically, self-interested and oblivious—attempts to hold herself accountable for her actions. For *her*, an Ivy League educated lawyer who gave up her partnership at a New York law firm to follow her high school crush to California, this individual act of sacrifice represents social justice. While her effort seems sincere it is still a small gesture compared to the legal and judicial issues less privileged individuals have navigated for centuries. *CXG* recognizes this and uses it strategically in season four.

Instead of settling for Rebecca's seeming act of personal sacrifice as the turning point, *CXG* pushes us further. Once incarcerated in a women's prison in season four in "I Want to Be Here" (4.1), she attempts to understand the fates of the numerous women, many of color, and fails miserably. As is common on *CXG* she fantasizes about the fates of the women in a song ("What's Your Story") patterned after the musical *Chicago*'s "Cell Block Tango." As the women sing their stories she realizes their stories fall beyond anything she can access, and the song ends abruptly. She is startled into a different reality she is unprepared for.

Shortly after, she is released from prison after the truth emerges, thanks to legal interventions by her friends, and a judge who will not let her *stay* in prison just so she can feel contrite. Rebecca persists in berating herself about being let out of prison while the other women remain incarcerated unfairly. Though she eventually (and naively) voices what is obvious to her friends ("Oh my God guys, I realize I'm privileged"), Heather and Valencia, unable to bear her naive recitals of White guilt, finally intervene. Notably, they advise her to stop feeling sorry for herself and lamenting her privilege and actually use it to fight the injustices her newfound imprisoned friends, largely coded as poor and working class, have navigated their *entire* lives.

Rebecca's forced awakening, and the follow-up scenes of Rebecca and her former law colleagues working to provide pro bono legal assistance to the women, symbolizes how White Americans *could* shift from guilt and shame toward something more palpable. As a television series *CXG*'s effort is hopeful but not naive enough to frame this as the solution to racism. It's gestural but astute in its way.

Though the scene is part of a broader moral metamorphosis Rebecca experiences in season four, it speaks to *CXG*'s tendency to continually defy expectations, including its audience's. By pivoting away from the witless White savior trope mid-song, it turns toward other possibilities. Just as it eschews the tropes of romantic comedies and reveals the slippery boundaries of television genre conventions, it uses comedy to mock White liberalism, negate "White saviorism," name privilege, and depict one strategy of cross-racial allyship among women. The disruptions of the song, and its aftermath, depict a useful proxy for the creative pivot in contemporary television that *Broads, Sisters, Exes* depicts to readers.

## Pivot and Impact

The 2010s to early 2020s clearly represent a pivot in the range of representations of women in comedic, dramatic, and dramedic television. For example, Hohenstein and Thalmann have referred to the 2010s as a "Golden Age of Feminist TV" characterized by "an increase in difficult women on screen, a greater and more diverse range of female and male writers, showrunners, and executives behind the scenes" and more feminist-oriented coverage of media in different forms.[1] The women-led, women-centric series this study addresses represent only a slice of the series that emerged during 2012–20. Most major US- and UK-based broadcasters premiered women-centric series featuring women-identified lead characters, produced or coproduced by women, that represented a range of women in a variety of settings. US examples include a White single-mother-led household (*Better Things*, 2016–22, FX); a single Mexican American woman working on her law career (*Cristela*, 2014–15, ABC); a high-powered Black Beltway political "fixer" (*Scandal*, 2012–18, ABC); a White trans woman who comes out to her family in late middle age (*Transparent*, 2014–19, Amazon Prime Video); and a neurotic self-identifying "fat, queer dyke" managing mental health and romantic intimacy (*Work in Progress*, 2019–22, Showtime), to name a few. Additionally, some women-created women-centric web series also garnered strong viewership and critical attention, such as Jen Richards's trans-women-focused *Her Story* (2016, YouTube) and Fatimah Asghar's women-of-color-focused *Brown Girls* (2017, Open TV), both nominees for the Primetime Emmy Award for Outstanding Short Form Comedy or Drama Series. The Millennial focus of *Broads, Sisters, Exes* has drawn out some of the ways select series depict distinctive elements of the generation's experiences with socioeconomic conditions, contemporary gender and racial dynamics, and notions of what constitutes viable household and living arrangements, among others.

Beyond the fact that different types of women were increasingly represented during this period, the roles of new generations of women as creators and storytellers are equally germane. Whereas some women producers have limited their production to one series or medium, several former showrunners have continued their careers writing and producing for television, film, and Broadway as well as acting. Issa Rae's production company Hoorae produced the Black women-centric HBO series *The Black Lady Sketch Show* (2019–23) and *Rap Sh!t* (2022–23), as well as reality programs. As of this writing the company will also produce several forthcoming feature films. Lena Dunham executive produced the HBO series *Camping* (2018) and *Genera+ion* (2021), and wrote, produced, and directed the 2022 films *Sharp Stick* and *Catherine Called Birdy*. *Broad City*'s Ilana Glazer was one of several coproducers of

Michael R. Jackson's Tony Award and Pulitzer Prize Award winning Black queer musical *A Strange Loop*, and Abbi Jacobson co-created and cowrote the television adaptation of *A League of Their Own* (2022, Amazon Prime Video). Phoebe Waller-Bridge executive produced the drama *Killing Eve* (2018–22, BBC America), and cowrote the screenplay for the 2021 James Bond film *No Time to Die*. In many ways the "good" and "complex" series they created were an opening to other creative endeavors.

Their artistic contributions include incorporating aspects of "indie" film's interventions into television production and, in the case of *Insecure* and *Shrill*, bringing a more culturally inclusive perspective to the storylines, characters, themes, and creative teams involved. Thus, they challenge White biases in the film industry and among other indie-oriented television. The emergence of comedies centered on women of color builds on these precedents, as does the casual incorporation of women of color on series with White female leads, such as Sasha Compère and Madison Shepard (*Single Drunk Female*) and Mercedes White (*Somebody Somewhere*). Trans women and gender nonconforming performers are also integral to this more expansive approach. For example, Bilal Baig is the creator, lead actor, coproducer, and cowriter of *Sort Of* (CBC/HBO, 2021–23), which depicts a Pakistani Canadian trans woman's personal and professional life. Lea Robinson (*A League of Their Own*, *Twenties*) and Peppermint (*Survival of the Thickest*, 2023–present, Netflix) also have substantive supporting roles on women-led series.

The use of a range of surreal techniques that interrupt genre conventions have also continued to inform women-centric stories. For example, temporal play, especially flashbacks, add depth to the present-day realities of characters struggling with addiction (*Feel Good*, *Single Drunk Female*), mental health issues (*Work in Progress*), and family trauma (*Tiny Beautiful Things*, 2023, Hulu). The use of the technique also shapes the narratives of series focused on adolescent women, produced by women creatives, including *Sex Education* (2019–23, Netflix), created by producer and writer Laurie Nunn, and *Never Have I Ever* (2020–23, Netflix) coproduced by Mindy Kaling and Lang Fisher. These series have a distinctive creative touch to them, reflecting greater creative and expressive freedom audiences began to see in the early first decade of the twenty-first century, a time Mizejewski and Sturtevant describe as "a remarkable moment in the history of American women's participation in stand-up, television, and film comedy."[2]

An essential part of what made the era remarkable is the expanded range of characters the series introduced. Issa Rae and Michaela Coel's depiction of the textures of Black Millennial life in southern California and London, respectively, as complex, varied, and unapologetic rather than "respectable" or didactic is a major progression for US and British television. Rae's desire to present Black experiences as layered speaks to Haggins's observation about contemporary Black creatives as "post-soul babies" whose "comic personae are inflected by complex tastes and cultural practices that emerged in the post-civil rights era, as well as by race, class, gender, and region," which often projects "hopeful cynicism (or cynical hopefulness)."[3] Hence the character Issa's "aggressive passiveness."

Similarly, Coel's authorship responds to a well-documented history of stereotypes and exclusions pervading British film and television.[4] In many ways she is part of an emerging vanguard of young Black British creatives seeking to follow up on the pioneering work of the 1980s Black British arts movement.[5] Malik's discussion about the need for a wider plane of Black British representation precedes *I May Destroy You* by decades but seems remarkably prescient in her argument that,

> Leaning too heavily on the "stereotypes/positive and negative image" rhetoric can be limiting for three main reasons: in the first place, "typing" has to be recognized as an inevitable and necessary system of representation; in the second, there can be no absolute agreement as to what "positive" and "negative" definitively constitute (can the image of a gold-medal winning Black sportsman only be considered as "positive"?); and in the third, the validity of "positive" and "negative" as racial categories of representation themselves need to be questioned since they do little to displace the assumptions on which the original stereotypes are based.[6]

Just as *OITNB* complicated stereotypes of imprisoned women through presenting a range of contexts and struggles, the "good" and "complex" series continually subverted stereotypes and forced audiences to question the utility and limitations of "positive" and "negative" distinctions. On *JTV* Jane is not choosing between an "outdated" traditional Latin culture or a "modern" American one; rather, she places multiple elements of her cultural heritage in conversation with each other. On *Shrill* Annie Easton embraces her fatness and uses her forum as a writer and her position within her personal relationships to challenge fat stigma. Further, her best friend Fran is not a "token" Black character; she is a developed character in her own right whose story speaks to Blackness, queerness, and immigrant experiences with authenticity and intelligence. Fleabag, Issa, Abbi, Ilana, Rebecca, and Hannah challenge the unspoken mandate that female comedic leads must be "likable" or well behaved, instead presenting flawed, idiosyncratic, and "unruly" characters whose trial-and-error experiences are part of adulthood rather than mere phases in the past covered up by age or education.

Finally, many series regularly depict characters who embrace variants of "queer time," which Halberstam characterizes as temporalities "allowing their participants to believe that their futures can be imagined according to logics that lie outside of those paradigmatic markers of life experience—namely, birth, marriage, reproduction, and death." In this context "queer" refers to challenges to repro-time, family time, and time of inheritance common to the "logic of reproductive temporality."[7] Numerous series conclude by emphasizing platonic connections between friends, including *Broad City*'s Abbi and Ilana and *Shrill*'s Annie and Fran. Other series (*CXG*, *Fleabag*, *I May Destroy You*) end with single leads in their early thirties whose willingness to reflect and develop aspects of self are more salient than their relationship status as "single." These endings do not foreclose the possibility of intimate relationships for the characters, but de-emphasize this as the only relevant storyline for women. I cite the commonality of "queer time" primarily to note how Millennial women characters tend to explore and embrace a wider range of intimate possibilities compared to their predecessors. Even less obviously "queer" series endings like Issa reuniting with her ex-boyfriend Lawrence (*Insecure*), Jane and Rafael marrying *and* managing blended families (*JTV*), and Hannah now a single mother (*Girls*) veer from marriage and children in a nuclear family setting as the natural "conclusion" for women's stories.

Collectively, these series have opened spaces for a wider range of women who vary in age, race, body type, geography, ambition, and other areas to comprise the focus of new comedic and dramedic series. For example, queer women are in lead or co-lead roles on *A League of Their Own*, *Feel Good*, *Harlem*, *Twenties*, *Work in Progress*, and their queerness intersects with numerous aspects of their experience. These range from the tension between queerness and Black elite familial expectations (the character Quinn Joseph in *Harlem*) to the ways White and Black women of the 1940s struggled to balance their authentic intimate desires with post–World War II gender and racial norms (the characters Maxine "Max" Chapman and Carson Shaw on *League*).

From a writing, directing, and producing perspective, multicultural women-led creative teams seem to have laid a blueprint that modeled the narrative possibilities available through greater inclusion in the production process. British Channel Four's adaptation of *Tales of the City* (1993–94) was coproduced by Anthony Root and Alan Poul, British and American White men, respectively. All six episodes were directed by Scottish director Alastair Reid and cowritten by Maupin and Richard Kramer, both White and American gay men. The miniseries queer content undoubtedly meant the presence of established writers and producers were integral to getting it produced. Despite critical acclaim and strong ratings, in the United States it aired at a time when PBS was targeted explicitly by conservative politicians. After PBS's *American Playhouse* series lost funding, premium cable network Showtime and Channel Four produced a 1998 sequel, and a 2001 sequel was produced by Showtime.[8]

Comparatively, the showrunner and executive producer of *Armistead Maupin's Tales of the City* of 2019 was Lauren Morelli, who began her career as a writer on *OITNB*. The production team also included seven other executive producers, including two women and six men. The series featured an all-LGBTQ writer's room, which included playwright Marcus Gardley, a Black cisgender man; Hansol Jung, a South Korean playwright; Thomas Page McBee, a White trans man writer; and Jen Silverman, a White nonbinary writer who uses they/them and feminine pronouns. Four cisgender women and two cisgender men were also part of the writing team. The directors of the ten episodes included four gay cisgender men, three White cisgender women, two trans men, and filmmaker Sydney Freeland, a Navajo cisgender woman. Though *Tales* has always entailed a large ensemble format and range of themes, the 2019 series featured a far wider range of characters embodying races, ethnicities, genders, sexualities, and related storylines beyond the initial series and sequels.[9] These include the nuances of coming out as transgender in contemporary society, the hostile climate for queer and gender nonconforming people in the 1960s, intergenerational tensions about HIV status in the age of pre-exposure prophylaxis (PrEp), and the challenges of aging as LGBTQ+ people, among others. A similarly expansive understanding of race, gender, and sexuality informs the casting and creative teams behind *League*.

The pivots in representation and production I have outlined briefly have clearly informed and influenced many women-centered, gender inclusive, and queer oriented television series of the late 2010s and early 2020s. This development is historically significant for television and forms the root of the cautious optimism I note in the preface. Because television as a medium must be understood in the context of trends in media industries, changes in technology, economic realities, and the larger sociocultural climate, I conclude with critical attention to enduring challenges for women-centric television and television in general.

## Challenges and Possibilities

At the macrolevel a nation's sociopolitical climate shapes perceptions of social norms and deviations, and media representations are integral to this process. Scholars can easily interpret the proliferation of women-centric series, many of which feature characters who are queer, racially minoritized, and otherwise marginal, as reflecting socially and politically liberal, and economically neoliberal paradigms associated with the Obama administration in the United States and the Cameron administration in the United Kingdom. As tempting as this line of thinking might appear, chapter 1 details the unique salience of shifting audience demographics and technological changes in reshaping contemporary concepts of what constitutes television as a medium, who has access to produce it, how it is distributed, and who constitutes its audiences. None of these factors negate the possibility of the sociopolitical climate making audiences more hospitable to more diversified programming, it merely suggests that political symbolism is one of many factors.

Equally relevant to these liberal, and neoliberal, administrations are the way they inspired political and cultural backlashes, which have also served as contexts for the content of the series. Norris and Inglehart trace the rise of authoritarian populism in the United States and Europe since the mid-2010s. Cultural backlash and economic grievances factor prominently in their transatlantic analysis. Their discussion of Britain's decision to exit the European Union (or "Brexit") is partially rooted in tensions between well-educated, geographically mobile "Anywheres," "who embrace new people and experiences, and define themselves by their achievements," and "Somewheres," who have more localized identities and "find rapid change unsettling, particularly that brought on by the flow of migrants, the growth of multiethnic cities, and more fluid gender identities."[10] They trace part of Trump's appeal as partially attributable to disillusioned White voters in the United States who "feel betrayed by 'line cutters'—black people, immigrants, women, and gays—who they see as jumping ahead in the queue for social mobility."[11] In both contexts a fear of changing gender dynamics, including the need for structural efforts to foster economic, social, and political power for women, and a more expansive understanding of gender and sexuality beyond heteronormative paths are strands of larger backlashes with judicial, legislative, and economic consequences.

For the sake of brevity, I focus on an especially precarious gender issue in the United States. Notably, tensions over reproductive rights, inaugurated by the Supreme Court of the United States' (SCOTUS) 1973 decision in *Roe v. Wade*. Reproductive rights were among the issues that mobilized the organizers of the 2017 Women's March staged in protest of the Trump administration (2016–20). Reproductive freedom was especially vulnerable under the new administration, which pledged to advance antichoice measures and to overturn *Roe*. As depicted in the 2018 documentary *Reversing Roe*, states had already begun dismantling access to reproductive choice since the 1970s.[12] According to Griffith, "At last count, between 2011 and 2020, Republican states had passed 480 restrictions on reproductive freedom," which included mandated waiting periods, fetal "personhood" laws, and more limited insurance coverage, among others.[13] The nomination and confirmation of Neil Gorsuch, Brett Kavanaugh, and Amy Coney Barrett, to the SCOTUS during the Trump administration from 2017–20 laid the foundation for June 24, 2022's SCOTUS decision in *Dobbs v. Jackson Women's Health Organization*, which eliminated the constitutional right to abortion and returned power to states to determine on access.[14]

While this radical judicial decision generated a spate of harsh legal restrictions in various states and was highly dispiriting for advocates of reproductive rights, it has reinvigorated segments of the liberal and progressive communities. For example, many journalists and pundits attributed Democratic victories in the 2022 midterm elections, which enabled the Democrats to maintain a majority in the Senate, and the underwhelming performance of Republican candidates, which resulted in a much slighter flip in Congress than predicted, to voters rejecting political extremism.[15] These brief examples of the shifting winds of politics depict historic vacillations between liberal and conservative ideologies as ongoing contexts media representations continuously respond to in different ways.

Even as woman-identified creatives have gained footing in certain industry roles, it is still remarkable, unusual, and noteworthy for a series centered on and/or created by people from minoritized backgrounds to be greenlit in the US and UK media industries. I will use two examples to illustrate these concerns. White and heteronormative biases continue to inform who has access to tell stories and have them greenlit and distributed widely. *Girls* is the most obvious example of how cultural biases can shape what gets produced and promoted in the US television industry, even when women-centric stories by women creators are supported.

Even Roxane Gay, who has written positively about *Girls*, noted, "While critics, in their lavish attention, have said Dunham's show is speaking to an entire generation of girls, there are many of us who recognize that that show is only speaking to a narrow demographic within a generation."[16] Integral to the success of *Girls* was its appeal to established White industry figures like Jenni Konner and Judd Apatow. While *Girls* is innovative and influential, and much of the positive critical responses are nuanced and astute, a lot of White critics tended to universalize its characters and storylines as generational stand-ins for Millennial women with minimal or no attention to its racial insularity.[17]

Acknowledging that *no* story is universal is important for critics and scholars, as is owning the potential and limitations of writing from one's own perspective. The enduring issue is a presumption that creators like Issa Rae have identified, which is the equation of "universal" or "relatable" characters as White and middle class. Dodai Stewart's observation is relevant in this regard: "*Girls* was meant to be different from what we usually see on TV: Highly current, thoroughly modern. But the casting choices are *not* different. Not modern. To be clear: It's fine that the show is about spoiled, delusional, narcissists. The idea that 'if a character isn't *exactly* like me, I can't relate' is bullshit. But that doesn't mean we don't desperately need diversity in the stories being told, characters being explored and actors being hired."[18]

If we can agree that Dunham captures the nuances of a very specific milieu, and this can be interesting and insightful, we can also acknowledge that the world she documents is narrow by definition. To that end I agree with Ta-Nehisi Coates's argument about Dunham, that "storytellers—first and foremost—must pledge their loyalty to the narrative as it comes to them. I don't believe in creating characters out a of [*sic*] desire to please your audience or even to promote an ostensible social good. I think good writing is essentially a selfish act—storytellers are charged with crafting the narrative they want to see. I'm not very interested in Lena Dunham reflecting the aspirations of people she may or may not know. I'm interested in her specific and individual vision; in that story she is aching to tell. If that vision is all-white, then so be it. I don't think a story-teller can be guilted into making great characters."[19] Well-educated, artsy, middle-class women of color exist; Dunham chose to not explore their experience or to hire writers who could. For Coates, the bigger structural issue is not Dunham, rather, it's HBO's reluctance to offer a wider range of writers' and directors' opportunities at that time. This gap tacitly made space for creatives of color to tell their stories, since no one else was telling them, and also pushed creators of White-centered shows to go beyond a White frame. The results are explicitly racialized series like *Orange Is the New Black*, *Insecure*, and *I May Destroy You*, and the more conscious inclusion of diverse voices in casting and production, on series like *CXG* and *Shrill*, which were exceptional at the time. These practices should become a norm rather than function as a sign of exceptional inclusion.

We can turn to the British television industry to see a parallel struggle with diversity and inclusion. As Hope notes, "much of the British television and film industry is publicly owned, overseen and funded by the Department for Digital Culture, Media and Sport and the British Film Institute, a charitable organization sponsored by the Department for Digital Culture, Media and Sport. The BBC, British Film Institute, and Channel 4 are all funded via a combination of national lottery funds, television licensing and taxes. This funding and oversight structure allow for a large segment of British television to avoid being beholden to shareholders and corporations, and attempts to evade the prioritization of profit, in lieu of 'public value.'"[20]

In British series, this matters because of the public advocacy work of numerous creatives regarding the lack of diversity and representation in the British television industry. In *Access All Areas: The Diversity Manifesto for TV and Beyond*, of 2021, actor Sir Lenny Henry and media industry consultant Marcus Ryder address the lack of racial and ethnic diversity in Britain's broadcast industries and conclude with the "96 Per Cent Majority Manifesto," an eight-point list of action items for making British media more inclusive behind the scenes and in front of the camera, including the following:

1. We are the 96 percent. We believe *we* are the majority.
2. We believe the best solutions are achieved together.
3. We believe the time is now.
4. We believe in the power of allies.
5. We believe in individuality.
6. We believe in structural change.
7. We believe in setting specific, measurable goals.
8. We are fighting for a power share, *not* a power grab.[21]

In the context of this study the two most salient of these, "structural change" and "individuality," note the following, respectively: "Structural solutions solve systemic problems. We are fighting against cosmetic changes that have no substantive impact. We reject lip service and demand real engagement," and "Those in power must realize that we are all human beings and not just convenient boxes to be ticked. As individuals demand recognition, and four our *true* potential to be realized and rewarded."[22]

These recommendations stand out for reinforcing the data the Directors UK group observed in their 2018 study of racial and ethnic representation among directors in *Adjusting the Colour Balance* and echoing Michaela Coel's observations in her 2018 MacTaggart lecture at the Edinburgh International Television Festival. For example, though *Adjusting* notes a rise in Black, Asian, and minority ethnic (BAME) directors in drama and comedy from 2.6 (2013) to 4.1 (2016), which are slight figures overall, these numbers do not speak to the quality of their experiences.[23] Did these directors have production credits? Were they able to tell BAME focused stories? Were they able to advocate for more diverse actors and television crews? Did they have the freedom to intervene when micro- and/or macroaggressions happen on set? In other words, the 1.5 percent increase suggests some tentative movement toward welcoming more diverse people in television but does not necessarily translate into creative license in the storytelling process or experiential differences for the creators involved.

Placing the *Manifesto* in conversation with *Adjusting*, and connecting them to Cole's lecture, illuminates a shared concern over a lack of racial, ethnic, and other forms of representation in television. Embedded in Coel's lament about the sheer lack of representation is a deeper discussion of the industry's superficial approach to what she terms "misfits." As she documents in her discussion of her experience working on 2015–2017's *Chewing Gum*, she was flattered by the producers' interest in her ideas, including the ideal of telling stories about Black working-class people, but also overwhelmed and perturbed by certain norms. The unequal way actors of color were treated, the isolation she experienced as head writer from the producers charged with making major decisions, her steadfast advocacy to be listed as an executive producer, which was downgraded to creative coproducer, and the exclusion of her when *Chewing Gum*'s online broadcast rights were secured reflect the industry's superficial understanding of "diversity." Unsurprisingly, she advocated to serve as executive producer and sole writer of *I May Destroy You*, and codirects nine of twelve episodes. She was better able to tell her story on her own terms creatively after a series of challenges and confrontations during *Chewing*.

Similarly, in 2020, Black British actor and writer Daniel Lawrence Taylor commented on the surge of global interest in antiracism through reiterating Coel's message about the media industry's superficial engagement with "diverse" talent, noting how he struggled to be trusted as a writer on the award-winning British series *Timewasters*. As he wrote in *The Guardian*, "But in order to show real solidarity understand you will need to enact genuine change. Nurture talent from people of colour—in front of and behind the camera. Stop trying to take black art without black artists; that's how you end up with Iggy Azalea. Trust and support rather than question and doubt our abilities to tell our stories. Be aware of overwhelming and unwelcoming white spaces as they are often experienced by people of colour, and take steps to change the environment and culture. You don't have to, but remember your solidarity black squares have been screengrabbed."[24] He was one of 4,000 BAME creatives to contribute to a letter demanding the UK film and television industry diversify personnel and stories funded, and support independent producers. Shortly after it was published, the BBC announced it would require its series to hire at least 20 percent of personnel from "diverse" communities, including those with BAME, disabled, and lower socioeconomic backgrounds.[25] The 2021–23 Diversity and Inclusion plan includes the following specification: "The new plan will enable the BBC to meet the 50:20:12 workforce targets—announced in September 2020—in the next three to five years. That's 50 percent women; at least 20 percent black, Asian or minority ethnic; and at least 12 percent disabled employees."[26] This is a promising start, and time will tell how these policies impact future productions.

These examples reflect historic struggles with racial, gender, and other biases, and a pivot toward solutions. In the United States, high visibility awareness campaigns have generated heightened public awareness of industry exclusions, changes in professional media organizations, and the generation of talent development programs. Alongside efforts to foster organizational and industrial accountability are talent development programs targeting underrepresented creatives in film and television. Numerous organizations, such as Women in Film Los Angeles founded in 1973, have advocated for equity and provided spaces for talent development in the screen industries for decades.[27] More recently, individuals in partnership with various entities have taken on some of this work. Programs heralded by successful showrunners like Ryan Murphy's HALF Directors Shadowing Program, founded in 2016, and Shonda Rhimes's The Producers Inclusion Initiative and The Ladder, launched in 2022, are examples of efforts to nurture talent from historically unrepresented communities. Murphy's program "provides an educational Director Shadowing Program in which professional episodic directors on every Ryan Murphy Television production mentor emerging and mid-career women, BIPOC, LGBTQ and minority directors (mentees)."[28] Rhimes's Initiative focuses on "indie producers, unit production managers, supervisors and first assistant directors," and the Ladder, launched from the United Kingdom, provides "opportunities for people from marginalized groups who are looking to gain the kind of on-set experience and training that's key to success in the film and TV business." Both Rhimes's programs are partially funded by Netflix's Fund for Creative Equity.[29]

Networks and streaming services have also launched development programs. The Directors Guild of American (DGA) lists programs targeting directors from various underrepresented communities sponsored by Apple Studios, Disney Entertainment, NBC Universal, Paramount, and Sony Pictures.[30] Collectively, these examples illustrate a range of approaches from independent organizations, powerful individual creatives, and corporations to expand the range of storytellers and participants in television and film. While none of these programs can guarantee emerging creatives work or career success, they are stepping stones and reflect the clear need to challenge significant creative gaps in the production side of screen industries.

The analyses throughout *Broads, Sisters, Exes* illustrate that representation is an issue of equity and one of *aesthetic significance*. The wide range of elements that define the series I examine as "good" and "complex" reflect the skills, insights, and approaches of their creative teams. The nature of the stories they sought to tell, the narrative and technical approaches they employed, and the constitution of their creative teams operated in tandem to produce these series. The ongoing tension between political progress and backlash dynamics, and the profit-driven nature of media industries are variables creatives will continue navigating. My discussion is less of a retrospective of a lost or stolen moment from the recent past than a signal that the conversations and creative possibilities these series opened—about race, gender, sexuality, desire, trauma, injustice—can no longer be ignored. There is no turning back from what we have been able to see even if the movement forward remains complex.

# NOTES

## Preface

1 Elana Levine, *Wallowing in Sex: The New Sexual Culture of 1970s American Television* (Durham, NC: Duke University Press, 2007).

2 *Mary Hartman, Mary Hartman*, seasons 1–2, featuring Louise Lasser, Greg Mullavey, and Mary Kay Place, 1976–77, Shout Factory, 2013, DVD.

3 Vincent L. Stephens, "Over*Flow: Whitelash in the Heartland: 1977 Speaks to Today through the Voice of *Mary Hartman, Mary Hartman*," *Flow: A Critical Forum on Media and Culture*, November 3, 2021. www.flowjournal.org/2021/11/whitelash-in-the-heartland/.

4 Piper Kerman, *Orange Is the New Black: My Year in a Women's Prison* (New York: Spiegel and Grau, 2010); Lindy West, *Shrill* (New York: Hachette Books, 2017).

5 Jeffrey Sconce, "What If? Charting Television's New Textual Boundaries," in *Television after TV: Essays on a Medium in Transition*, ed. Lynn Spiegel and Jan Olsson (Durham, NC: Duke University Press, 2004), 94, 95.

6 Joy Press, *Stealing the Show: How Women Are Revolutionizing Television* (New York: Atria, 2018).

## Introduction

1 Aymar Jean Christian, *Open TV: Innovation beyond Hollywood and the Rise of Web Television* (New York: New York University Press, 2018).

2 Stacy L. Smith, Marc Choueti, and Katherine Pieper, 2016, *Inclusion or Invisibility? Comprehensive Annenberg Report on Diversity in Entertainment*, Institute for Diversity and Empowerment at Annenberg (IDEA). https://annenberg.usc.edu/sites/default/files/2017/04/07/MDSCI_CARD_Report_FINAL_Exec_Summary.pdf.

3 Stella M. Rouse and Ashley D. Ross, *The Politics of Millennials: Political Beliefs and Policy Preferences of America's Most Diverse Generation* (Ann Arbor: University of Michigan Press, 2018), 29.
4 Kristen Bialik and Richard Fry, "Millennial Life: How Young Adulthood Today Compares with Prior Generations," Pew Research Center, February 14, 2019, www.pewresearch.org/social-trends/2019/02/14/millennial-life-how-young-adulthood-today-compares-with-prior-generations-2/.
5 Sarah Cardwell, "Is Quality Television Any Good? Generic Distinctions, Evaluations and the Troubling Matter of Critical Judgment," in *Quality TV: Contemporary American Television and Beyond*, ed. Janet McCabe and Kim Akass (London: I. B. Tauris, 2007), 20; Jason Mittell, *Complex TV: The Poetics of Contemporary Television Storytelling* (New York: New York University Press, 2015), 35.
6 Fien Adriaens and Sofie Van Bauwel, "*Sex and the City*: A Postfeminist Point of View? Or How Popular Culture Functions as a Channel for Feminist Discourse," *Journal of Popular Culture* 47, no. 1 (2014): 174–95, https://doi.org/10.1111/j.1540-5931.2011.00869.x; Jessalynn Keller and Maureen E. Ryan, "Introduction: Mapping Emergent Feminisms," in *Emergent Feminisms: Complicating a Postfeminist Media Culture*, ed. Jessalynn Keller and Maureen E. Ryan (New York: Routledge, 2018), 14.
7 Merri Lisa Johnson, "Introduction: Ladies Love Your Box: The Rhetoric of Pleasure and Danger in Feminist Television Studies," in *Third Wave Feminism and Television: Jane Puts It in a Box*, ed. Merri Lisa Johnson (London: I. B. Tauris, 2007), 19–20.
8 Francesca Sobande, "Awkward Black Girls and Post-Feminist Possibilities: Representing Millennial Black Women on Television in *Chewing Gum* and *Insecure*," *Critical Studies in Television* 14, no. 4 (2019): 446, https://doi.org/10.1177/1749602019870298.
9 Amanda D. Lotz, "Postfeminist Television Criticism: Rehabilitating Critical Terms and Identifying Postfeminist Attributes," *Feminist Media Studies* 1, no. 1 (2001): 105–21, https://doi.org/10.1080/14680770120042891; Ashley Sayeau, "As Seen on TV: Women's Rights and Quality Television," in *Quality TV: Contemporary American Television and Beyond*, ed. Kim Akass and Janet McCabe (New York: I. B. Tauris, 2007), 52–61; Janet McCabe and Kim Akass, "Feminist Television Criticism: Notes and Queries," *Critical Studies in Television: The International Journal of Television Studies*, no. 1 (2010): 108–20.

10 McCabe and Akass, "Feminist Television Criticism," 110, 111, 115.

11 Sayeau, "As Seen on TV," 53; Mary Beth Haralovich, "Sitcoms and Suburbs: Positioning the 1950s Homemaker," in *Critiquing the Sitcom: A Reader*, ed. Joanne Morreale (Syracuse, NY: Syracuse University Press, 2003), 69–85; Robert Deming, "*Kate and Allie*: 'New Women' and the Audience's Television Archive," in *Private Screenings: Television and the Female Consumer*, ed. Lynn Spigel and Denise Mann (Minneapolis: University of Minnesota Press, 1992), 203–14.

12 Linda Blum, "Feminism and the Mass Media: A Case Study of *The Women's Room* as Novel and Television Film," *Berkeley Journal of Sociology* 27, no. 1 (1983): 1–26; Bonnie J. Dow, *Prime Time Feminism: Television, Media Culture, and the Women's Movement since 1970* (Philadelphia: University of Pennsylvania Press, 1996), 38; Lauren Rabinovitz, "Sitcoms and Single Moms: Representations of Feminism on American TV," *Cinema Journal* 29, no. 1 (1989): 3–19; Valerie Bryson, *Feminist Political Theory: An Introduction* (New York: Paragon House, 1992), 3.

13 Lotz, "Postfeminist Television Criticism," 108; Sayeau, "As Seen on TV," 58; Julie D'Acci, *Defining Women: Television and the Case of "Cagney & Lacey"* (Chapel Hill: University of North Carolina Press, 1994); Kathleen Rowe, *The Unruly Woman: Gender and Genres of Laughter* (Austin: University of Texas Press, 1995).

14 McCabe and Akass, "Feminist Television Criticism," 115; Julia Havas, *Woman Up: Invoking Feminism in Quality Television* (Detroit: Wayne University Press, 2022), 1–3, 53–136; Faye Woods, "Too Close for Comfort: Direct Address and the Affective Pull of the Confessional Comic Woman in *Chewing Gum* and *Fleabag*," *Communication, Culture and Critique* 12, no. 2 (2019): 199–200, https://doi.org/10.1093/ccc/tcz014.

15 Lotz, "Postfeminist Television Criticism," 114–16.

16 Henry Jenkins, "Welcome to Convergence Culture," *Pop Junctions*, June 19, 2006, http://henryjenkins.org/blog/2006/06/welcome_to_convergence_culture.html. Also see Jenkins's *Convergence Culture: Where Old and New Media Collide* (New York: New York University Press, 2006), 3, 15–16.

17 See pages 176–77 in Adriaens and Van Bauwel, "*Sex and the City*: A Postfeminist Point of View?"

18 McBeal related examples include Julie Brown, "*Ally McBeal*'s Postmodern Soundtrack," *Journal of the Royal Music Association* 126, no. 2 (2001): 275–303; Rachel Moseley and Jacinda Read, "'Having It Ally': Popular

Television (Post-)Feminism," *Feminist Media Studies* 2, no. 2 (2002): 231–49, https://doi.org/10.1080/14680770220150881; Elwood Watson, ed., *Searching the Soul of "Ally McBeal": Critical Essays* (Jefferson, NC: McFarland, 2006). *Sex and the City* related examples include Jane Arthurs, "*Sex and the City* and Consumer Culture: Remediating Postfeminist Drama," *Feminist Media Studies*, 3, no. 1 (2003): 83–98, https://doi.org/10.1080/1468077032000080149; Janet McCabe and Kim Akass, "Introduction: Welcome to the Age of Un-Innocence," in *Reading "Sex and the City,"* ed. Kim Akass and Janet McCabe (London: I. B. Tauris, 2006), 1–14; Jane Gerhard, "*Sex and the City*: Carrie Bradshaw's Queer Post Feminism," *Feminist Media Studies* 5, no. 1 (2005): 37–49, https://doi.org/10.1080/14680770500058173.

19 The Combahee River Collective, "A Black Feminist Statement," in *All the Women Are White, All the Blacks Are Men, but Some of Us Are Brave: Black Women's Studies*, ed. Gloria T. Hull, Patricia Bell, and Barbra Smith (New York: Feminist Press at the City University of New York, 1982), 13–22; Cherríe Moraga, "La Güera," in *This Bridge Called My Back: Writings by Radical Women of Color*, ed. Cherríe Moraga and Gloria Anzaldúa (New York: Kitchen Table, Women of Color Press, 1983), 27–34; Mitsuye Yamada, "Invisibility Is an Unnatural Disaster: Reflections of an Asian American Woman," in Moraga and Anzaldúa, *This Bridge Called My Back*, 35–40.

20 Adriaens and Van Bauwel, "*Sex and the City*," 175, 178–80, 190.

21 Sarah Hagelin and Gillian Silverman, *The New Female Antihero: The Disruptive Women of Twenty-First-Century US Television* (Chicago: University of Chicago Press, 2022), 17, 18.

22 Claire Snyder, "What Is Third-Wave Feminism? A New Directions Essay," *Signs* 34, no. 1 (2008): 175–96; Rebecca Munford, "'Wake Up and Smell the Lipgloss': Gender, Generation, and the (A)Politics of Girl Power," in *Third Wave Feminism: A Critical Exploration*, ed. Stacy Gillis, Gillian Howie, and Rebecca Munford (New York: Palgrave Macmillan, 2004), 148–53; Melissa Klein, "Duality and Redefinition: Young Feminism and the Alternative Music Community," in *Third Wave Agenda: Being Feminist, Doing Feminism*, ed. Leslie Heywood and Jennifer Drake (Minneapolis: University of Minnesota Press, 1997), 207–25.

23 Nicola Rivers, *Postfeminism(s) and the Arrival of the Fourth Wave* (Cham, Switzerland: Palgrave Macmillan, 2017); Rebecca Wanzo, "Precarious-Girl

Comedy: Issa Rae, Lena Dunham, and Abjection Aesthetics," *Camera Obscura* 31, no. 2 (2016): 26–59; Jorie Lagerwey, Julie Leyda, and Diane Negra, "Female Centered TV in an Age of Precarity," *Genders* 1, no. 1 (2016), www.colorado.edu/genders/2016/05/19/female-centered-tv-age-precarity; Meredith Nash and Ruby Grant, "Twenty-Something *Girls* v. Thirty-Something *Sex and the City* Women," *Feminist Media Studies* 15, no. 6 (2015): 976–91, https://doi.org/10.1080/14680777.2015.1050596; Hagelin and Silverman, *New Female Antihero*; Sarah Banet-Weiser, *Empowered: Popular Feminism and Popular Misogyny* (Durham, NC: Duke University Press, 2018); Catherine Rottenberg, *The Rise of Neoliberal Feminism* (New York: Oxford University Press, 2018); Sarah Banet-Weiser, Rosalind Gill, and Catherine Rottenberg, "Postfeminism, Popular Feminism and Neoliberal Feminisms? Sarah Banet-Weiser, Rosalind Gill and Catherine Rottenberg in Conversation," *Feminist Theory* 21, no. 1 (2020): 1–22, https://doi.org/10.1177/1464700119842555.

24 Emile Lawrence and Jessica Ringrose, "@NOFEMINISM, #FEMINISTSAREUGLY, and Misandry Memes: How Social Media Feminist Humor Is Calling Out Antifeminism," in *Emergent Feminisms: Complicating a Postfeminist Media Culture*, ed. Jessalynn Keller and Maureen E. Ryan (New York: Routledge, 2018), 213.

25 Patricia Pender, "'I'm Buffy and You're . . . History': The Postmodern Politics of Buffy," in *Fighting the Forces: What's at Stake in "Buffy the Vampire Slayer,"* ed. Rhonda V. Wilcox and David Lavery (Lanham, MD: Rowman and Littlefield, 2002), 38.

26 Hagelin and Silverman, *New Female Antihero*, 20; Johnson, "Introduction: Ladies Love Your Box," 12.

27 Dow, *Prime Time Feminism*, 214.

28 Hagelin and Silverman, *New Female Antihero*, 19.

29 Amanda D. Lotz, *The Television Will Be Revolutionized* (New York: New York University Press, 2007).

30 Robert J. Thompson, *Television's Second Golden Age: From "Hill Street Blues" to "ER"* (Syracuse, NY: Syracuse University Press, 1996), 12–16.

31 Cardwell, "Is Quality Television Any Good?," 20, 26; Mittell, *Complex TV*, 211.

32 Cardwell, "Is Quality Television Any Good?," 23.

33 Mittell, *Complex TV*, 212.

34 Cardwell, "Is Quality Television Any Good?," 21.

35 Michael Z. Newman and Elana Levine, *Legitimating Television: Media Convergence and Cultural Status* (New York: Routledge, 2012), 34, 40, 45–57.

36 Brett Mills, "What Does It Mean to Call Television 'Cinematic'?," in *Television Aesthetics and Style*, ed. Jason Jacobs and Steven Peacock (London: Bloomsbury, 2013), 58–63; Deborah L. Jaramillo, "Rescuing Television from 'The Cinematic': The Perils of Dismissing Television Style," in *Television Aesthetics and Style*, ed. Jason Jacobs and Steven Peacock (London: Bloomsbury, 2013), 64, 67, 72–74.

37 Helen Wheatley, *Spectacular Television: Exploring Televisual Pleasure* (London: I. B. Tauris, 2016); Jessica Ford, "Women's Indie Television: The Intimate Feminism of Women-Centric Dramedies," *Feminist Media Studies* 19, no. 7 (2019): 928–43, https://doi.org/10.1080/14680777.2019.1667060.

38 Mittell, *Complex TV*, 217–26.

39 Cardwell, "Is Quality Television Any Good?," 30.

40 Mittell, *Complex TV*, 217–26.

41 Newman and Levine, *Legitimating Television*, 53–55; Mittell, *Complex TV*, 86–117.

42 For example, in 2019 *Fleabag* won Primetime Emmy Awards for Outstanding Comedy Series, Actress, Directing, and Writing. *Girls* was nominated for Outstanding Comedy Series in 2012 and 2013; *Orange Is the New Black* was nominated for Outstanding Comedy Series in 2014 and Outstanding Drama Series in 2015; *Insecure* was nominated for Outstanding Comedy Series in 2020. In 2021 Michaela Cole won an Emmy for Outstanding Writing for a Limited or Anthology Series or Movie for *I May Destroy You*. See www.emmys.com/awards/nominees-winners for show specific information.

43 Roz Kaveney, "'She Saved the World. A Lot.' An Introduction to the Themes and Structure of *Buffy* and *Angel*," in *Reading the Vampire Slayer: The Unofficial Critical Companion to "Buffy" and "Angel,"* ed. Roz Kaveney (London: Tauris Parke Paperbacks, 2001), 1–36; Rhonda V. Wilcox and David Lavery, eds., *Fighting the Forces: What's at Stake in "Buffy the Vampire Slayer"* (Lanham, MD: Rowman and Littlefield, 2002); Michelle Byers, "*Buffy the Vampire Slayer*: The Next Generation of Television," in *Catching a Wave: Reclaiming Feminism for the 21st Century*, ed. Rory Dicker and Alison Piepmeier (Boston: Northeastern University Press, 2003), 171–87.

44 Accusations against *Buffy*'s showrunner Joss Whedon for problematic relationships with actresses on the series, tensions with women writers on its staff, and toxic dating relationships with women while he was married have tarnished perceptions of *Buffy* as a feminist series among many fans. Though *Ally* showrunner David E. Kelley's series (e.g., *L.A. Law*, *The Practice*) have prominently featured women, the hyperfeminine and highly sexualized appearance and demeanor of the *Ally McBeal* character led many critics to question Kelley's sensitivity toward contemporary feminism. Lila Shapiro, "The Undoing of Joss Whedon," *New York Magazine*, January 17, 2022, www.vulture.com/article/joss-whedon-allegations.html; David Payson, Introduction to *Searching the Soul of "Ally McBeal,"* ed. Elwood Watson (Jefferson, NC: McFarland, 2006), 7, 13.

45 Kimberly Springer, "Divas, Evil Black Bitches, and Bitter Black Women," in *Interrogating Postfeminism: Gender and the Politics of Popular Culture*, ed. Yvonne Tasker and Diane Negra (Durham, NC: Duke University Press, 2007), 249.

46 Julia Havas and Maria Sulimma, "Through the Gaps of My Fingers: Genre, Femininity, and Cringe Aesthetics in Dramedy Television," *Television and New Media* 21, no. 1 (2018): 1–20, https://doi.org/10.1177/1527476418777838; Wanzo, "Precarious-Girl Comedy," 26–59; Ford, "Women's Indie Television," 928–43.

47 Kristyn Gorton, "(Un)Fashionable Feminists: The Media and *Ally McBeal*," in *Searching the Soul of "Ally McBeal,"* ed. Elwood Watson (Jefferson, NC: McFarland, 2007), 216–17, 220–21; Sayeau, "As Seen on TV," 60; Mary Jo Lodge, "Beyond 'Jumping the Shark': The New Television Musical," *Studies in Musical Theatre* 1, no. 3 (2007): 293–305.

48 Nash and Grant, "Twenty-Something *Girls*," 980.

49 Gerhard, "*Sex and the City*," 37.

50 Emily Nussbaum, *I like to Watch: Arguing My Way through the TV Revolution* (New York: Random House, 2019), 301.

51 Author and advocate Tarana Burke, who originated the #MeToo hashtag before actress Alyssa Milano popularized it, chronicles her advocacy in *Unbound: My Story of Liberation and the Birth of the Me Too Movement* (New York: Flatiron Books, 2021). Numerous journalists commented on the episode's incisive approach, for example: Amanda Hess, "Lena Dunham and Matthew Rhys on the Latest *Girls* Provocation," *New York*

*Times*, February 24, 2017, www.nytimes.com/2017/02/24/arts/television/lena-dunham-and-matthew-rhys-on-the-latest-girls-provocation.html; Caroline Framke, "'American Bitch' Is One of *Girls*' Most Challenging Episodes to Date," *Vox*, February 27, 2017, www.vox.com/culture/2017/2/25/14725960/girls-american-bitch-recap-review-dunham-rhys.

52 Wanzo, "Precarious-Girl Comedy," 26–59; Lagerwey, Leyda, and Negra, "Female Centered TV"; Hagelin and Silverman, *New Female Antihero.*

53 Mikki Kendall, *Hood Feminism: Notes from the Women That a Movement Forgot* (New York: Penguin Books, 2020), 3.

54 Taylor Nygaard and Jorie Lagerwey, *Horrible White People: Gender, Genre, and Television's Precarious Whiteness* (New York: New York University Press, 2020), 6.

55 Taylor Nygaard, "'I'm Cool with It': The Popular Feminism of *Inside Amy Schumer*," in *Emergent Feminisms: Complicating a Postfeminist Media Culture*, ed. Jessalynn Keller and Maureen E. Ryan (New York: Routledge, 2018), 69.

56 Johnson, "Introduction: Ladies Love Your Box," 11.

57 Ford, "Women's Indie Television," 932, 935.

58 Scott R. Olson, "Meta-Television: Popular Postmodernism," *Critical Studies in Mass Communication* 4, no. 3 (1987): 284–300; Brian L. Ott, *The Small Screen: How Television Equips Us to Live in the Information Age* (Malden, MA: Blackwell Publishing, 2007).

59 Katy Steinmetz, "The Transgender Tipping Point," *Time*, May 29, 2014, https://time.com/135480/transgender-tipping-point/.

60 Caroline Framke, "'I Just Wanted It to Be a Regular Story about Black People': Issa Rae on Creating and Starring in HBO's *Insecure*," October 9, 2016, *Vox*, www.vox.com/culture/2016/10/7/13176104/issa-rae-insecure-hbo-interview.

61 Press, *Stealing the Show*, 73–102, 103–36, 137–49.

62 "On Strike," SAG-AFTRA, last modified July 13, 2023, www.sagaftrastrike.org/; "Writing Is Our Home," Writers Guild of America, last modified July 26, 2023, www.wgacontract2023.org/videos/writing-is-our-home; The WGA's strike ended on September 27, 2023, and SAG-AFTRA's on November 9, 2023, due to updated agreements between the industry and their members. Dominic Patten and Anthony D'Alessandro, "The Strike Is Over! SAG-AFTRA and Studios Reach Tentative Deal on New Three-Year Contract," November 8, 2023, *Deadline*, https://deadline.com/2023/11/sag-strike-ends-actors-studios-deal-contract-1235566470/.

## Chapter 1

1 Amanda Lotz, "Unpopularity and Cultural Power in the Age of Netflix: New Questions for Cultural Studies' Approaches to Television Texts," *European Journal of Cultural Studies* 24, no. 4 (2021): 890, https://doi.org/10.1177/1367549421994578.

2 Chris Anderson, *The Long Tail: Why the Future of Business Is Selling Less of More* (New York: Hyperion, 2006), 5, 6, 181–82; Michelle Hilmes, *Network Nations: A Transnational History of British and American Broadcasting* (London: Routledge, 2011), 1–25; Sam Ward, "Branding Bridges: Sky Atlantic, 'Quality' Imports, and Brand Integration," in *Transatlantic Television Drama: Industries, Programs, Fans*, ed. Matt Hills, Michele Hilmes, and Roberta Pearson (New York: Oxford University Press, 2019), 87–102.

3 Robert D. Putnam, *Bowling Alone: The Collapse and Revival of American Community* (New York: Simon and Schuster, 2001).

4 Alain Sylvain, "Why Buying into Pop Culture and Joining a Cult Is Basically the Same Thing," *Quartz*, March 10, 2020, www.yahoo.com/video/why-buying-pop-culture-joining-165002256.html.

5 Anderson, *Long Tail*, 4–5, 181; Kyle Chayka, "Can Monoculture Survive the Algorithm? And Should It?," *Vox*, December 17, 2019, www.vox.com/the-goods/2019/12/17/21024439/monoculture-algorithm-netflix-spotify.

6 Lotz, *Television Will Be Revolutionized*, 97–99; Horace Newcomb, *TV: The Most Popular Art* (New York: Anchor Books, 1974), 218–24; Newman and Levine, *Legitimating Television*, 23.

7 Newman and Levine, *Legitimating Television*, 25–29.

8 Lotz, *Television Will Be Revolutionized*, 103–4, 118.

9 As Joy Press notes, "despite the recent spate of high-profile, Zeitgeist-defining shows conceived, written, and starring women, television remains a male dominated industry. Anecdotal evidence suggests that female showrunners earn less than their male counterparts, and there are still few women in those positions of power," *Stealing the Show*, 3.

10 Nussbaum, *I like to Watch*, 50, 53.

11 Elana Levine, "Introduction: Feminized Popular Culture in the Early Twenty-First Century," in *Cupcakes, Pinterest, and Ladyporn: Feminized Popular Culture in the Early Twenty-First Century*, ed. Elana Levine (Urbana: University of Illinois Press, 2015), 7; Yael Levy, "Girls' Issues: The Feminist Politics of *Girls*'s Celebration of the 'Trivial,'" in *HBO's*

*"Girls" and the Awkward Politics of Gender, Race, and Privilege*, ed. Elwood Watson, Jennifer Mitchell, and Marc Edward Shaw (Lanham, MD: Lexington Books, 2015), 68.

12 Heather Hundley, "The Evolution of Gendercasting: The Lifetime Television Network—'Television for Women,'" *Journal of Popular Television and Film* 29, no. 4 (2002): 174–81.

13 Stacy L. Smith, Marc Choueti, and Katherine Pieper, *Inclusion or Invisibility? Comprehensive Annenberg Report on Diversity in Entertainment*, Institute for Diversity and Entertainment at Annenberg (IDEA), 2016, https://annenberg.usc.edu/sites/default/files/2017/04/07/MDSCI_CARD_Report_FINAL_Exec_Summary.pdf.

14 Christian, *Open TV*, 4.

15 Christian, *Open TV*, 12–13.

16 Christian, *Open TV*, 123.

17 Diana Scholl, "Issa Rae on *The Mis-Adventures of Awkward Black Girl* and Creating the Black Liz Lemon," *Vulture*, December 14, 2011, www.vulture.com/2011/12/issa-rae-on-the-mis-adventures-of-awkward-black-girl-and-creating-the-black-liz-lemon.html.

18 Jada Yuan, "*Awkward Black Girl* Goes to Hollywood," *Vulture*, October 9, 2016, www.vulture.com/2016/10/awkward-black-girl-issa-rae-hollywood-c-v-r.html.

19 Margaret Lyons, "*Awkward Black Girl*'s Issa Rae Lands ABC Sitcom," *Vulture*, October 2, 2012, www.vulture.com/2012/10/awkward-black-girl-issa-rae-sitcom-shonda-rhimes.html; Bradford Evans, "HBO Developing a Series from Larry Wilmore and *Awkward Black Girl*'s Issa Rae," *Vulture*, August 6, 2013, www.vulture.com/2013/08/hbo-developing-a-series-from-larry-wilmore-and-awkward-black-girls-issa-rae.html; Yuan, "*Awkward Black Girl*."

20 Nick Marx, "Expanding the Brand: Race, Gender, and the Post-Politics of Representation on Comedy Central," *Television and New Media* 17, no. 3 (2016): 273, 278. https://doi.org/10.1177/1527476415577212.

21 Christian, *Open TV*, 64–66, 98–99.

22 See *Broad City*, Internet Movie Database (IMDb), www.imdb.com/title/tt2578560/, for information on the awards and nominations the series received.

23 The issues are archived currently at www.lennyletter.com/.

24 Banet-Weiser, *Empowered: Popular Feminism*, 1, 2.

25 Anderson, *Long Tail*, 190–91.

26 Lotz, *Television Will Be Revolutionized*, 123–26; Kelly Kessler, *Broadway in the Box: Television's Lasting Love Affair with the Musical* (New York: Oxford University Press, 2020), 194–224; Mittell, *Complex TV*, 7–8, 27, 261–91.

27 Banet-Weiser, *Empowered: Popular Feminism*, 32–33.

28 Erec Smith, *Fat Tactics: The Rhetoric and Structure of the Fat Acceptance Movement* (Lanham, MD: Lexington Books, 2018), 58.

29 Lindy West, *Shrill* (New York: Hachette Books, 2017), 195–212.

30 Margaret Tally, *The Limits of #MeToo in Hollywood: Gender and Power in the Entertainment Industry* (Jefferson, NC: McFarland, 2021), 3–15.

31 Josef Adalian and Lane Brown, "Binge Purge," *New York*, June 15–18, 2023, 36–41, 96.

32 *Wanda at Large* (2003, FOX) and *Cristela* (2014–15, ABC).

33 racheldoesstuff, "Fuck Me, Ray Bradbury—Rachel Bloom," written by Rachel Bloom and Jack Dolgen, YouTube, August 15, 2010, www.youtube.com/watch?v=e1lxOS4VzKM.

34 Kate Hahn, "Showtime Mixes Internet Sensation Rachel Bloom with Seasoned Writer for *Crazy Ex-Girlfriend*," *Variety*, October 21, 2014, https://variety.com/2014/tv/news/showtime-crazy-ex-girlfriend-rachel-bloom-1201334777/.

35 Lausch notes, "the CW's declared target audience has been young women between the ages of 18 and 34. Most nightly ratings reports on the five networks include either this demographic or women ages 18–49 in their consideration of how the network is performing . . . the network is able to stay afloat because of its ability to successfully court the advertiser-coveted young female audience." Kayti Adaire Lausch, "The Nice Network: Gender, Genre, and the CW Brand" (master's thesis, University of Texas at Austin, 2013), 53, http://hdl.handle.net/2152/22453.

36 Lotz, *Television Will Be Revolutionized*, 5; For some writers *CXG* exemplifies how niche series survive in the post-network climate. See Rick Porter, "TV Long View: *Crazy Ex-Girlfriend*'s Unique Ratings History," *Hollywood Reporter*, April 6, 2019, www.hollywoodreporter.com/live-feed/crazy-girlfriends-unique-tv-ratings-history-1199892.

37 Richard Yao, "The End of TV Monoculture as We Know It," *Medium*, May 23, 2019, https://medium.com/ipg-media-lab/the-end-of-tv-monoculture-as-we-know-it-de9da18949dc.

38 Bryan Sandberg, "It's Official: Netflix, the CW Reach New Streaming Pact," *Hollywood Reporter*, July 5, 2016, www.hollywoodreporter.com/tv/tv-news/official-netflix-cw-reach-new-908442/.

39 Lotz, *Television Will Be Revolutionized*, 97–98.

40 Megan Garber, "*Crazy Ex-Girlfriend* and the Rise of the TV Musical," *The Atlantic*, October 11, 2015, www.theatlantic.com/entertainment/archive/2015/10/crazy-ex-girlfriend-and-the-rise-of-the-tv-musical/409792/; Isobel Lewis, "How *Crazy Ex-Girlfriend* Revived the TV Musical—And Liberated Its Heroine," *The Atlantic*, April 5, 2019, www.theatlantic.com/entertainment/archive/2019/04/crazy-ex-girlfriend-revived-tv-musical-the-cw/586555/; Willa Paskin, "*Crazy Ex-Girlfriend* Is Peak #PeakTV," *Slate*, October 8, 2015, https://slate.com/culture/2015/10/crazy-ex-girlfriend-on-cw-reviewed-this-show-is-peak-peaktv.html; James Poniewozik, "Review: *Crazy Ex-Girlfriend*, a Musical with Twisted Songs," *New York Times*, October 11, 2015, www.nytimes.com/2015/10/12/arts/television/review-crazy-ex-girlfriend-a-musical-with-twisted-songs.html.

41 Susan Dominus, "Rachel Bloom's Twisted Comedy: *Crazy Ex-Girlfriend*—the Subversive Series That Just Won the Actor a Golden Globe—Somehow Manages to Set Women's Uncomfortable Truths to Music," *New York Times*, January 19, 2016, www.nytimes.com/2016/01/24/magazine/make-em-laugh.html; Andrea Morabito, "*Crazy Ex-Girlfriend* Has Some Serious Broadway Pedigree," *New York Post*, October 17, 2015, https://nypost.com/2015/10/17/crazy-ex-girlfriend-has-some-serious-broadway-pedigree/.

42 Rachel Bloom, interview by Kevin Jacobsen, "Rachel Bloom (*Crazy Ex-Girlfriend*) on This Being a 'Parody of the Career I Dreamed of Having,'" Goldderby, July 10, 2019, www.goldderby.com/article/2019/rachel-bloom-crazy-ex-girlfriend-cw-network-video-interview-transcript/.

43 Amanda D. Lotz, "Unpopularity and Cultural Power in the Age of Netflix: New Questions for Cultural Studies' Approaches to Television Texts," *European Journal of Cultural Studies* 24, no. 4 (2021): 891, https://doi.org/10.1177/1367549421994578.

44 Yao, "End of TV Monoculture."

45 Chayka, "Can Monoculture Survive."

46 Michael Newman, "The Rom-Com/Sitcom/YouTube Musical: *Crazy Ex-Girlfriend*," *Film Criticism* 40, no. 3 (2016), http://dx.doi.org/10.3998/fc.13761232.0040.311.

47 Lotz, *Television Will Be Revolutionized*, 68, 81.
48 Lotz, "Unpopularity and Cultural Power," 895.
49 Stars in the House, "*Crazy Ex-Girlfriend* Reunion!" YouTube, July 17, 2020, www.youtube.com/watch?v=Zc0O2haFGhM.
50 Rachel Bloom, *I Want to Be Where the Normal People Are* (New York: Grand Central Publishing, 2020).
51 See, for example, Amanda Konkle and Charles Burnetts, eds., *Perspectives on "Crazy Ex-Girlfriend": Nuanced Postnetwork Television* (Syracuse, NY: Syracuse University Press, 2021).
52 See, for example, Adrienne Trier-Bieneiek, ed., *Feminist Theory and Pop Culture*. Rotterdam: Sense, 2015; April Kalogeropolous Householder and Adrienne Trier-Bieneiek, eds., *Feminist Perspectives on "Orange Is the New Black": Thirteen Critical Essays* (Jefferson, NC: McFarland, 2016).
53 Callie Holtermann, "Why Are So Many People Rewatching *Girls*? Viewership of Lena Dunham's HBO Dramedy Is Surging as Many Millennials Reassess Their 20s and a Show That Defined Them," *New York Times*, March 16, 2023, www.nytimes.com/2023/03/16/style/girls-show-hbo-lena-dunham.html.
54 Simon Reynolds, "Streaming Has Killed the Mainstream: The Decade That Broke Popular Culture," *The Guardian*, December 18, 2019, www.theguardian.com/culture/2019/dec/28/overload-ambush-and-isolation-the-decade-that-warped-popular-culture-simon-reynolds.

## Chapter 2

1 Ford, "Women's Indie Television," 928–43.
2 Ford, "Women's Indie Television," 930, 939–40.
3 Ford, "Women's Indie Television," 931–32.
4 Lawrence and Ringrose, "@NOFEMINISM, #FEMINISTSAREUGLY, and Misandry Memes," 213.
5 Notable discussions of racial representations on *Girls* include the following: Nisha Chittal, "A Reaction to the Backlash against Mindy Kaling," *Jezebel*, September 21, 2012, https://jezebel.com/a-reaction-to-the-backlash-against-mindy-kaling-5945075; Roxane Gay, *Bad Feminist: Essays* (New York: Harper Perennial, 2014), 56–57; Elwood Watson, "Lena Dunham: The Awkward/Ambiguous Politics of White Millennial Feminism," in *HBO's "Girls" and the Awkward Politics of Gender, Race, and Privilege*, ed. Elwood Watson, Jennifer Mitchell, and Marc Edward Shaw (Lanham,

MD: Lexington Books, 2015), 145–65; Eesha Pandit, "The Unending Heartbreak of Great Expectations: Why I Can't Watch *The Mindy Project* Anymore," in *The Crunk Feminist Collection*, ed. Brittney C. Cooper, Susana M. Morris, and Robin M. Boylorn (New York: The Feminist Press at the City University of New York, 2017), 223–26; Kendall, *Hood Feminism*, 5; Nygaard and Lagerwey, *Horrible White People*, 6.

6 Jeffrey Sconce, "Irony, Nihilism, and the New American Smart Film," *Screen* 43, no. 4 (2002): 349–69.

7 Michael Z. Newman, *Indie: An American Film Culture* (New York: Columbia University Press, 2011), 3.

8 Allyson Nadia Field, Jan-Christopher Horak, and Jacqueline Najuma Stewart, "Introduction: Emancipating the Image: The L.A. Rebellion of Black Filmmakers," in *L.A. Rebellion: Creating a New Black Cinema*, ed. Nadia Field, Jan-Christopher Horak, and Jacqueline Najuma Stewart (Oakland: University of California Press, 2015), 3.

9 Emanuel Levy, *Cinema of Outsiders: The Rise of American Independent Film* (New York: New York University Press, 1999), 2, 5.

10 Newman, *Indie*, 1, 2, 9.

11 Newman, *Indie*, 4.

12 Levy, *Cinema of Outsiders*, 6.

13 Newman, *Indie*, 10.

14 Sconce, "Irony, Nihilism, and the New," 351, 359.

15 Ford, "Women's Indie Television," 936–38, 940.

16 Levy, *Cinema of Outsiders*, 386.

17 Christina N. Baker, *Contemporary Black Women Filmmakers and the Art of Resistance* (Columbus: Ohio State University Press, 2018), 39–40.

18 Yuan, "*Awkward Black Girl*."

19 *Love Jones*, directed by Theodore Witcher (1997; New York: New Line Cinema, 2006), DVD; *Hav Plenty*, directed by Christopher Scott Cherot (1997; Los Angeles: Miramax, 2002), DVD; *Medicine for Melancholy*, directed by Barry Jenkins (2008; New York: IFC Films, 2009), DVD.

20 Yuan, "*Awkward Black Girl*."

21 *Insecure*, HBO.com, www.hbo.com/insecure.

22 Joel Stein, "Millennials: The Me Me Me Generation," *Time*, May 20, 2013, https://time.com/247/millennials-the-me-me-me-generation/.

23 Wanzo, "Precarious-Girl Comedy," 26–59; Lagerwey, Leyda, and Negra, "Female Centered TV in an Age of Precarity."

24 Jeffrey Jensen Arnett, "Emerging Adulthood(s): The Cultural Psychology of a New Life Stage," in *Bridging Cultural and Developmental Approaches to Psychology: New Syntheses in Theory, Research, and Policy*, ed. Lee Arnett Jensen (New York: Oxford University Press, 2011), 255–56; Jeffrey Jensen Arnett, *Emerging Adulthood: The Winding Road from the Late Teens through the Late Twenties*, 3rd ed. (New York: Oxford University Press, 2024), 190.
25 Ford, "Women's Indie Television," 929.
26 Sconce, "Irony, Nihilism, and the New American Smart Film," 361.
27 Ford, "Women's Indie Television," 929.
28 Bialik and Fry, "Millennial Life"; Jean A. Twenge, *The Real Differences between Gen Z, Millennials, Gen X, Boomers, and Silents—And What They Mean for America's Future* (New York: Atria, 2024), 280.
29 Lynn C. Spangler, "A Historical Overview of Female Friendships on Prime-Time Television," *Journal of Popular Culture* 22, no. 4 (1989): 21–22.
30 *Shrill* S2, E5.
31 Ford, "Women's Indie Television," 934.
32 Amy Erdman Farrell, *Fat Shame: Stigma and the Fat Body in American Culture* (New York: New York University Press, 2011), 5; Laura Fraser, *Losing It: False Hopes and Fat Profits in the Diet Industry* (New York: Plume, 1998), 224.
33 West, *Shrill*, 86–107, 108–23, 165–94.
34 Karen Lumsden and Heather Morgan, "Media Framing of Trolling and Online Abuse: Silencing Strategies, Symbolic Violence, and Victim Blaming," *Feminist Media Studies*, 17, no. 6 (2017): 927, 932–35, https://doi.org/10.1080/14680777.2017.1316755.
35 In the chapter "Discussion," in Gina Dent, ed., *Black Popular Culture* (Seattle: Bay Press, 1992), 270, cultural critic Greg Tate describes the "black familiar" as the following: "It encapsulates the notion that there's a cultural base, an incredible body of knowledge and information which, if you want to function at all as a black thinker or writer or artist, you have to have at least passing familiarity with. If you come up in a certain black communal context, there are a lot of experiences and emotional responses, vernacular, and so forth that you have access to."
36 Derald Wing Sue defines microaggressions as "the everyday verbal, nonverbal, and environmental slights, snubs, or insults, whether intentional or unintentional, that communicate hostile, derogatory, or negative messages to target persons based solely upon their marginalized group

membership," "Microaggressions, Marginality, and Oppression: An Introduction," in *Microaggressions in Everyday Life: Race, Gender, and Sexual Orientation*, ed. Derald Wing Sue (Hoboken, NJ: John Wiley & Sons, 2010), 3.

37 In this respect *Insecure* exemplifies what Beretta E. Smith-Shomade terms "an 'insider creation'" expressing the worldview of a minoritized culture, *Shaded Lives: African-American Women and Television* (New Brunswick, NJ: Rutgers University Press, 2002), 34–35.

38 Scholl, "Issa Rae."

39 Julia Ioffe, "Issa Rae: 'I Never Identified as a Nerd'; Talking to *Insecure*'s Creator about Her TV Ambitions, L.A. Gentrification, and Her Awkward Public Persona," May 2018, *The Atlantic*, www.theatlantic.com/magazine/archive/2018/05/issa-rae-insecure/556880/.

40 *Insecure*, "Insecure: In the Room," season 1, aired October 9, 2016, HBO.

41 Joan Morgan, *When Chickenheads Come Home to Roost: A Hip-Hop Feminist Breaks It Down* (New York: Simon and Schuster Paperbacks, 1999), 86–87.

42 Smith-Shomade, *Shaded Lives*, 56.

43 Reniqua Allen, "From Love to Melancholy: The Evolution of the Black Bohemian Identity in Black Indie Love Films from Gen-X to Gen-Y," *Journal of Black Studies* 44, no. 5 (2013): 508–28, https://doi.org/10.1177/0021934713496570.

44 Yuan, "*Awkward Black Girl*."

45 Felix Gillette and John Koblin, *It's Not TV: The Spectacular Rise, Revolution, and Future of HBO* (New York: Viking, 2022), 298–300.

46 *Girls*, HBO.com, www.hbo.com/girls; Nussbaum, "It's Different for *Girls*."

47 Claire Perkins, *American Smart Cinema* (Edinburgh: Edinburgh University Press, 2012), 32–34.

48 Biographical and professional information drawn from the following: Nico Lang, "Samantha Irby Is Coming Out—Again," INTO, August 17, 2017, https://web.archive.org/web/20180315003710/https://intomore.com/culture/samantha-irby-is-coming-outagain/ee6b146cb5494e58; "Shaka King," IMDb, www.imdb.com/name/nm3489851/; Reggie Ugwu, "Shaka King Goes to Hollywood," *New York Times*, February 12, 2021, www.nytimes.com/2021/02/12/movies/shaka-king-judas-black-messiah.html; Race Forward, "#Raceand: Hye Yun Park," YouTube, May 15, 2016, www.youtube.com/watch?v=7OPf49u5sEU; "Sudi Green," IMDb, www.imdb.com/name/nm6003622/; Naomi Ekperigin and Andy Beckerman, "Sudi

Green," episode 222, September 27, 2022, in *Couples Therapy*, podcast, 94:00, https://shows.acast.com/couplestherapy/episodes/sudi-green.

49 "Prentice Penny," IMDb, www.imdb.com/name/nm1079781/; "Laura Kittrell," IMDb, www.imdb.com/name/nm3308450/; https://www.amyaniobi.com/; https://daynalynnenorthwriteaway.teachable.com/; "Ben Dougan," IMDb, www.imdb.com/name/nm3684607/; https://thembibanks.com/; http://www.laceyduke.com/.

50 Matt Donnelly, "Lena Waithe's Hillman Grad Launches Mentorship Lab for Writers, Actors, Executives," *Variety*, December 16, 2020, https://variety.com/2020/film/news/lena-waithe-hillman-grad-mentorship-lab-1234864079/.

51 See https://att-hellolab.com/.

## Chapter 3

1 Marx, "Expanding the Brand," 273, 278.

2 Hahn, "Showtime Mixes Internet Sensation"; Lausch, "Nice Network."

3 For examples of broad romantic comedy definitions, see Tamar Jeffers McDonald, *Romantic Comedy: Boy Meets Girl Meets Genre* (London: Wallflower, 2007), 9; Claire Mortimer, *Romantic Comedy* (London: Routledge, 2010), 4; Leger Grindon, *The Hollywood Romantic Comedy: Conventions, History, Controversies* (Malden, MA: Wiley-Blackwell, 2011), 2.

4 Celestino Deleyto, *The Secret Life of Romantic Comedy* (Manchester: Manchester University Press, 2009), 45–46.

5 Mortimer, *Romantic Comedy*, 5–6.

6 Hilary Radner, *The New Woman's Film: Femme-Centric Movies to Smart Chicks* (New York: Routledge, 2017), 17–18.

7 *Crazy Ex-Girlfriend*, season 1, episode 14, "Josh Is Going to Hawaii!," directed by Erin Ehrlich, written by Sono Patel, aired March 7, 2016, CW.

8 Paula Marantz Cohen, "What Have Clothes Got to Do with It? Romantic Comedy and the Female Gaze," *Southwest Review* 95, nos. 1 and 2 (2010): 78–88.

9 Martin Barker and Thomas Austin, *From Antz to Titanic: Reinventing Film Analysis* (London: Pluto Press, 2000), 145.

10 Scott McMillin, *The Musical as Drama: A Study of the Principles and Conventions behind Musical Shows from Kern to Sondheim* (Princeton, NJ: Princeton University Press, 2006), 21.

11 Olson, "Meta-Television," 287.

12 racheldoesstuff, "You Stupid Bitch (feat. Rachel Bloom)—*Crazy Ex-Girlfriend*," written by Rachel Bloom and Adam Schlesinger, YouTube, February 9, 2016, www.youtube.com/watch?v=zgUKQCVieWM.
13 David Metzer, *The Ballad in American Popular Music: From Elvis to Beyoncé* (Cambridge: Cambridge University Press, 2017), 135.
14 Metzer, *Ballad in American Popular Music*, 135–36.
15 Melissa Klein, "Duality and Redefinition: Young Feminism and the Alternative Music Community," in *Third Wave Agenda: Being Feminist, Doing Feminism*, ed. Leslie Heywood and Jennifer Drake (Minneapolis: University of Minnesota Press, 1997), 208; Jennifer Baumgardner and Amy Richards, *Manifesta: Young Women, Feminism, and the Future* (New York: Farrar, Straus and Giroux, 2000), 52; Lisa Jervis and Andi Zeisler, eds., Introduction to *Bitchfest: Ten Years of Cultural Criticism from the Pages of "Bitch" Magazine* (New York: Farrar, Straus and Giroux, 2006): xxi.
16 Whitney Houston, "Whitney Houston—'Greatest Love of All,'" YouTube, September 27, 2010, www.youtube.com/watch?v=IYzlVDlE72w; Mariah Carey, "Mariah Carey—'Hero' (Official Video)," YouTube, November 24, 2009, www.youtube.com/watch?v=0IA3ZvCkRkQ.
17 Diane Railton and Paul Watson, *Music Video and the Politics of Representation* (Edinburgh: Edinburgh University Press, 2011), 58.
18 Nick Paumgarten, "Id Girls: The Comedy Couple behind *Broad City*," *New Yorker*, June 16, 2014, www.newyorker.com/magazine/2014/06/23/id-girls.
19 Wanzo, "Precarious-Girl Comedy," 26–59; Lagerwey, Leyda, and Negra, "Female Centered TV."
20 Callie Holtermann, "Why Are So Many People Rewatching *Girls*?," *New York Times*, March 16, 2023, www.nytimes.com/2023/03/16/style/girls-show-hbo-lena-dunham.html.
21 Paumgarten, "Id Girls."
22 Marx, "Expanding the Brand," 277–81.
23 For more on stoner comedy elements and the classics in the genre, see the following: Marisa Meltzer, "Leisure and Innocence: The Eternal Appeal of the Stoner Movie," *Slate*, June 26, 2007, https://slate.com/news-and-politics/2007/06/the-eternal-appeal-of-the-stoner-movie.html; Bradford Evans, "A Definitive Guide to Stoner Comedies," *Vulture*, April 5, 2011, www.vulture.com/2011/04/a-definitive-guide-to-stoner-comedies.html; Scott Meslow, "High Art: The Subversive History of Stoner Comedies," *The Atlantic*, November 3, 2011, www.theatlantic.com/entertainment/

archive/2011/11/high-art-the-subversive-history-of-stoner-comedies/247838/.

24 *Broad City*, season 4, episode 4, "Mushrooms," directed Nicolas Jasonovec, written by Abbi Jacobson and Ilana Glazer, aired October 11, 2017, Comedy Central.

25 Rowe, *Unruly Woman*, 31.

26 Paumgarten, "Id Girls."

27 See Katrin Horn, "'Period Sex': *Crazy Ex-Girlfriend* and the Feminist Politics of Offence," in *Media and the Politics of Offence*, ed. Anne Graefer (Birmingham, UK: Palgrave Macmillan, 2019), 127–45, and Jennifer Caplan, "Rachel Bloom's Gaping MAAW: Jewish Women, Stereotypes, and the Boundary Bending of *Crazy Ex-Girlfriend*," *Journal of Modern Jewish Studies*, 19, no. 1 (2020): 93–109, https://doi.org/10.1080/14725886.2019.1703629.

28 Jonathan Branfman, "'Plow Him like a Queen!': Jewish Female Masculinity, Queer Glamor, and Racial Commentary in *Broad City*," *Television and New Media* 21, no. 8 (2020): 846, https://doi.org/10.1177/1527476419855688.

29 Havas and Sulimma, "Through the Gaps of My Fingers," 1–20.

30 *Broad City*, season 1, episode 5, "Fattest Asses," directed John Lee, written by Abbi Jacobson and Ilana Glazer, aired February 19, 2014, Comedy Central.

31 Missy Elliott, "Missy Elliot—'The Rain (Supa Dupa Fly)' [Official Video]," YouTube, October 26, 2009, www.youtube.com/watch?v=hHcyJPTTn9w; The Notorious B.I.G., "The Notorious B.I.G.—'Mo Money Mo Problems' (Official Music Video)," YouTube, September 6, 2011, www.youtube.com/watch?v=gUhRKVIjJtw.

32 McMillin, *Musical as Drama*, 21.

33 Ash Kinney d'Harcourt, "Queer Romance in *Take My Wife*: How the Television Rom-Com Sitcom Gives New Life to the Genre," in *After "Happily Ever After": Romantic Comedy in the Post-Romantic Age*, ed. Maria San Filippo (Detroit: Wayne State University Press, 2021), 102.

34 *Jane the Virgin*, IMDb, October 13, 2014, www.imdb.com/title/tt3566726/.

35 Evelyn P. Stevens, "Marianismo: The Other Face of Machismo in Latin America," in *Female and Male in Latin America*, ed. Ann Pescatello (Pittsburgh: University of Pittsburgh Press, 1973), 91.

36 Linda G. Castillo, Flor V. Perez, Rosalinda Castillo, and Mona R. Ghosheh, "Construction and Initial Validation of the Marianismo Beliefs Scale,"

*Counselling Psychology Quarterly* 23, no. 2 (2010): 164, https://doi.org/10.1080/09515071003776036.

37 Stevens, "Marianismo," 96.

38 Ann Mari Cauce and Melanie Domenech-Rodríguez, "Latino Families: Myths and Realities," in *Latino Children and Families in the United States: Current Research and Future Directions*, ed. Josefina M. Contreras, Kathryn A. Kerns, and Angela M. Neal-Barnett (Westport, CT: Praeger Publishers/Greenwood Publishing Group, 2002), 15, 17.

39 Castillo, Perez, Castillo, and Ghosheh, "Construction and Initial Validation," 164–65.

40 Sandberg, "Netflix, the CW Reach New Streaming Pact."

41 Robert C Allen, Introduction to *To Be Continued . . . Soap Opera around the World*, ed. Robert Allen (New York: Routledge, 1995), 2; Elana Levine, *Her Stories: Daytime Soap Operas and US Television History* (Durham, NC: Duke University Press, 2020), 7.

42 Levine, *Her Stories*, 9, 12.

43 Allen, Introduction, 18–20.

44 Levine, *Her Stories*, 96–103.

45 Levine, *Her Stories*, 5–6, 12.

46 Joseph Straubhaar, Melissa Santillana, Vanessa de Macedo Higgins Joyce, and Luiz Guilherme Duarte, *From Telenovelas to Netflix: Transnational, Transverse Television in Latin America* (Cham, Switzerland: Palgrave Macmillan, 2021), 53; Ana M. Lopez, "Our Welcomed Guests: Telenovelas in Latin America," in *To Be Continued . . . Soap Opera around the World*, ed. Robert Allen (New York: Routledge, 1995), 258; June Carolyn Erlick, *Telenovelas in Pan-Latino Context* (New York: Routledge, 2018), 5.

47 Erlick, *Telenovelas*, 5.

48 Allen, Introduction, 22; Lopez, "Our Welcomed Guests," 258.

49 Erlick, *Telenovelas*, 7–8.

50 Allen, Introduction, 22; Straubhaar et al., *From Telenovelas to Netflix*, 54.

51 Hugo O. Benavides, *Drugs, Thugs, and Divas: Telenovelas and Narco-Dramas in Latin America* (Austin: University of Texas Press, 2008), 11.

52 Benavides, *Drugs, Thugs, and Divas*, 10.

53 Jason Mittell, *Genre and Television: From Cop Shows to Cartoon in American Culture* (New York: Routledge, 2004), 164–65, 171; Elana Levine, *Wallowing in Sex: The New Sexual Culture of 1970s American Television* (Durham, NC: Duke University Press, 2007), 202–7; Erin Lee Mock, "'The

Soap Opera Is a Hell of an Exciting Form': Norman Lear's *Mary Hartman, Mary Hartman* and the 1970s Viewer," *Camera Obscura*, 28, no. 2 (2013): 109–49, https://doi.org/10.1215/02705346-2209934; Mittell, *Complex TV*, 240–43.

54 Mittell, *Genre and Television*, 160–78; Levine, *Wallowing in Sex*, 200–202, 205; Mittell, *Complex TV*, 242–43.

55 Erlick, *Telenovelas*, 12–13.

56 Levine, *Her Stories*, 227–28, 230–32.

57 Benavides, *Drugs, Thugs, and Divas*, 211.

58 *Jane the Virgin*, season 1, episode 7, "Chapter Seven," directed by Janice Cooke, written by David S. Rosenthal, aired November 24, 2014, CW.

59 Sconce, "What If?," 95, 106.

60 Mittell, *Complex TV*, 38, 50.

61 Payson, Introduction to *Searching the Soul of "Ally McBeal,"* 8, 10–11.

62 *Ally McBeal: Season Five*, produced by David E. Kelley (2001–2; Los Angeles: 20th Century Fox, 2010), DVD.

63 *Woori the Virgin*, IMDb, May 9, 2022, www.imdb.com/title/tt20227130/.

## Chapter 4

1 McMillin, *Musical as Drama*, 21.

2 Yael Levy, *Chick TV: Antiheroines and Time Unbound* (Syracuse, NY: Syracuse University Press, 2022), 74.

3 Kathleen A. McHugh, "Giving Credit to Paratexts and Parafeminism in *Top of the Lake* and *Orange Is the New Black*," *Film Quarterly* 68, no. 3 (2015): 20.

4 Levy, *Chick TV*, 22–24.

5 Hagelin and Silverman, *New Female Antihero*, ix.

6 Anna Bogutskaya. *Unlikeable Female Characters: The Women Pop Culture Wants You to Hate* (Naperville, IL: Sourcebooks, 2023), 27–34, 41–46, 49–50.

7 Nussbaum, *I like to Watch*, 49; Hagelin and Silverman, *New Female Antihero*, 4, 5, 9, 118.

8 Rowe, *Unruly Woman*, 50–91; Hagelin and Silverman, *New Female Antihero*, 133–39.

9 Framke, "I Just Wanted It to Be a Regular Story."

10 Leo Barraclough, "Amazon Acquires Comedy Series 'Fleabag' from 'Broadchurch's' Phoebe Waller-Bridge," *Variety*, May 19, 2016.

11 Information is from https://www.emmys.com/shows/fleabag.
12 Rowe, *Unruly Woman*, 31.
13 In episodes 3 and 4 of season 2, *Fleabag* further disrupts the form when the priest Fleabag develops affection for, and eventually sleeps with, sees her look off into the fourth wall space and asks her what she is doing. See *Fleabag*, season 2, episode 3, directed by Harry Bradbeer, written by Phoebe Waller-Bridge, aired April 8, 2019, Amazon Prime. A similarly transgressive moment occurs in the finale of *CXG* when Paula sees Rebecca pivot to break into song and Rebecca allows her into her musical imagination. See *Crazy Ex-Girlfriend*, season 4, episode 17, "I'm in Love," directed by Aline Brosh McKenna, written by Aline Brosh McKenna and Rachel Bloom, aired April 5, 2019, CW.
14 Holtermann, "Why Are So Many People Rewatching *Girls*?"
15 Nygaard and Lagerwey, *Horrible White People*, 216–17.
16 Woods, "Too Close for Comfort," 195.
17 Woods, "Too Close for Comfort," 197, 208.
18 Hagelin and Silverman, *New Female Antihero*, 22–23.
19 Nygaard and Lagerwey, *Horrible White People*, 39–47.
20 Nygaard and Lagerwey, *Horrible White People*, 40–41.
21 "Michaela Coel: MacTaggart Lecture in Full," Broadcast, August 23, 2018, www.broadcastnow.co.uk/broadcasters/michaela-coel-mactaggart-lecture-in-full/5131910.article.
22 E. Alex Jung, "Michaela the Destroyer: How a Young Talent from East London Went from Open-Mic Nights to Making the Most Sublimely Unsettling Show of the Year," *Vulture*, July 6, 2020, www.vulture.com/article/michaela-coel-i-may-destroy-you.html.
23 Caetlin Benson-Allott, "How *I May Destroy You* Reinvents Rape Television," *Film Quarterly* 74, no. 2 (2020): 103, https://doi.org/10.1525/fq.2020.74.2.100.
24 Marc Prensky, "Digital Natives, Digital Immigrants Part 1," *On the Horizon: The Strategic Planning Resource for Education Professionals* 9, no. 5 (2001): 3–4.
25 Rouse and Ross, *Politics of Millennials*, 29.
26 Benson-Allott, "How *I May Destroy You* Reinvents," 100.
27 Jung, "Michaela the Destroyer."
28 "Rape and Sexual Assault Statistics," Rape Crisis England and Wales, https://rapecrisis.org.uk/get-informed/statistics-sexual-violence/.

29 "Victims of Sexual Violence: Statistics," RAINN, https://rainn.org/statistics/victims-sexual-violence.

30 Hannah Yelin and Laura Clancy, "Doing Impact Work While Female: Hate Tweets, 'Hot Potatoes,' and Having 'Enough of Experts,'" *European Journal of Women's Studies* 28, no. 2 (2021): 177, https://doi.org/10.1177/1350506820910194.

31 Bolu Babalola, "The Innate Black Britishness of *I May Destroy You*," *Vulture*, August 30, 2020, www.vulture.com/article/i-may-destroy-you-black-britishness.html.

32 *I May Destroy You*, season 1, episode 8, "Line Spectrum Border," directed by Sam Miller and Michaela Coel, written by Michaela Coel, aired July 27, 2020, HBO.

33 Sarah J. Jackson, Moya Bailey, and Brooke Foucault Welles, *#Hashtag Activism: Networks of Race and Gender Justice* (Cambridge, MA: MIT Press, 2020), xxviii.

34 Kaitlynn Mendes, Jessica Ringrose, and Jessalynn Keller, "#MeToo and the Promise and Pitfalls of Challenging Rape Culture through Digital Feminist Activism," *European Journal of Women's Studies* 25, no. 2 (2018): 238, https://doi.org/10.1177/1350506818765318.

35 Jackson, Bailey, and Foucault Welles, *#Hashtag Activism*, 4–8, 24–27.

36 Briony Anderson and Mark A. Wood, "Harm Imbrication and Virtualised Violence: Reconceptualising the Harms of Doxing," *International Journal for Crime, Justice, and Social Democracy* 11, no. 1 (2022): 196, https://doi.org/10.5204/ijcjsd.2140.

37 Stine Eckert and Jade Metzger-Riftkin, "Doxxing, Privacy, and Gendered Harassment: The Shock and Normalization of Veillance Cultures," *Medien & Kommunikationswissenschaft* 68, no. 3 (2020): 285, http://dx.doi.org/10.5771/1615-634X-2020-3-273.

38 Svana M. Calabro, "From the Message Board to the Front Door: Addressing the Offline Consequences of Race- and Gender-Based Doxxing and Swatting," *Suffolk University Law Review* 51, no. 1 (2018): 61–62.

39 Candi S. Carter Olson and Victoria LaPoe, "'Feminazis,' 'Libtards,' 'Snowflakes,' and 'Racists': Trolling and the Spiral of Silence Impact on Women, LGBTQIA Communities, and Disability Populations before and after the 2016 Election," *Journal of Public Interest Communications* 1, no. 2 (2017): 116; Sarah Beresford, "From Scolds to Trolls: Social and Legal Responses to Visible and Audible Women—a Conference Blob," Lancaster University

Law School, 2015, www.lancaster.ac.uk/law/blogs/staff/from-scolds-to-trolls-social-and-legal-responses-to-visible-and-audible-women/; F. Vera-Gray, "'Talk about a Cunt with Too Much Idle Time': Trolling Feminist Research," *Feminist Review* 115, no. 1 (2017): 67; Lumsden and Morgan, "Media Framing," 927, 932–35, https://doi.org/10.1080/14680777.2017.1316755.

40 Katelyn Burns, "The Rise of Anti-Trans 'Radical' Feminists, Explained: Known as Terfs, Trans-Exclusionary Radical Feminist Groups Are Working with Conservatives to Push Their Anti-Trans Agenda," *Vox*, September 5, 2019, www.vox.com/identities/2019/9/5/20840101/terfs-radical-feminists-gender-critical.

41 Jessica Bennett, "What If Instead of Calling People Out, We Called Them In? Prof. Loretta J. Ross Is Combating Cancel Culture with a Popular Class at Smith College," *New York Times*, November 19, 2020, www.nytimes.com/2020/11/19/style/loretta-ross-smith-college-cancel-culture.html.

42 Steve Bellovin, "Yes, 'Algorithms' Can Be Biased. Here's Why. Op-Ed: A Computer Scientist Weighs in on the Downsides of AI," Ars Technica, January 24, 2019, https://arstechnica.com/tech-policy/2019/01/yes-algorithms-can-be-biased-heres-why/.

43 Yelin and Clancy, "Doing Impact Work While Female," 188.

44 Lumsden and Morgan, "Media Framing," 936; Anastasia Powell and Nicola Henry, *Sexual Violence in a Digital Age* (London: Palgrave Macmillan, 2017), 12.

45 Paul Booth, "Memories, Temporalities, Fictions: Temporal Displacement in Contemporary Television," *Television and New Media* 12, no. 4 (2011): 374, https://doi.org/10.1177/1527476410392806.

46 April Terry, "Surveying Issues That Arise in Women's Prisons: A Content Critique of *Orange Is the New Black*," *Sociology Compass* 10, no. 7 (2016): 553–66, https://doi.org/10.1111/soc4.12388.

47 Jane Caputi, "The Color Orange? Social Justice Issues in the First Season of *Orange Is the New Black*," *Journal of Popular Culture* 48, no. 6 (2015): 1130–50; Anna Marie Smith, "Review Essay: *Orange* Is the Same White," *New Political Science* 37, no. 2 (2015): 276–280, http://dx.doi.org/10.1080/07393148.2014.995401; Shannon O' Sullivan, "Who Is Always Already Criminalized? An Intersectional Analysis of Criminality on *Orange Is the New Black*," *Journal of American Culture* 39, no. 4 (2016): 409–11, https://doi.org/10.1111/jacc.12637; Christina Belcher, "There Is No Such Thing

as a Post-Racial Prison: Neoliberal Multiculturalism and the White Savior Complex on *Orange Is the New Black*," *Television and New Media* 17, no. 6 (2016): 498–500, https://doi.org/10.1177/1527476416647498.

48 Lesley Henderson, *Social Issues in Television Fiction* (Edinburgh: Edinburgh University Press, 2007), 25; Allen, Introduction, 18, 21.

49 Henderson, *Social Issues in Television Fiction*, 173.

50 Rachel E. Silverman and Emily D. Ryalls, "'Everything Is Different the Second Time Around': The Stigma of Temporality on *Orange Is the New Black*," *Television and New Media* 17, no. 6 (2016): 521, https://doi.org/10.1177/1527476416647496.

51 Jason Demers, "Is a Trojan Horse an Empty Signifier? The Televisual Politics of *Orange Is the New Black*," *Canadian Review of American Studies / Revue canadienne d'études américaines* 47, no. 3 (2017): 403–22, https://doi.org/10.3138/cras.2017.023; Anne Schwan, "Postfeminism Meets the Women in Prison Genre: Privilege and Spectatorship in *Orange Is the New Black*," *Television and New Media* 17, no. 6 (2016): 478–81, https://doi.org/10.1177/1527476416647497.

52 Suzanne M. Enck and Megan E. Morrissey, "If *Orange Is the New Black*, I Must Be Color Blind: Comic Framings of Post-Racism in the Prison-Industrial Complex," *Critical Studies in Mass Communication* 32, no. 5 (2015): 303–17, https://doi.org/10.1080/15295036.2015.1086489.

53 Edward Schiappa, *Beyond Representational Correctness: Rethinking Criticism of Popular Media* (Albany: State University of New York Press, 2008), 9–10.

54 Henderson, *Social Issues in Television Fiction*, 174.

55 Booth, "Memories, Temporalities, Fictions," 376, 379.

56 Neil Postman, *Amusing Ourselves to Death: Public Discourse in the Age of Show Business* (New York: Penguin Books, 1985), 159–60.

57 Sconce, "What If?," 95.

58 Henderson, *Social Issues in Television Fiction*, 174, 176; Allen, Introduction, 21.

59 Press, *Stealing the Show*, 250; Nussbaum, *I like to Watch*, 298, 299.

60 www.emmys.com/shows/orange-new-black.

61 McHugh, "Giving Credit to Paratexts and Parafeminism," 22.

62 Jaspreet K. Nijjar, "Female Masculinity and Transgressive Temporality: How *Orange Is the New Black* Recontextualizes Prisoner Agency," *Communication, Culture and Critique* 15, no. 3 (2022): 419–24, https://doi.org/10.1093/ccc/tcab059; Ashley Ruderman-Looff, "Looking beyond

the Lesbian: The Intersectionality of Death on Netflix's *Orange Is the New Black*," *Journal of Lesbian Studies* 23, no. 4 (2019): 490–503, https://doi.org/10.1080/10894160.2019.1652084; Marta Fernández-Morales and María Isabel Menéndez-Menéndez, "Seeing Red: An Analysis of Age within the Intersectional Paradigm of *Orange Is the New Black*," *Frontiers: A Journal of Women Studies* 43, no. 2 (2022): 107–38, https://doi.org/10.1353/fro.2022.0014; Victoria E. Thomas, "Gazing at 'It': An Intersectional Analysis of Transnormativity and Black Womanhood in *Orange Is the New Black*," *Communication, Culture and Critique* 13, no. 4 (2020): 519–35, https://doi.org/10.1093/ccc/tcz030; Clare Kim, "The Blindspot: Asian Misrepresentation in *Orange Is the New Black*," *Elements* 12, no. 2 (2016): 77–81, http://dx.doi.org/10.6017/eurj.v12i2.9380; Jessica Scott, "Hillbilly Horror and the New Racism: Rural and Racial Politics in *Orange Is the New Black*," *Journal of Appalachian Studies* 23, no. 2 (2017): 221–38, https://doi.org/10.5406/jappastud.23.2.0221.

63 *Orange Is the New Black*, season 2, episode 12, "It Was the Change," directed by Phil Abraham, written by Sara Hess, aired June 6, 2014, Netflix.

64 Booth, "Memories, Temporalities, Fictions," 384.

65 Melissa Ames, ed., *Time in Television Narrative: Exploring Temporality in Twenty-First Century Programming* (Jackson: University of Mississippi Press, 2012); Levy, *Chick TV*.

## Coda

1 Svenja Hohenstein and Katharina Thalmann, "Difficult Women: Changing Representations of Female Characters in Contemporary Television Series," *Zeitschrift für Anglistik und Amerikanistik: A Quarterly of Language, Literature, and Culture* 2019, no. 2 (2019): 119.

2 Linda Mizejewski and Victoria Sturtevant, Introduction to *Hysterical! Women in American Comedy*, ed. Linda Mizejewski and Victoria Sturtervant (Austin: University of Texas Press, 2017), 8.

3 Bambi Haggins, Introduction to *Laughing Mad: The Black Comic Persona in Post-Soul America* (New Brunswick, NJ: Rutgers University Press, 2007), 5.

4 Sarita Malik, *Representing Black Britain: Black and Asian Images on Television* (London: SAGE Publications, 2001), 7–34, 91–106, 173–86; Stephen Bourne, *Black in the British Frame: The Black Experience in British Film and Television* (London: Bloomsbury, 2005), 142–52.

5 Kobena Mercer, *Welcome to the Jungle: New Positions in Black Cultural Studies* (London: Routledge, 1994), 53–96; Sarita Malik, "Reflections on Representing Black Britain," *Journal of Cultural Economy* (2022), https://doi.org/10.1080/17530350.2022.2138502.

6 Malik, *Representing Black Britain*, 29.

7 J. Jack Halberstam, *In a Queer Time and Place: Transgender Bodies, Subcultural Lives* (New York: New York University Press, 2005), 11–12.

8 Steven Capsuto, *Alternate Channels: The Uncensored Story of Gay and Lesbian Images on Radio and Television, 1930s to the Present* (New York: Ballantine Books, 2000), 317–25.

9 *Armistead Maupin's Tales of the City*, IMDb, June 7, 2019, www.imdb.com/title/tt7087260/?ref_=nv_sr_srsg_0_tt_7_nm_1_q_tales%2520of%2520the%2520city; Lesley Goldberg, "*Armistead Maupin's Tales of the City*: Ellen Page Joins Laura Linney, Olympia Dukakis in Netflix Sequel," *Hollywood Reporter*, April 24, 2018, www.hollywoodreporter.com/tv/tv-news/armistead-maupins-tales-city-ellen-page-joins-laura-linney-olympia-dukakis-netflix-sequel-1105348/.

10 Pippa Norris and Ronald Inglehart, *Cultural Backlash: Trump, Brexit, and Authoritarian Populism* (Cambridge: Cambridge University Press, 2019), 396.

11 Norris and Inglehart, *Cultural Backlash*, 340.

12 *Reversing Roe*, directed by Ricki Stern and Anne Sundberg, aired September 13, 2018, Netflix.

13 Elisabeth Griffith, *Formidable: American Women and the Fight for Equality; 1920–2020* (New York: Pegasus, 2022), 363.

14 Adam Liptak, "In 6-to-3 Ruling, Supreme Court Ends Nearly 50 Years of Abortion Rights," *New York Times*, June 24, 2022, www.nytimes.com/2022/06/24/us/roe-wade-overturned-supreme-court.html.

15 Eric Levitz, "David Shor's (Premature) Autopsy of the 2022 Midterm Elections," November 10, 2022, *New York Magazine*, https://nymag.com/intelligencer/2022/11/election-results-who-won-the-midterms-david-shor.html; Ally Mutnick and Jessica Piper, "Republicans Flip the House: Republicans Are on Track for a Tiny Majority despite Predictions That a Red Wave Was Coming," Politico, November 16, 2022, www.politico.com/news/2022/11/16/house-control-midterm-elections-results-2022-00066546.

16 Gay, *Bad Feminist*, 57.

17 Gillette and Koblin, *It's Not TV*, 230–31.

18 Dodai Stewart, "Why We Need to Keep Talking about the White Girls on *Girls*," Jezebel, April 19, 2012, https://jezebel.com/why-we-need-to-keep-talking-about-the-white-girls-on-gi-5903382.

19 Ta-Nehisi Coates, "*Girls* through the Veil," *The Atlantic*, April 20, 2012, www.theatlantic.com/entertainment/archive/2012/04/girls-through-the-veil/256154/.

20 Jeanelle Hope, "An Ode to Black British Girls: Black British Feminism, Black Girl Surrealism, and Michaela Cole's *Chewing Gum*," *View: Journal of European Television History and Culture* 10, no. 20 (2021): 3.

21 Lenny Henry and Marcus Ryder, *Access All Areas: The Diversity Manifesto for TV and Beyond* (London: Faber, 2021), 167–69.

22 Henry and Ryder, *Access All Areas*, 168.

23 "Adjusting the Colour Balance: A Report on BAME Representation among Directors Working in UK TV," Directors UK, September 18, 2020, https://directors.uk.com/news/adjusting-the-colour-balance; "Michaela Coel: MacTaggart Lecture in Full."

24 Daniel Lawrence Taylor, "As a Black TV Writer in a White Industry, We Need Support—Not Doubt," *The Guardian*, June 26, 2020, www.theguardian.com/tv-and-radio/2020/jun/26/trust-and-support-us-rather-than-doubting-us-tales-from-a-black-tv-writer.

25 Jim Waterson, "BAME Creatives Urge UK Film and TV to Do More to Tackle Racism," *The Guardian*, June 22, 2020, www.theguardian.com/media/2020/jun/22/bame-creatives-urge-uk-film-and-tv-to-use-diverse-content.

26 "BBC Sets Out Plans to Become Industry Gold Standard for Workplace Diversity and Inclusion," BBC, February 23, 2021, www.bbc.com/mediacentre/2021/bbc-plans-industry-gold-standard-workplace-diversity-inclusion.

27 "Advocacy," Women in Film, https://womeninfilm.org/advocacy/.

28 "Programs," HALF Initiative, www.halfinitiative.com/programs.

29 Lacey Rose, "Shonda Rhimes Launches Two New DEI Initiatives with Netflix (Exclusive)," *Hollywood Reporter*, May 31, 2022, www.hollywoodreporter.com/tv/tv-news/shonda-rhimes-launches-two-new-dei-initiatives-netflix-1235153753/.

30 "The Guild: Diversity," Directors Guild of America, www.dga.org/The-Guild/Diversity/TV-Studio-Directors-Development-Programs.aspx.

# INDEX

*Note:* Page numbers appearing in *italics* refer to figures.